HOPE CIRCUITS

HOPE CIRCUITS

*Rewiring Universities
and Other Organizations
for Human Flourishing*

JESSICA RIDDELL

McGill-Queen's University Press
Montreal & Kingston • London • Chicago

ISBN 978-0-2280-2066-0 (cloth)
ISBN 978-0-2280-2067-7 (paper)
ISBN 978-0-2280-2068-4 (ePDF)
ISBN 978-0-2280-2069-1 (ePUB)

Legal deposit first quarter 2024
Bibliothèque nationale du Québec

Reprinted 2024

Printed in Canada on acid-free paper that is 100% ancient forest free
(100% post-consumer recycled), processed chlorine free

Funded by the   Financé par le   Canada Council   Conseil des arts
Government   gouvernement   for the Arts   du Canada
of Canada   du Canada

Canada

We acknowledge the support of the Canada Council for the Arts.
Nous remercions le Conseil des arts du Canada de son soutien.

McGill-Queen's University Press in Montreal is on land which long served as a
site of meeting and exchange amongst Indigenous Peoples, including the Haudenosaunee and Anishinabeg nations. In Kingston it is situated on the territory of
the Haudenosaunee and Anishinaabek. We acknowledge and thank the diverse
Indigenous Peoples whose footsteps have marked these territories on which
peoples of the world now gather.

Library and Archives Canada Cataloguing in Publication

Title: Hope circuits : rewiring universities and other organizations for human
    flourishing / Jessica Riddell.
Names: Riddell, Jessica, author.
Description: Includes bibliographical references and index.
Identifiers: Canadiana (print) 20230550673 | Canadiana (ebook) 20230550843 |
    ISBN 9780228020660 (cloth) | ISBN 9780228020677 (paper) | ISBN 9780228020691
    (EPUB) | ISBN 9780228020684 (ePDF)
Subjects: LCSH: Education, Higher—Canada. | LCSH: Educational change—
    Canada.
Classification: LCC LA417.5 .R53 2024 | DDC 378.71—dc23

To all the wyrdos who challenge the actual in the name of the possible.

Contents

Acknowledgments

I am not here by myself. I am here in conversation with a multitude of generous and generative humans, each of whom start their work and shape their lives from the foundational principle of love.

I had the guidance and help, relentless love, and daily inspiration from my wyrd sisters, Shannon Murray and Lisa Dickson. We have howled into the abyss, sat in wonder, and moved into creative spaces since the day we first met on a bus in Vancouver in June 2015; that day, in retrospect, was a tipping point into a new paradigm that has shaped my journey in profound ways.

I have hope because of them.

Literary scholar and coach extraordinaire Bassam Chiblak has been instrumental in the creation of this book. I hired him as my "book butler," and yet he has been so much more: an accountability partner, incisive editor, insightful guide, treasured sounding board – and cherished friend. He has pushed me to reach farther, think harder, roar louder. Bassam showed me what hopeful collaboration looks like in real time.

I finished this book because of him.

Cécilia Alain has been an exceptional wyrd apprentice for both *Shakespeare's Guide to Hope, Life, and Learning* (University of Toronto Press, 2023) and now *Hope Circuits*. She built the back end of this book: the endnotes, bibliography, and index are all hers while the errors remain mine. James Baldwin once said, "Talent is insignificant. I know a lot of talented ruins. Beyond talent lie all the usual words: discipline, love, luck, but, most of all, endurance." Cécilia brings both talent *and* endurance to every contribution.

I want to write books because of her.

My book buddy Jeff Hennessy has been a tireless supporter and crucial thought partner. Throughout the writing process he helped me work out the stickiest concepts with a generosity of spirit that eschews ego in favour of genuine curiosity. Watching him operationalize hope within institutional systems confirms that we can do this messy work of rewiring imperfect systems together.

I know hope circuits work because of him.

Heather Lawford has gifted me Gaudí and generativity, Marvel and mentorship. She helps unlock superhero powers for so many, including me. Maybe, just maybe, I have convinced her of the value of hope, and yet I suspect she has transformed me more, and for the better, in this generative relationship.

I have generativity because of her.

When I first talked about Hope University, Susie Andrews dusted off her cv. "Where is it and how do I apply?" she demanded, even as Hope University was still an emerging thought. Her persistence willed Hope University into the world, and her insistence that "this better be real because I need it" moved this project from thought experiment to reification. In every single conversation with Susie, Hope University comes into being.

I have Hope University because of her.

To help us become our best selves, early modern writer Baldassare Castiglione uses an apiary metaphor whereby we are bees and our friends are flowers. If we surround ourselves with the most beautiful flowers, Castiglione instructs, their pollen (exceptional qualities) helps us create our own unique honey. For me, this pedagogy of intellectual friendship captures the otherwise ineffable qualities of the 3M National Teaching Fellowship. I owe so much to my 3M Fellows 2015 cohort – Veselin Jungic, Etienne Coté, David Creelman, Pam Toulouse, Jin-Sun Yoon, Sara Harris, Ann Bigelow, Steve Joordans, and Peter Ostafichuk – and to fellows Sarah-Myriam Martin-Brûlé, Georges-Philippe Gadoury-Sansfaçon, Angie Kolen, Pat Maher, Sufia Langevin, Théo Soucy, and Oorja Gonepavaram.

I have honey because of them.

I have benefitted from numerous guides and sponsors in my career development: Michael Goldbloom and Michael Childs were the most formative. As a junior faculty, too green to know better, I booked meetings with them to pitch a passion project for which I had no experience or expertise. And yet, both Michaels (the principal and the vp academic) made the time and space for me to build the earliest prototypes of hope circuits. Their investment in me took me to places I would never have gotten to otherwise. I have opportunity because of them.

To my long-term rumblers, whom I adore, admire, and often just sit in awe of, thank you: Corinne Haigh, Neil Silcox, Scott Stoddard, David Hornsby, Gabrielle Donnelly, Jasmeen Sidhu, Toni Roberts, Peter Felten, Claire Hamshire, Paul Taylor, Rachel Forsyth, Heather Smith, Charlene Marion, Jock Phippen, Brad Weuthernick, Bryan Dewsbury, Shawna Garrett, Katie Bibbs, Royal Orr, Elizabeth Wells, Sandy McIver, Lynn Aylward, Jean-Marc Drouet. I have yes/and because of them.

Special thanks to my elder guides, the luminaries in higher education who have forged paths for us to hope harder and dream bigger: Lynn Pasquerella, David Sylvester, Ross Paul, Tom Chase, Marie Battiste, Sheila Cote-Meek, Gabrielle Starr, Leo Charbonneau, David Graham, David Scobey, Frederick Lawrence, Jeffrey Buller, David Kwabena Wilson, Squee Gordon, Scott Griffin. We have generous legacy because of them.

To those who were willing to sit with me with their hearts open: you are the gold threads that weave together the tapestry of the book. Throughout the writing process I heard your stories and tried to listen hard to your generous souls: Juan Carlos Lopez, Cheryl Foy, Mary Sweatman, Rachel Hurst, Joy Mighty, Duncan Cross, Fiona Rawle, Erin Austen, Jamie Sedgwick, Alice Cohen, Jeffrey Buller, Katie Edwards, Linda Pearse, Tara Taylor, Sarah Bunnell, Ivan Joseph, Amy Abe, Vicky Boldo, Vicki Chartrand, Jesse Dymond, Mark Caduc, Angela Pratt, Ginger Grant, Earle Abrahamson, Peter D'Sena, Fortunate Madondo, Andy Kasi, Helen Barefoot, David Pace, Maria Thistle, Anna Redden, Mark Adam, Kailin Wright, Tim Loreman, Anne Berthold, Emily Keenlyside, Kiera Galway, Justin Liefer, Tracy Everitt, Larissa Strong, Hans Rouleau, Mark Bishop, Mark Caduc, Stine Linden-Andersen, Anne Comfort. I have intentional community because of them.

And to the members of the focus groups, summits, workshops, and the 2022 and 2023 Maple League micro-certificate cohorts: my eternal gratitude. I have extra special appreciation for students in ENG205, "The Art of Rhetoric," ENG224, "Shakespeare's Guide to Critical Hope," and ENG237, "Metaphors, Mentors, and the Marvel Cinematic Universe," for reading and rumbling on various versions of these chapters. With permission, Jayna Renaud, Elsa Marina Lamontagne, Arianne Rainville, Ryan LeBlanc, William Nicolas, Kelly-Ann Bousquet, Kamille Longchamps, and Sarah Alguire-Cartier shared their reflections in the mentorship chapter. And a special shout out to my OLTC crew Loch Baillie, Sally Cunningham, Alisha Winter, Sonoma Brawley, Matthew Dunleavy, and so many others who showed me what authentic co-design looks like.

I teach and learn because of them.

Leo Charbonneau, my thoughtful editor at *University Affairs* for almost six years, gave me the chance to write regularly about higher education and became my first platform for what would eventually become this book. He helped me find my wobbly voice to explore ideas and issues related to navigating higher education with a very forgiving audience.

I have a genealogy for Hope University because of him.

One day, my friend the historian David Webster retweeted a post from Emily Andrew, newly returned to Canada, that exclaimed, "DOOR'S OPEN, AUTHORS! Want to confer about a book project, discuss the thesis-into-book transition, explore the process of writing a compelling proposal? I am available every Tuesday, 10am–1pm EST. Sign up here (and pass it on)." He knew the generosity of this offer because he models generosity himself. Emily was, from the first meeting, the person I wanted to write for and speak with.

I have this book because of her.

Philanthropist and investor Mr Stephen A. Jarislowsky is generativity-in-action. His patronage has shaped the higher education and public service sectors in ways we may never be able to measure and yet his impact is everywhere. His insistence on maintaining the independence of the Jarislowsky chairships, insulating them from the micromanagement of university bureaucracy within which they are housed, gave me the space to build. His exhortation that we must be bolder, louder, and more responsive to combat fascism and champion human rights gave me the urgency to write. He challenged me to engage people in conversations who might not otherwise be included.

I have moral courage because of him.

Thank you to the funders of this project: the Bishop's University Research Office, SSHRC Insight Development Funding, and the Jarislowsky Foundation. This book would not be in the world without this support.

Emily Andrew @eandreweditor · Apr 19, 2022   ···
DOOR'S OPEN, AUTHORS! Want to confer about a book project, discuss the thesis-into-book transition, explore the process of writing a compelling proposal? I am available every Tuesday, 10am–1pm EST. Sign up here (and pass it on):

calendly.com
Emily Andrew
Welcome to my scheduling page. Please follow the instructions to add an event to my calendar.

♡ 2   ⇄ 21   ♡ 30   ılıl   ⤴

Dr. Jessica Riddell   ···
@DrJRiddell

Replying to @eandreweditor

Oh my goodness: thank you for this incredibly generous and generative invitation. I have signed up fir a slot in May and am so grateful for any guidance on an emerging book project called Hope University. Thanks for the nudge @dwebsterhist 🖤🖤🖤🖤🖤

8:54 AM · Apr 20, 2022

In *A Hidden Wholeness: The Journey towards an Undivided Life*, Parker Palmer talks about the "soul work done in community." He says, "When we catch sight of the soul … we are called back to our 'hidden wholeness' amid the violence of the storm." It is in community that we find the "integrity that comes from being what you are." My wealth lies in my beloved community – my dear friends who do soul work with belly laughs and open hearts, to those named above and below: Tara MacDonald, Nadine Majaess, Laura Vail, Amanda Cockburn, Andrea Drumheller, Steve Cole, Amber Rommens, Leigh Hortop-DiMascio, Kristen Moulton, Anthony DiMascio, Mike Teed, Jordan Tronsgard.

I am myself with them.

My parents raised me with bottomless love and the unrelenting belief that I could achieve whatever I set out to do – and that the best work is done in service to and for others. Their life-long commitment as volunteers and social change-makers gave me the earliest model of civic engagement and servant leadership.

I have possibility because of them.

My husband indulges me when I whine over wine – and then asks me to shake it off and make the world better. He quietly tends to the home fires because he believes I can set the world on fire. And of course, my most beloved hope warriors – my children Sophie and Henry Burns – teach me every day what it looks like to stay with the trouble, to sit in the discomfort, and to appreciate that the longer-term benefit of being broken open is to experience deep and enduring love.

I would not be me without them.

HOPE CIRCUITS

Pandemic Prologue

> We want lives of meaningful engagement, of membership in civil
> society, and how much societal effort goes into withering us away
> from these fullest, most powerful selves. But people return to those
> selves, those ways of self-organizing, as if by instinct when the
> situation demands it. Thus a disaster is a lot like a revolution when
> it comes to disruption and improvisation, to new roles and an
> unnerving or exhilarating sense that now anything is possible.
> – Rebecca Solnit[1]

This is not a book about the impact of the pandemic on post-secondary education.

This is not a book that attempts to predict what a post-pandemic university sector will resemble.

This is not a book that offers a series of prescriptions (do this) and proscriptions (do not do that).

This is a book that was written at a particular moment in time.

This is a book written at a time when the pandemic forced us to pause long enough to see the otherwise imperceptible things that surround us in new and startling ways.

This is a book that rumbles, in real time, with surfaced systems and uncomfortable truths that had hitherto been invisible or latent.

Time has its own logic in the post-secondary education (PSE) sector at the best of times: imagining the future of higher education amidst tremendous social upheaval and prophesying what is yet to come is increasingly fraught and troublesome. Moreover, when this book is published, many of the insights and contexts gleaned from the global pandemic will be outmoded.

And yet, it feels disingenuous to overlook the global pandemic because Hope University was forged during the COVID-19 lockdowns and rolling re-entries of 2020–23. Failing to acknowledge the context that gave rise to Hope University contradicts what makes this project most helpful, which is that context matters.

How does one straddle the paradox between timely and timelessness?

Shakespeare comes to the rescue.

This early modern author lived through a different pandemic and dealt with numerous outbreaks that shuttered theatres and other public gathering spaces whenever mortality rates hit epidemic thresholds.

Shakespeare knows what lockdown feels like. And yet, he rarely mentions the plague directly.[2]

How can this be?

Shakespeare offers us a body of work that is both timely and timeless because he offers us a radical invitation to participate in "gappiness."

In *This Is Shakespeare*, Oxford professor Emma Smith proposes the concept of "gappiness" as a quality of "radical uncertainty": Shakespeare's plays offer ambiguity, pose questions that are never resolved, and leave room for many holes (in motivation, plotting, or description). As spectators, we must "get in there and complete the plays in a way that works with our experience or our sense of the world."[3]

If Shakespeare gives us "a body of writing which has got room for us,"[4] Hope University also offers a spaciousness to adopt and adapt for our own diverse contexts and situatedness.

The Hope University project creates room for each of us to find what Smith calls "air holes ... that we can breathe in, we can think in, we can take part in, and that [are] only complete when we are there."

In this way, Hope University is both a mindset and a movement that is created in conversation with others who have diverse lived experiences. Just as Emma Smith suggests that Shakespeare's "plays only happen if we're there to complete them,"[5] Hope University comes into being when we can identify the conceptual tools necessary to rewire the systems within which we exist, and then apply these tools to our own practices to engage in structural change.

If Hope University offers a blueprint for a new paradigm in higher education, hope circuits are the tools we use to build it.

That is the spirit of this project.

This book does not attempt to be universal, monolithic, or comprehensive.

Instead, this is a book that makes space for gappiness.

Stay with the trouble

There is an old joke that academics write books they need to read – which certainly rings true here. I needed to write my way into hope because I struggled with despair.

COVID was a time of horror and heartbreak for so many, and the stories of individual and community grief were palpable. Writing before the pandemic, Rebecca Solnit captured the spirit when she remarked, "this is an extraordinary time full of vital, transformative movements that could not be foreseen. It's also a nightmarish time. Full engagement requires the ability to see both."[6]

COVID is inextricably bound up in the origin story for this book, which in retrospect, I can trace back to an op-ed I wrote on 1 June 2020.

In the early days of the global pandemic, I was particularly interested in how leaders – particularly higher education leaders – talked about the COVID-19 crisis. I identified two notable narratives that were circulating, which imagined very different futures and in turn exposed invisible power structures:

1 Toxic positivity
2 Critical hope

Toxic positivity promises us that everything is going to be okay. We are encouraged to shelter in place to eventually return to "business as usual" and look back on the global pandemic with a twinge of nostalgia for pajama pants and pandemic puppies. Likewise, we are reassured that life will return to normal in no time – that our institutions can pivot seamlessly to online delivery without diluting the student experience if we stick together and look for the silver linings.

Critical hope acknowledges that the world as we know it is changing rapidly. We ask ourselves how we might remake a world that is more just, equitable, and inclusive, while acknowledging that our institutions cannot "pivot" easily because changing technology without changing mindsets (e.g., moving to online delivery without reflecting on pedagogy) transforms relationships – and with them our ability to connect meaningfully. We double down on collaboration and community just as we understand that silver linings are rarely afforded to the most vulnerable and marginalized populations. We are willing to open ourselves up to imagine a new model of education that moves us into a future that is better than our present and more humane than our past.

Toxic positivity effaces conflict and does not allow room for disagreement or discontent. This narrative denies that we are in the midst of radical transformation and advocates for a return to normalcy. In contrast, critical hope understands complexity and discomfort as a necessary transformation process and holds spaces for candid and uncomfortable conversations as a way forward. This narrative recognizes that "normal" was a system based on inequity and injustice that benefitted a privileged few.

One narrative threatens to break us apart because it denies the fact of our transformation. The other narrative offers us a way to be broken open, to occupy the position of learner, to embrace empathy, and to relinquish authority in favour of collaboration – with students, colleagues, and communities.

Theorizing these two narratives was not merely a pedagogical or professional exercise. It was deeply personal.

In March 2020, as the world was shutting down, my forty-something-year-old husband (a smoothie-drinking, salad-eating former varsity athlete) was diagnosed with lung cancer. In a strange twist of fate, the path to a diagnosis began the day public schools closed in our region for the first time due to COVID: our small children (at that time four and six years old) were sent home abruptly, and the world as we knew it changed irrevocably overnight.

Toxic positivity and critical hope were not merely an intellectual exercise; rather, they were narratives I oscillated between as I figured out how to talk to our kids about what was happening. It would have been easier to erase their (and our) discomfort with reassuring platitudes. I wondered: if I said "everything is going to be fine" enough times, maybe I could believe it too? It was much harder to be candid and careful about making room for not knowing all the answers.

Perhaps because children are in a constant state of transformation, our kids responded calmly and with curiosity to the messiness and disorientation – and trusted us enough to believe we could live in the questions and eventually live into the answers together.

They taught me everything I know about hope as something you do as a daily practice.

Stay with the trouble

In her *Dare to Lead* podcast, Brené Brown asks all her conversation partners the same question: what lesson does the universe ask you to learn repeatedly? One of my (many) lessons is the reminder that despair is not the antithesis of hope; rather, that it is a critical component of hope circuits.

Right before the 2020 lockdown, my co-authors Lisa Dickson and Shannon Murray and I had just finished the first draft of a book on critical hope and Shakespeare. We were jubilant – even smug – with our shiny new theoretical frameworks for critical hope, critical empathy, and critical love. The trinity of virtues we could identify in Shakespeare's canon unlocked the plays and our classrooms while also making room for new scholarly voices where we could finally sound like ourselves.

It was a heady time.

And then the universe intervened.

The confluence of personal and global disruptions tested my theoretical frameworks to their limits. I howled into the abyss – a lot. I hid under the covers. And then I re-read the manuscript for *Shakespeare's Guide to Hope, Life, and Learning* and found that critical hope, critical love, and critical empathy were robust in the midst of trauma and became a crucial lifeline.

On 1 June 2020, as my husband was on the operating table having a lobectomy to remove a large tumour, I started writing my way into hope – and what would become *Hope Circuits*. As I finish this manuscript, I am not much closer to a final destination as much as I am clearer on the value of the journey. This book, rather than striving to be complete, aspires to be a conversation starter, an entry point, a different starting place for discussions that already have long genealogies – of hope and purpose, systems and individuals, higher education and society.

Quaker philosopher Parker Palmer says that "wholeness does not mean perfection, it means embracing brokenness as an integral part of your life."[7] Thus, this book has, by design (and by accident), many gaps, holes, and oversights; rather than pursuing perfection, this project might help us consider embracing the brokenness of ourselves and the systems within which we are immersed as a whole-hearted invitation rather than an indictment.

It will always be imperfect because we are imperfect.

Surface the systems

I interviewed hundreds of people in the making of this book, and one of my favourite aspects of being in conversation with diverse thought partners was the beauty of the rumble. I discovered this concept on my long walks during COVID lockdown when I began listening to the *Daring to Lead* podcast series from American social worker Brené Brown. She defines "rumbling" in the following way:

> A rumble is a discussion, conversation, or meeting defined by a commitment to lean into vulnerability, to stay curious and generous, to stick with the messy middle of problem identification and solving, to take a break and circle back when necessary, to be fearless in owning our parts, and, as psychologist Harriet Lerner teaches, to listen with the same passion with which we want to be heard. More than anything else, when someone says, "Let's rumble," it cues me to show up with an open heart and mind so we can serve the work and each other, not our egos.[8]

My interview style was profoundly informed by the rumble, where I endeavoured to sit in a learner position, holding my opinions lightly and my values firmly, willing to be convinced, persuaded, transformed in conversation with humans who shared a commitment to generosity and generativity. As we rumbled – on Zoom, via email, through Teams, on Twitter – I had to decentre and recentre what I thought I knew and what I sought to learn in every conversation.

This process knocked me on my butt regularly as I confronted the limits and parameters of this project. As one of my thought partners, Canadian university president Jeff Hennessy, notes,

> Well I think maybe the limitation [of your book] is also a boundary. You are working on systems. That is very valuable work. The X factor of course is that people are people with their own triumphs, disappointments, traumas etc. and every system has individuals as inputs; this means every pathway is individual. We can create the most supportive system in the world and someone still may not be able to flourish because they have individual work to do.[9]

Yes.

And.

We have individual and institutional work to do and recognizing the people factor is paramount. This is why an investment in compassion, consent, and community is so important both as individual acts and as a collective mindset. The responsibility as individuals to reflect, rewire, and renew, and how that work interacts within and informs higher level systems, is a tension that runs throughout the book.

There are many philosophical traditions that seek to reconcile the individual and the collective that would take us beyond the scope of this project; what this project necessitates, however, is a relentless commitment to humanity and its infinite capacities to create systems that recognize individual sovereignty and self-determination while also binding us together in symbiosis. *Ubuntu*, a concept popularized by South African spiritual leader Archbishop Desmond Tutu, offers us a valuable model of social connectedness:

> Ubuntu is the essence of being human. It speaks of how my humanity is caught up and bound up inextricably with yours … I can be me only if you are fully you. I am because we are, for we are made for togetherness, for family. We are made for complementarity. We are created for

a delicate network of relationships, of interdependence with our fellow human beings, with the rest of creation.[10]

This belief in humanity finds many expressions and finds resonance with the fourteenth Dalai Lama's teachings:

Real change in the world will only come from a change of heart. What I propose is a compassionate revolution, a call for radical reorientation away from our habitual preoccupation with the self. It is a call to turn toward the wider community of beings with whom we are connected, and for conduct which recognizes others' interests alongside our own.[11]

COVID gave us a master class in interdependency. None of us live in isolation from one another or from the systems within which we are immersed, systems that are largely invisible until they stop working. The global pandemic invited (and sometimes forced) us to engage in radical reorientation.

What got me out of bed every morning was the invitation from South Asian author and Booker Prize winner Arundhati Roy to locate choice over stagnation and helplessness. In an op-ed published in the *Financial Times* on 1 April 2020, Roy challenged us to think about COVID as a portal:

Coronavirus has made the mighty kneel and brought the world to a halt like nothing else could. Our minds are still racing back and forth, longing for a return to "normality," trying to stitch our future to our past and refusing to acknowledge the rupture. But the rupture exists. And in the midst of this terrible despair, it offers us a chance to rethink the doomsday machine we have built for ourselves. Nothing could be worse than a return to normality. Historically, pandemics have forced humans to break with the past and imagine their world anew. This one is no different. It is a portal, a gateway between one world and the next. We can choose to walk through it, dragging the carcasses of our prejudice and hatred, our avarice, our data banks and dead ideas, our dead rivers and smoky skies behind us. Or we can walk through lightly, with little luggage, ready to imagine another world. And ready to fight for it.[12]

The portal offers us a metaphor for crossing from one state of being into another. As we grapple with paradigmatic change – at different rates and with varying degrees of rupture to our social institutions – we can choose to transform with all the discomfort that change necessitates. The challenge becomes, how do we remain attentive to our current conditions, become more mindful about the systems and structures that no longer serve us and others, and be willing to fight for systems that foster human, ecological, and inter-species flourishing? Arundhati Roy asks us to summon the courage to walk through a portal and to imagine what is possible.

What the world looks like on the other side is up to us.

Build intentional community

This book project would not have emerged if the world had not gone into lockdown. Many of us reached out as we were shut in, seeking the balm of human connection in virtual spaces. Pinned to the present moment with others who were also processing radical reorientation, the façade of the everyday fell away, and we had conversations that were tender and vulnerable, raw and unprocessed, candid and unfiltered.

Amid my disorientation, I started writing my way out of despair and into Hope University. However, writing alone was not enough: I needed to be in a dynamic and ongoing conversation for Hope University to be more than just a thought project.

As Brené Brown says, "stories are data with a soul."[13]

Therefore, I set about gathering stories.

My first port of call was to rumble with partners across the Maple League of Universities, a consortium of four primarily undergraduate universities in Eastern Canada. As the executive director, I had spent the two years before the pandemic focused on building communities of practice: people with shared professional or disciplinary kinship met regularly to benchmark, share leading practices, and howl into the abyss in equal measure. From IT to athletic directors, registrars to VPs of student affairs, these thoughtful humans met in safe and brave spaces to talk about what kept them up at night and what got them out of bed in the morning.

Conversations extended into sessions with the three Maple League committees – academic, research, and teaching and learning – that had broad representation from faculty and staff with interdisciplinary and intergenerational perspectives. From there, I started interviewing award-winning educational leaders across the four universities in a series of one-on-one interviews about Hope University.

In these focus groups, I provided people with a primer and a series of thought prompts:

- How do we align values and practices so that universities fulfill their social contract to the broader society?
- How do we design hopeful and resilient systems for ourselves and others?
- What are the uncomfortable truths and discomfort we need to sit with to transform?
- Where do we fall on the spectrum of "no need to panic" on one end and "existential crisis" on the other?
- Have you ever wondered about what it might look like to start a brand-new university? What would it look like? What would we teach and learn? Who would we hire? How would we govern? How would we research?
- And what happens when we realize we don't have the luxury of a brand-new model? What does it look like to inherit and then renovate existing systems?

By engaging in conversations that took a deep dive into the local and the disciplinary, the visionary and the practical, I gathered a myriad of insights and strategies that formed the basis of this book.

I then started to reach out to people beyond the Maple League to interview university presidents, provosts, junior faculty, educational leaders, 3M National Teaching Fellows, undergraduate students, and staff members. As my thinking deepened, I started to ask more specific questions related to the topics that animated the chapters – rumbling on governance or leadership, teaching or funding – and that harnessed the interests and expertise of my interviewees.

In a parallel project on failure, Arctic researcher Pat Maher, also a 3M National Teaching Fellow, and I started interviewing national teaching fellows from Canada and around the world to understand the relationship between failure and hope. Talking with people from South Africa, New Zealand, the UK, and Sweden helped me think more deeply about universities' roles in democratic societies. We asked this group the following questions:

- Tell us your story – how did you get here?
- What keeps you up at night and/or what gets you out of bed in the morning? (And are they the same thing?)
- How do we identify the sources of hope and its shadow value, despair?
- If you could build Hope University, what would it look like?
- Can you talk to us about your relationship with failure and if/how you've grown from those experiences?
- How do these two concepts – of failure and hope – overlap/interact for you?
- How would you position vulnerability in your experiences (work, leadership, classroom, life, etc.)? What leads you to growth/hope in relation to failure and vulnerability?
- Has any of this changed from pre-COVID, to present circumstances, to post-COVID?

In addition to one-on-one interviews, I hosted focus groups and summits in virtual spaces. When we returned to in-person gatherings I led pre-conference workshops and delivered presentations at international conferences that rumbled on these questions in different contexts.

The idea of hope circuits – the tools we need to build Hope University – emerged when I delivered a series of keynotes and plenaries in June 2022. In these talks I was able to kick the tires on these concepts in real time with hundreds of people in communal gathering spaces to see what resonated – and what did not.

My research team – made up of undergraduate students and recent graduates – worked on a bibliography dashboard to ensure this project engaged with various voices, scholars, perspectives, and experiences. As a list of conceptual tools developed, I consulted previous thought partners and sought new ones to rumble and reflect. I asked regularly, whose voices am I missing, what have I overlooked, what gaps do I need to fill?

I tested the conceptual tools in my classes, in committees, at conferences, and in less formal spaces – over a beer, on a walk, during a school drop-off, in hallways, and at playgrounds and community pools. I reached out to people I knew and to perfect strangers via Twitter, email, texts, and Teams chats. And as these chapters emerged, I shared the rough drafts with generous humans, from all ages and stages, who guided me in innumerable ways.

And all the while I kept revising and reflecting, rumbling and reporting.

Commit to unlearning and relearning

Conversations with more than three hundred people generated one thousand pages of transcripts that captured the silly and serious, playful and pedantic, tearful and boisterous. Nothing was off limits. And nothing was wasted. This project was animated by the stories and souls of so many hopeful humans.

What struck me in the interviews was that the return to work and "normality" exposed several pain points we will have to process and reconcile for many years. The uneven social and institutional responses to the pandemic, and the varying degrees in the ethics of care for our communities, meant that latent feelings came to the surface in conversation. Holding space for that discomfort was both a privilege and a responsibility to ensure that we design better systems for human flourishing.

When we did deep dives into the despair and discomfort, it was increasingly clear from the interviews that COVID-19 was not the cause of our discomfort; instead, it was a reckoning. Even as we "go back to normal" – and our selves and systems try to spring back to pre-pandemic default settings – the interviewees were clear that there is no return. Rather, we must move forward – with the hope Rebecca Solnit articulates of "new roles and an unnerving or exhilarating sense that now anything is possible."[14]

One key takeaway from my interviews was a deepening appreciation of consent – and how to build it into every time we gather.[15]

This book is animated by consent as I gathered multiple voices in the interviewing and writing process. The named interviewees provided enthusiastic consent for their quotations and the context within which their words appear. I anonymized many contributions to honour confidentiality, to make room for candid comments, and to mitigate the risk for those brave souls who said the quiet parts aloud. I cited contributors in the summits and public events we hosted and where the material is shared in the public domain. There were a few examples where three or more comments offering the same or similar insights were combined and anonymized to provide a vignette of a common or shared perspective. With more than one thousand pages of transcripts, rich material has been left out but will continue to inform future books in this series as we build, prototype, and reflect on hope circuits in conversation with others.

Exercising consent, paired with critical empathy, feels more urgent in the work ahead as we rebuild intentional communities that are healthy, inclusive, and just. John D. Caputo defines empathy as a way of doing relationships, making "community with the unknowable other" that recognizes our "common strangeness" in which "we concede that we do not know each other, and that, because of this, we can only speak *to* each other, not *about* each other."[16]

Therefore, we included quotations from interviews in text boxes to highlight distinct voices without paraphrasing or editorializing them. I wanted to preserve the energy and insights of these contributions, which offer an added dimension to the main argument within which they live. I wanted to emphasize, in textual form, the importance of polyvocality and the richness of conversation, including digressions, divergences, and disagreement. The space in conversation created between and amongst interlocuters is, after all, where the magic happens.

The conceptual tools that emerged and were tested in the global pandemic will serve us in new spaces as we reconfigure social institutions at the systems level.

This is not a book about the impact of the pandemic on post-secondary education.

This is a book that was made possible by the pandemic.

This is a project built in gappiness.

Hope circuits take us from a moment to a mindset into a movement. The work of building new paradigms for higher education amid rupture is daring even as it is daunting. The good news is that so many humans are already doing this work; finding the connections and convergences will be essential for building new and yet unimagined worlds.

American civil rights activist Loretta Ross defines "a group of people thinking the same thing and moving in the same direction [as] a cult. A group of people thinking different things and moving in the same direction is a movement."[17]

Let's build a movement.

Chapter 1

How Do We Hope? An Introduction

You do not rise to the level of your goals. You fall to the level
of your systems.
James Clear[1]

We now find ourselves at the precipice of a higher-education paradigm shift.

After many years of incremental change and deferral, we need substantial change. What we do now will inform how we, as individuals, institutions, and society, experience revolutionary change. It is an extraordinary time that challenges us to go back to the fundamentals and ask:

What is higher education?

What is the social contract universities have with a broader society?

And, how can we fulfill this contract at the systems- and sector-wide levels?

Canadian university president David Sylvester argues that universities are anchors of hope in our communities.[2]

I agree.

The university is a provocative system to study. Universities are complex organizational systems with robust social missions to a democratic society: rewiring systems for flourishing will enable us to better fulfill this social contract at a time when human and biotic spheres are endangered.

As members of the academy, we are hard-wired for hope – to teach it, to share it, and to imagine a better future.

The central metaphor of this book – hope circuits – relies heavily on the concept of electrical circuits and was originally inspired by the work of American psychologist Martin Seligman and neuroscientist Steven Maier, who were curious about mapping electrical pathways in the brain with its complex neural networks. Metaphor invites us to imagine the superimposable possibilities of how multiple systems operate simultaneously; if we can understand the logic of how an electrical circuit is wired, how a brain uses wiring to transmit information that shapes behaviour, and by extension how we live and work within systems that wire us in certain ways, then we can begin to illuminate where and how we might go about rewiring systems for human flourishing.

We need to peel back the façade and get into the walls. That is where hope circuits are activated.

Those with experience in relational, human-centred organizations that have a social purpose and fiscal constraints – government, not-for-profits, corporate sectors, or other K–12 educational systems – might also find the thought prompts in this book resonate or discover some of the conceptual tools come in handy to support organizational change in their own contexts.

We can all ask:

What does it look like if we can build hopeful systems where individuals and communities flourish?

The work ahead constitutes a brand of hope that is inexorably difficult, unrelentingly hard.

Birthing new paradigms is the work of hard hope. And it is, fundamentally, an act of love.

What the new paradigm looks like is not yet clear. We are in the early stages of emergence that will only come into focus in retrospect. Nevertheless, when we have adequate tools, mindset, and purpose to design better systems, we can claim a degree of agency in determining what this new paradigm looks like. To do so, we must be willing to surface the rot, stay with the trouble, and build our capacities for daring imagination: this is what a commitment to rewiring for systemic flourishing looks like.

We are overdue for a new model: what shape will it take?

When I think about the paradigmatic shifts occurring in higher education and in other sectors, I am struck by a meme that is making the rounds on social media: "The person who invented electricity did so by candlelight."

When you delve into the origin story of electricity, this is a tale of incremental discoveries over a long period of time by many people (which includes a scandalous footnote about Nikola Tesla's love of a white pigeon he wished to marry). Small, incremental changes accumulated over time until a tipping point ushered forth a revolutionary, innovative technology.

The invention of an entirely new paradigm was achieved without existing frameworks: it had to be imagined. And then it had to be created.

Nothing really changed until it *really* did.

We are building a new and yet-to-be articulated paradigm in higher education. How much influence we have in determining what that might look like requires diverse people from different spheres willing to occupy learner positions, sit in the discomfort of transformation, and imagine something new and reconfigured.

We need luminous thinkers willing to rewire systems – and themselves – in the process.

Members of universities are some of the best-trained and best-wired humans to do this work of systems-level renewal and re-invention. The irony, though, is that while many of us entered the academy as messy, emergent, curious learners, over time the systems have dismembered people by reinforcing siloed thinking and compartmentalization. Indeed, Parker Palmer, in *The Courage to Teach*, reflects,

> Academics often suffer the pain of dismemberment. On the surface, this is the pain of the people who thought they were joining a community of scholars but find themselves in distant, competitive, and uncaring relationships with colleagues and students. Deeper down, this pain is more spiritual than sociological: it comes from being disconnected to our own truth, from the passion that took us into teaching, from the heart that is the source of all good work.[3]

Many of our existing systems have disconnections between institutional values and what we incentivize and reward. The antidote to dismemberment is a re-membering of our selves and our origins as learners illuminated by wonder and curiosity. "Re-membering" works against the siloed thinking that has divided our work into parts, and instead moves us towards wholeness and incorporation.[4] This approach is informed by Quaker philosopher

Parker Palmer, who also reminds us that wholeness does not mean perfection; instead, it is an invitation to embrace brokenness.

While Parker Palmer's invitation resonates at an individual level, we must also extend this to organizational and sector-wide spheres if we are to build greater possibilities for change. This project is predicated on a deep and abiding faith in the capacity of the individual – as a coherent and viable entity capable of self-determination and collective action animated by ideals and driven by purpose – that must be paired with systems-level thinking about how institutional structures impose rules and conventions that shape behaviours. Understanding how systems operate – and how they create order and determine interaction between otherwise diverse or distinct components that produces behaviours over time – is worthy of our attention as we undergo paradigmatic shifts in the social institutions that both reflect and shape our communities.

As American First Lady "Lady Bird" Johnson reflected in 1968, "I know that the nature we are concerned with ultimately is human nature. That is the point of the beautification movement, and that finally is the point of architecture. Winston Churchill said, 'First we shape our buildings, and then they shape us.' The same is true of our highways, our parks, our public buildings, the environment we create. They shape us."[5]

Systems are not neutral: they form and inform behaviours, mindsets, actions, and perspectives – often for the better and sometimes for the worse. It is tricky to figure out how systems are wired, where the disconnects are, when we need circuit breakers, and what rewiring must occur so that our journeys as individuals and institutions are purposeful and just.

Some of the best guides on this journey are students: as they navigate systems, they encounter the structural barriers and opportunities that have become internalized and often invisible to those of us who have been in these systems longer. Students have powerful lived experiences and can model for us the exhilaration and exhaustion of reconfiguring and reconstituting selves and structures. Looking with fresh eyes at aging systems gives us new ways of understanding ourselves, our disciplinary fields, and our organizations.

To move past what is rotten at the systems level, we must be willing to re-member and unlearn.

To decolonize the systems we have inherited and internalized, we must re-member and unlearn.

For our institutions to help solve wicked problems, we must re-member and unlearn.

As we live in the questions, we live our way into building Hope University.

This book, the first in a series, identifies tools to create hope circuits in your own contexts. It is an invitation to build, illuminate, dream, and scheme towards Hope University. The challenge ahead is understanding the forces that converge upon us in this moment, finding the tools necessary to build a new mindset, and creating an intentional community where we inspire a movement.

What Kind of Book Is This?

Do I contradict myself?
Very well then, I contradict myself,
(I am large, I contain multitudes.)
…
Looking with side-curved head curious what will come next,
Both in and out of the game and watching and wondering at it.
– Walt Whitman[1]

Who could possibly be an expert on hope?

In the process of writing this book, I talked myself into and out of the project many times. Who has the audacity, I often wonder (usually at 3 a.m.), to undertake such a project? No single person could claim the experience, knowledge, insight, and creativity necessary to understand a university's complex and multi-faceted structures, much less be able to identify the design principles and levers of change to renovate and renew the broken systems we have inherited. A singular person cannot accomplish this Herculean feat nor would it be an interesting or helpful read.

The prospect of writing a book on Hope University has felt Sisyphean.

Whitman's poem appeared just as I had talked myself into imposter syndrome for the umpteenth time. Books and poems often have a habit of finding us when we are most in need of insight or guidance. I found myself at a critical juncture, and these lines captured the in-between spaces we occupy when we write about systems we live within: critical reflection requires us to be "both in and out of the game" with attentiveness and curiosity. And with a love big enough to challenge a social institution we cherish to be better.

Whitman asks us to live in "Yes. And."

So, what kind of book is this?

A book proposal submitted to an editor for review might read something like this:

> The Hope University project is animated by a combination of thought pieces, interviews with a wide range of partners, research (applied, theoretical, literary, grounded), and practical advice. However, most importantly, this project represents people in conversation with one another. As such, this project is inspired by hopeful and resilient leaders, learners, and community clusters in the post-secondary sector that dare to reimagine high-quality education for a twenty-second-century context.

Yes. And. It is more than this.

The book contains multitudes, contradictions, and competing opinions, because the people I interviewed are themselves under development, contradictory, and perfectly imperfect.

Just as I am. Just as our systems are.

When ideas are put in conversation with one another, we create something greater than the sum of its parts, countering assimilation in favour of collision and convergence. It is nothing short of radical to work in communion with others, to build hopeful and resilient systems where individuals flourish because the structures and policies are designed for thriving, not surviving.

This book weaves together conversations with thought partners through formal interviews (one-on-one, panel discussions, focus groups), communal events (campus tours, town halls, talks and workshops, keynotes and plenaries), engaging communities of practice (through strategic visioning, regular meetings, benchmarking), and teaching (engaging students through content, problem-based learning, summits, and work-integrated learning experiences).

I have had the privilege of listening to and conversing with hundreds of humans as we dreamed and schemed our way into hope.

And, I realized relatively late into this project, I spent five years unwittingly building Hope University with a diverse range of guides, mentors, collaborators, and possibility models as the executive director of the Maple League of Universities (an academic consortium of four primarily undergraduate universities in Eastern Canada). In this role, I had a unique opportunity to listen intently to a range of people whose experiences cut across disciplines and departments, silos and services. I had the privilege of seeing the inside of four universities. I sat at tables and gained insights into how policies, systems, and structures operate and how they inform, shape, and reflect deep cultures. I have benefitted from a master class in policy development and implementation.

The dynamic simultaneity of seeing four universities in action at once – as they all pursued differentiation and authenticity – has been extraordinary. Working with partners as diverse as faculty and staff, students and alumni, presidents and provosts, registrars and deans, directors of athletics and information technology, leads in student affairs and recruitment, has been revelatory. The experience has offered me a nuts-and-bolts understanding of systems – and constraints – and a greater understanding of how universities strive to fulfill their mandate to contribute to the broader society. All the while trying – in some cases literally – to keep the lights on.

While the four universities I worked with are especially precarious (they have resisted national trends of massification and stayed small at their financial peril), scarcity resonates for all Canadian universities and colleges: financial exigency is now a present and real danger.

Later I will outline, at length, the downsides of working within institutions that have experienced long-term, chronic austerity. Nevertheless, I have seen some of the most generous and generative examples of what hopeful practice can look like in research, teaching, and educational leadership. Despite (and sometimes because of) narratives of scarcity and crisis, I have seen what happens when space is carved out for abundance.

Indeed, an abundance mindset drives innovation and creativity. In the interstitial spaces of four universities, I have sought out the outliers, innovators, and early adopters who are often creating things *despite* – not *because of* – the conditions within which they are working. Together we have beta-tested concepts, designed projects and initiatives, and facilitated structural change through diverse communities of practice. The insights yielded by superimposing four universities onto a wider landscape of higher education would not have been possible had I been constrained to work within one institution's structures or operate within a singular, unique ecosystem.

So, some readers might still be wondering, what exactly is this book?

At its core, it is an open-hearted invitation to dream and scheme, imagine and build, challenge and reflect, illuminate and invent.

It is a decentring and reorientation of systems and structures to look with fresh eyes at old systems.

It is building the architecture for a new paradigm of higher education that is only just emerging.

It is a calling in, at a critical juncture, to walk gently and bravely into a future that takes a systems-level approach to human flourishing.

This book is a collection of short essays. Each essay takes, as its starting point, a central question, which is then explored through theoretical frameworks, research, literary and historical lenses, and multiple voices in conversation with one another.

Hope Circuits is a *bricolage*, a term drawn from French anthropologist Claude Lévi-Strauss who suggests we reuse available resources and artefacts to solve new problems.

Hope Circuits is an *essai* inspired by the spirit of sixteenth-century French writer Michel de Montaigne and his invention of the essay as a genre whose core function is "to attempt."

Hope Circuits is a culmination of many disciplines and fields – formal and informal, traditional and emerging, established and irreverent – to invite in multiple and sometimes contradictory perspectives that, ideally, free up our thinking and engage us in the imaginative, curious, and creative work necessary for the task at hand.

In a time when our attention spans are limited and our bandwidth is spotty, this book is designed so that readers can pick it up with curiosity and browse a chapter. Each chapter is a stand-alone piece that can be read in any order, and yet, when read in its entirety, the book provides the conceptual tools necessary to conceive a plan for your own space and place – to create a blueprint for a new paradigm.

This book, therefore, aims to empower readers as social architects in creating renewed and rewired systems.

I will draw on, for inspiration and guidance, a diverse body of authors and artists that includes writers like Marie Battiste, Audre Lorde, James Baldwin, Parker Palmer, and many others. There are books dedicated to hope that I rely upon heavily, especially from bell hooks and Paulo Freire – both of whom authored books with *Pedagogy of Hope* in their titles. I also turn to books on hope in higher education, such as *Radical Hope* by American historian Kevin Gannon and those written by activist writers such as *Hope in the Dark* by American essayist Rebecca Solnit.

Hope – as an essential human quality – lives in many places and means many things. As such, this is not a comprehensive book of hope nor will it provide a history of hope. This book is about rewiring hope circuits so we can *do* hope within the spaces we inhabit.

Later in this chapter I introduce the critical framework for hope not via an academic definition or a theoretical lens; instead, we begin with a poem. Emily Dickinson's metaphor of a bird is an invitation to pause, reflect, and engage in affective experience. Since this project seeks to rewire, which by extension asks us to reimagine ways of being and doing in the academy, metaphors are a crucial conceptual tool. We approach old ideas with fresh eyes when we create correlational meaning through metaphor.

Post-critical hope

When we use old tools to address new problems, anomalies arise that expose the current status quo as unsustainable and untenable. How we engage with one another in the creation and sharing of knowledge is worth serious consideration as we decolonize Western knowledge and value different ways of knowing.

American sociologist Eboo Patel laments that universities train people in the pursuit of "telling other people what they are doing wrong." Patel argues that "right now, we have enough critics. What we need are more builders, more people who know how to create concrete instantiations of a fair, just and inclusive social order."[2]

Many are already moving into a post-critical state of knowledge making. American writing instructor John Warner theorizes the difference between an illuminator and a debater in a Twitter thread: he defines "an illuminator" as someone who "is interested in shining a light on a phenomenon in order to increase the sum total of our collective understanding of that phenomenon." A debater, in contrast, "wants to 'win' an argument, winning being gauged by moving people toward your position, or receiving approval or what have you. Winning may require obscuring as much or more than illuminating."[3]

In building a social movement, we must acknowledge that we cannot build new systems that address the complexities of our reality through specialized language that alienates the very humans with whom we need to partner. Similarly, we cannot afford *not* to build at all. Thus, we must understand building and illumination in tandem.

Warner gives us a framework for understanding new ways of knowledge creation and sharing: "The biggest difference between an illuminator and a debater is that the debater is trying to get you to adopt their judgement and opinion as your own. The illuminator is trying to better arm you to figure stuff out for yourself. Illuminators want you to think." With a systems-level approach, Warner points out, "illumination would almost certainly reveal a complex, more nuanced situation likely involving some measure of institutional failure."[4]

When reading Warner, I ask myself, "Have students inherited a legacy of illumination in my classrooms? Or, have I replicated the debate-centric model instilled in me as an undergraduate?"

My hope is the former. And, if I commit to staying with the trouble, I must admit that unintentionally (and sometimes intentionally), I have trained students to debate, deconstruct, and dismantle. We reward them for producing often scathing critiques of arguments that have come before. I have unreflectively reproduced systems that never truly served me and no longer serve students.

We have all witnessed the negative consequences of a debater-centric academic milieu.

When I was in graduate school, we were expected to all show up for the tenure-stream job talks. An ancient Anglo-Saxonist would sit in the front row, take off his shoes, rub his feet on the carpet, and promptly fall asleep. When the question period rolled around, he would rouse himself rather noisily and ask – unfailingly – a question on etymology. He designed his question – cruel in its worst iterations, ungenerous at best – to challenge the foundation of the job candidate's argument on what he considered an incorrect use of a word or phrase. "Checkmate!" you could almost hear him chortle to himself. The candidate had no recourse: respond with frustration and the department would close ranks; respond with curiosity and the department would dismiss the candidate as too soft.

As a graduate student, I watched and internalized these harmful practices, terrified of the prospect of ever being in the job candidate's position.

My anecdote is not particularly original. It has become cliché. It has become the stuff of satirical fiction surrounding academic job candidates and the search for that increasingly elusive tenure-track job.

If our systems reward an insatiable appetite for debate and critique-centric models, they also have, consequentially, marginalized and punished the illuminators who think, write, and research differently. How knowledge is valued and rewarded in the current system runs counter to the promises we make for post-secondary education: to build a society of future leaders.

There is, as Shakespeare cautions us, something rotten in the state of Denmark.

When oppositional arguments and methodologies are deployed for the sole purpose of winning an argument rather than coming to a greater understanding, we are capable of violent rhetoric and real harm.

And yet, in Aristotelian terms, rhetoric has the power to engage everyone in debate to reach greater understanding and illumination. As Canadian journalist and long-time thought partner Royal Orr reflects,

> I suspect what we're aiming at is a "debate" that challenges participants to persuade with *ethos* more than with *pathos* or *logos* (though these need to be marshalled as well) and to attempt to show to an audience "where they're coming from" (my favorite translation of *ethos* as a rhetorical proof). And beyond that, I think the emphasis within *ethos* discourse (in A[ristotle]'s three-way division of it) would be on *eunoia* [good will] as opposed to *arete* [virtue] and *phronesis* [wisdom]. A debate that was aimed at participants creating *eunoia* with their audience ("beautiful thinking" or "the seeds of friendship") would be radically different in aim and experience.[5]

Rigorous arguments are still needed to build Hope University, and the book engages in research, scholarship, and literary criticism and deploys various forms of evidence to make the case that we can and should rewire our systems from a starting point of human flourishing rather than from a foundational premise of unfettered growth or transaction. Universities are overrun with neoliberal ideas and commercialized assumptions that deserve careful and sustained critiques.

Nevertheless, criticism alone cannot usher in new ways of being driven by social mission and vision. As such, this project focuses on the building side of hope instead of critical deconstruction as a primary strategy. Put differently, we must teach students – and learn ourselves – how to design timely, equitable systems with robust hope circuits.

Appetite for change

Are we courageous enough to take action?

Are our institutional systems strategically and sustainably conceived to stay with the trouble and be willing to transform?

It depends on whom you ask. As you will see in this project, I have asked many people. One of the emerging themes is the increasing awareness that we need to shift our focus from resilience at an individual level to a systems-wide approach that imagines a renewed focus for higher education.

Otherwise, as James Clear reminds us, "You do not rise to the level of your goals. You fall to the level of your systems."[6]

Yes.

And.

Change-resistant narratives are plentiful, and one can imagine sceptics and critics chiming in here to say something along the lines of, "operations, implementation timelines, annual budgets, and pressing issues make this concept of hope all very well and good but not pragmatic. We don't have time."

This book is not for them.

Or, more precisely, this book is not engaged in combat with critics who start from a place of cynicism or skepticism without an intention of being transformed; instead, this book is in conversation with builders and illuminators, people willing to work along edges and in margins as we navigate the seismic shift our sector (and society more generally) is experiencing.

I have had to suppress the desire to write this book defensively and in response to attacks from the realists and cynics whose voices I hear as I write. I have had to unlearn my scholarly training that anticipates a refutation at every turn; I have had to resist my impulse to shore up every statement with counterarguments and footnotes; I have had to catch myself every time I was tempted to flex my expertise or weaponize complex theories or write in esoteric language or bombard imagined detractors with a million citations.

By design, the holes in this book are places where the reader can breathe into, think into, dream into. In any endeavour that seeks to invent electricity by candlelight, imperfection and incompletion are features, not flaws. As such, this book leaves room for the "gappiness" discussed in the prologue.

I will say this:

Yes: we need to be fiscally responsible, accountable, and transparent – and I explore this in greater detail in the chapter "How Do We Fund."

And: we cannot use financial sustainability as an excuse for diluting the social contract we have with communities or at the expense of the health of individuals.

Moreover, the challenge ahead invites us to adopt a mindset of abundance and possibility even as we acknowledge the realities of scarcity and declining funding in the existing systems.

The rhetoric of building resilient universities cannot simply be a euphemism for financial sustainability so often deployed to justify spending cuts or reliance on a precarious workforce. We have relied for too long on a system whose financial survival necessitates asking individuals to work harder under deteriorating conditions. We need to stop the double-speak of strategic plans with taglines like "Growth with Focus"[7] that thinly disguise blood-on-the floor budgets.

Moreover, what does a system look like where we eradicate the need to talk about individual grit or academic buoyancy because the systems are designed to be hospitable, inclusive, and built for human flourishing?

I want to live into that question.

American scholar and emergent strategist adrienne maree brown works on paradigm shifts and has this to say: "'Octavia [Butler] said '[t]here's nothing new / under the sun, / but there are new suns.' We are in a time of new suns. We have no idea what we could be, but everything that we have *been* is falling apart. So it's time to change."

adrienne maree brown also reminds us that "emergence is our inheritance as a part of the universe; it is how we change."

In this context, she challenges us to practise "radical imagination" by asking, "what does it look like to imagine beyond the constructs? What does it look like to imagine a future where we all get to be there, not causing harm to each other, and experiencing abundance?"[8]

We can work our way across microcosms of classrooms to mesocosms of curriculum and middle management to macrocosms of the institutions to the ecosystem of the post-secondary education sector to ask, How can our systems and structures actively facilitate flourishing?

What this book is NOT

It is important to highlight what this book is NOT: it is not a comprehensive plan or an authoritative guide to building a new bricks-and-mortar university. Neither is this a purely theoretical exercise. Moreover, this book will overlook countless angles and aspects of running a university.

My intersectionality – as a white, cis-gendered settler, a mother of two young children, educated with a PhD in Shakespeare grounded in Western traditions, and employed as a full professor at a primarily undergraduate university in rural Quebec, Canada – means I will not be the expert on many things. Nevertheless, that is the very reason why this book might be helpful.

I am not the expert.

I am not an expert in hope or systems thinking or organizational behaviour.

I am something else, though. I am an insatiable learner.

And being a learner is a superhero power that we can summon as we stretch the limits of our known knowledge and endeavour to peek over the edge into the unknown with wonder and curiosity.

Instead of a book about solutions, this is a how-to guide to develop the conceptual tools to rewire circuitry – in our selves and our systems – that can issue forth Hope University.

There is more work to be done on systemic hope via topics such as sustainable funding and finances, recruitment and retention, internationalization and global competencies, faculty associations and collective bargaining, and a host of worthy topics that should be written by more qualified people.

We also need to have a serious conversation about the precarious and contingent workforce, which I address in various chapters – though it will not be nearly enough. Intersectionality and the interdependency of race, class, gender, sexuality, geography informs where and how we engage with systems – and more attention needs to be paid to the systematic exclusion of a whole group of economically marginalized working-class students from post-secondary institutions. Rural, poor, first-generation, racialized, queer, disabled humans deserve better blueprints that are committed to radical invitation and relentless welcome – which I explore throughout in *Hope Circuits* but dedicate more time, resources, and conversations to in the books in the series.

Furthermore, this project does not offer in-depth solutions for wicked problems like improving mental health, leading efforts on decolonization, harnessing educational technology, eradicating gendered violence, or the myriad other complex challenges we face.

This book is not about solving specific problems because the tension between timely and timeless runs means that by the time this is published, the answers will already be obsolete or so general that they will be helpful to no one. Instead, this project is about developing the framework and conceptual tools so that people can solve problems in their own contexts and spheres. We can and must build hope circuits on our campuses and identify interventions to deploy in our contexts – wherever we are and whatever role we occupy.

How do we empower humans to think and feel their way through this difficulty without getting overwhelmed and stuck? I ask this with genuine curiosity because I often despair when encountering significant, complex, grand challenges. The complexity is overpowering and oftentimes I feel like lying down on the ground until the world stops spinning so quickly.

How do we get unstuck?

In conversation with others, I have identified ten conceptual tools that have helped me – as an individual and in community – move into spaces of action and intervention. Deploying these tools to build hope circuits better equips us to metabolize the otherwise jarring and difficult encounters with people and systems that arise in change work within complex organizational structures.

Edges and centres

This book will be too radical for some and not nearly radical enough for others. Some want to burn it all to the ground and start fresh, while others want to preserve the legacies and traditions of publicly funded social institutions.

I explore later in this chapter how Audre Lorde's oft quoted phrase, "the master's tools will never dismantle the master's house,"[9] favours demolition over rewiring; Sara Ahmed's response – that we can "rebuild the master's house so that it can accommodate those for whom it was not intended"[10] – deploys renovation to push the architectural metaphor into more hopeful spaces that are nothing short of radical.

Rethinking the blueprint of higher education is architectural and requires us to outline, conceive, plan, design, and build complex, three-dimensional systems. Architecture invokes the act of building and creating, which we can trace to classical Greek traditions: Aristotle argued that "the architect is held to be wiser than other workers," while Greek historian Herodotus proposes that "an architect was not only a builder of temples and houses, but he … could be involved in other projects whose extraordinary dimensions called for the skills of a tekton mastering his métier."[11]

We often think of buildings – and, by extension, any system with "extraordinary dimensions" – as monolithic, fixed, and impervious once they are in place, and yet, buildings just like systems can be designed to evolve, change shape, and undergo transformative renovations.

Two striking architectural metaphors emerged in interviews that illuminate the dynamic nature of rewiring and reconfiguring that lies at the heart of this project.

The first architectural model emerged in my conversations with Canadian researcher on youth engagement Heather Lawford. She shared her experience touring Antoni Gaudí's La Sagrada Família in Barcelona, Spain, through the lens of her work on generativity and inter-generational partnerships; for her, this basilica – started 141 years ago and still unfinished – is a stunning metaphor for generativity, a concept coined by German psychoanalyst Erik Erikson as a "concern for the future, a need to nurture and guide younger people and contribute to the next generation."[12]

Heather Lawford was struck by the generative nature of the design, which intentionally left gaps in the building: Antoni Gaudí believed that the next generation would build from the current system and yet *not be in* the system. The blueprints are, therefore, unfinished by design. Gaudí conceived of the building to be imagined differently by future users who would engage in the spaces and structures in ways he could not anticipate, so he created the plans to be undone and redone over generations. He left space for gappiness.

American historian David Pace, the founder of a project called *Decoding the Ivory Tower*, shared his thoughts on hope during a Hope University focus group through another architectural metaphor:

It's funny that you should ask that question about hope today. It's going to take a minute to explain this but for the last several days I've been struggling with a problem in my mind because I've been so over-whelmed by the way that information is conveyed to us in ways that prevent action; that separates us from one another to disempower us … [In your presentation of Hope University] you actually imagined how you could convey information in a way that can lead to action and bring [people] together. I'm on vacation right now and I'm in Paris. And it's a fantastic day here and my wife and I went out for a walk. We went to see what Notre Dame looks like since the fire four years ago. Across the [construction] barrier they created a space for artists, writers, and others. One was from Togo. One had grown up in the '80s during the crisis, some space was given to French writers [past and present] … and what they had done – I can't capture exactly what was happening. And it was beautiful. It was people coming together work-ing with a common goal. Using their knowledge and expertise coordi-nating. I thought wow, that's it. Right in front of the cathedral. In a bunch of pictures. Yeah, there it is.[13]

These two architectural examples prompt us to ask, "how can we build a university to recognize value that is outside the reproducing of standards?"

How do we design for a system that is willing to be unmade and remade?

How do we create systems that account for – in their conception – adap-tation for future generations we cannot imagine and yet we know will think and live differently than the original social architects?

How do we envision an institutional structure that can produce something that is not itself?

These are big questions that might leave us with more questions than answers.

That's okay. That's enough. For now.

American yoga instructor Adriene Mishler, who shot to fame during the COVID pandemic for her virtual yoga challenges, provides the following guidance: "take what you need and leave the rest on the mat."[14]

Adriene Mishler's statement is simple in its elegance and relevant to our purposes; it is inclusive for her millions of followers of all ages, stages, and abilities. Building on Adriene's all-embracing language, I place ideas, frameworks, definitions, and voices side by side without the pressure of reconciling them.

For my purposes, hope is a theoretical framework and a verb, a moment and a mindset.

Likewise, hope takes shape through the contestation of meaning and finds animation in conversations without requiring consensus. In that way, hope is as much a thought prompt as a call to action. It will be different for each reader.

As Parker Palmer and Arthur Zajonc write, in *The Heart of Higher Education*, "sometimes good conversations are ends in themselves, good simply because they are enjoyable and edifying. At other times, something stirs in the participants, and larger forms of dialogue and action begin to take shape."[15]

I encourage you to take what is helpful for your context and leave the rest on the mat.

Something Is Rotten in the State of Denmark

Shakespeare gives us a master class on systems-level approaches and design thinking that we can adapt to our contexts.

In *Hamlet*, it is not Hamlet's fault that he fails to thrive; instead, the play instructs us that the interests of the "state" (the systems, structures, policies, governance, deep culture) always trump individual resilience. Hamlet cannot survive because the systemic core is deeply flawed.

Something is rotten in the state of Denmark.

Hamlet falls to the level of the system within which he lives.

Unless we are willing to go to the root of the rot, individual agency – and the joy, delight, purpose, and flourishing of human potential – is untenable.

Still, we blame Hamlet. Dismiss him in popular culture as a moody teenager. Because that is easier than taking responsibility for systems and structures that we inherit, internalize, reproduce …

… and through which many of us benefit.

Ay, there's the rub.

This book seeks out the rot as an invitation, not an indictment. If we can locate what is rotten in the state of higher education, we can expose it, name it, reflect, and then begin to rewire the systems within which we live.

There is a gap between *what we say* and *what we do* at institutions of higher learning. That gap is wide and widening.

On one side, we have the *actual*: systems, structures, and policies that shape individual and group behaviour, which determines what is valued and how value circulates.

On the other side, we have the *possible*: ideas, values, and vision that call people into the academy, which connects individuals and groups to purpose within and beyond existing structures, which fuels hope and social action.

The actual and the possible will never fully align, overlap, converge. They are not supposed to.

And yet, the energy is palpable when organizations focus on closing the gap between the actual and the possible. Humans flourish: they tap into their purpose more easily and often; they feel a keen sense of corporate steward- ship with shared values; they experience renewal and replenishment.

Conversely, when organizations experience widening gaps between the actual and the possible, we see a loss of trust, manifesting in dissonance, dis- comfort, disengagement, and despair. The size, scope, and directional drift of that gap informs the health of (or harm to) the university as a whole – and has a tremendous impact on individuals and communities.

We must mind the gap.

We have tweaked and retweaked the current higher education system for fifty years and have reached the limits of a maintenance approach.

> Consider the point made by Tom Chase, long-time provost and educational leader:
>
> "It's fascinating that, apart from occasional decades (say the '70s in Canada) of stability or rapid growth, higher education seems to be in a more or less permanent state of inflection, or indeed dysfunction and even crisis.
>
> "To me, that's because universities, by the very nature of the community of students, faculty, and staff they house, are acutely sensitive to currents of social change and tension. Indeed, they are often petri dishes for the latter.
>
> "But what we are facing now is unlike anything I've lived through. We are in a period that I think is qualitatively and quantitatively different from anything we've seen over the past few generations, perhaps even over the past century.
>
> "The potential for melioration (and I've always been a card- carrying meliorist!) certainly remains in the air. But looming ever larger is the potential for large-scale warfare, climate-change-driven economic and social disruptions, and a breakdown of the social fab- ric driven not just by these macro-level factors but by the countless micro-damages to society. These are fuelled by social media and the fragmentation of truth and civil society into competing worldviews, most of which are demonstrably false."

Stay with the trouble

Perhaps the least visible yet most profound risk to higher education is the deferred maintenance of the systems, policies, and structures that comprise the governance and systems-wide infrastructure.

Simply put, the difference between what we say and what we do is increasingly untenable. We have lost integrity. We must be willing to imagine a new architecture – and determine a blueprint – for the future of universities and then develop the tools necessary to rebuild the systems that deliver higher education.

First, though: what is rotten in the state of Denmark?

The answer is complex. When we look, clear-eyed, at the current systems, we must acknowledge realities that can be decentring:

- Our systems are built on mystification and exclusion.
- Our systems are built on precarity and insecurity.
- Our systems are built to be siloed and hierarchical.
- Our systems are built on conditions of austerity and scarcity.

We can start by sitting in the discomfort of these unsettling acknowledgments. However, this book is not designed as a prolonged howl into the abyss. Instead, it is a love letter to higher education – to its potential and power to make the world better, more equitable, and just. The goal of Hope University is to unbuild and rebuild – unlearn and learn – systems to develop the conceptual tools necessary to engender lasting hope in the face of complexity.

This book will ask many things. At the core, though, are two guiding questions.

How do we align values and practice so universities fulfill their ethical (moral, social) contract to the broader society?

And, at the same time,

How do we design hopeful and resilient systems to take the pressure off individuals and put our energy towards renovation and renewal of the structures upon which our communities are built?

How do we move forward?

In order to fulfill the social mission of publicly funded institutions, universities have to respond to pressing human rights issues while also *leading* in the following areas:

- Fulfilling the recommendations of the Truth and Reconciliation Commission and decolonizing the academy.
- Tackling gender-based violence on our campuses.
- Combatting ableism by redesigning learning landscapes forged in disability justice and accessibility.
- Creating more inclusive spaces that are welcoming to historically excluded and equity-deserving groups.
- Addressing the climate crisis and climate emergencies largely caused by "settler colonialism and global capitalism."[1]

In the next decade, the onus is on all of us to ensure universities are places where we think carefully, responsibly, and ethically about the significant issues of our time – social, economic, philosophical, and beyond.

Moreover, we must grasp the complexity of these issues as they evolve. We must deploy interventions and develop solutions to *wicked problems* – these messy, confusing, unstable, ill-structured, and ambiguous problems where there is no single solution and that resist resolution.[2]

Here, again, is the gap between what we *say* and what we *do*.

The academy *should* be uniquely situated to lead in tackling wicked problems:

- Because of its fundamental values of curiosity, knowledge creation, and sharing.
- Because of its members' highly specialized skill sets in data collection, analysis, and application.
- Because of its emphasis on multi-disciplinary expertise.
- Because transdisciplinary expertise is a superhero power that should – in theory – enable us to learn, adapt, and innovate at exponential rates.

In practice, though, we don't tap into these strengths in design and operationalization.

The current systems – this bears repeating – are built on mystification and exclusion, predicated on colonization, racism, ableism, classism, and other forms of discrimination. The structures and policies are inhospitable and alienating, perpetuating systemic imposter syndrome for even the most privileged, leaving equity-deserving and historically excluded groups even further disenfranchised. Many policies no longer serve our communities, and many more never served equity-deserving and historically excluded groups.

At many of our institutions, innovation, delight, and transformation happen despite the conditions in which we work and learn, not because of them.

Why is this happening?

We have inherited nineteenth-century systems of higher education that are now floundering in twenty-first-century contexts. Our understanding of what a twenty-first-century university looks like has shifted under intense pressures accelerated and exacerbated by COVID-19.

Tom Fletcher, principal of Hertford College, Oxford, and former UK ambassador, suggests,

> The lockdowns exposed a greater truth, and one that had already been introducing itself pre-COVID: namely, that an industrial education model created in the 19th Century and updated for the mass market of the 20th Century is no longer delivering in the 21st. The social, political, and economic contexts have changed dramatically. Yet universities have not kept pace even as they preach the now ubiquitous buzzword "innovation."[3]

Higher education faces an acute resource, mission, and legitimization crisis amid our increasingly complex world.

As individuals, institutions, and nations we must be equipped to respond to various ethical challenges in the twenty-first century, including wars and geopolitical conflict, globalization, economic instability, emergent technologies, and endangered natural environments.

And yet, we are often unable to find an entry point into these challenges precisely because of the predominantly transactional systems of our institutions, which cannot sustainably coexist with our well-intentioned visions and missions.

Or can they?

To ask the question is to move toward possible answers.

Our institutions are not, for the most part, strategically integrated. The compartmentalization of knowledge, the silos of practice, and the administrative quagmires deflate even the sturdiest souls of change-makers.

I confess somewhat sheepishly that I have a Word document on my computer titled "This is why we can't have nice things." Addressed at various times to the academy at large or university presidents, provosts or faculty colleagues, middle managers or policymakers, this running account of missed opportunities, administrative hurdles, needless gatekeeping, and short-sightedness marks an undeniable pattern: universities do not seize their purpose and the opportunities made available to them.

The systems (and system guardians) even actively block them.

In contrast, countless pockets of delight exist despite, not because of, the conditions within which they live at the *individual or grassroots levels.*

This reality significantly impacts students, who, in turn, internalize harmful and outmoded systems. Students are the biggest losers in vicious cycles of normalized apathy at both the institutional and individual levels.

We cannot fulfill the social contract to a broader society by ignoring the systemic struggles that have set our most important learners behind.

Is there a risk reduction paradox?

As I mentioned earlier, one of the fundamental conundrums faced by post-secondary education is the systems-wide fixation with risk reduction. There are two different approaches to risk and change management emerging from post-pandemic strategic planning.

The first approach insists we will return to normal as soon as possible. The argument invokes risk reduction as a form of institutional resilience.

Indeed, the etymology of resilience comes from the Latin verb *resilire,* meaning "to jump back" or "to recoil." The desire to return to normal is both human and systemically reinforced. We assume that if we return to pre-COVID times, the hurts will hurt less, while the systems will snap back into place and we can carry on as before.

However, the definition of pre-pandemic "normal" benefitted a privileged few at the expense and exclusion of many. Looking back with longing at older systems erases all the lessons we have learned about who has been excluded, harmed, and erased. *New York Times* contributor John Hodgman reminds us, "I consider nostalgia to be a toxic impulse. It is the twinned, yearning delusion that (a) the past was better (it wasn't) and (b) it can be recaptured (it can't)."[4]

Normal is not healthy; it is just the default.

Indeed, John D. Caputo points out that "the merely external fact that it is now a past event does not annul the truth that when it happened this event could have been otherwise."[5] In other words, the fallacy of necessity should not trap us into a position of resignation that the way things are now is how they have to be.[6] This world is not the only one we could have ever had. Choices were made. There are still many choices to make.

A Reddit post making the rounds on social media captures this perfectly: "When people talk about traveling to the past, they worry about radically changing the present by doing something small, but barely anyone in the present really thinks that they can radically change the future by doing something small."[7]

We cannot and must not go back to the way it was. Being risk averse, protecting systems that "snap back" to the status quo, and believing we can fix the current problems by returning to the old normal are mindsets that now pose the most significant risk to universities.

In the next decade, some institutions will fail even as (because) they strive to endure. The old tools and traditional approaches will increase institutional risk even as they are used to mitigate it.

> As one senior university leader notes, "As we do with any highly valorized social function (the law, religion, medical knowledge and care), we rhetorize volubly about universities. But we (that's us academics and administrators) tend to back away from radical critique leading to radical and necessary change ... I think we've reached a juncture where postsecondary institutions will start to fail in large numbers, first slowly and then at an accelerated pace."

We must acknowledge the significant risk of deferred maintenance to the systems, structures, and policies shaping our behaviours, mindsets, and perspectives. Prior challenges have been largely ignored or neglected as people scrambled to respond to the relentless urgency of the permacrisis.

So, let us turn to the second and rarer approach to risk management whereby institutions change to survive; it imagines a strategic approach where risk reduction and transformative change are synonymous. Foundational to this understanding is that the global pandemic exposed several pre-existing fissures in institutions, cultures, and communities that we ignore at our peril.

Universities and humans will flourish when we dare to rethink the systems built to endure and instead make decisions based on enduring values.

We must be willing to ask, "Do these policies and structures still serve us, our social mission, and our communities?"

The more damning question is, "Did they ever serve some of us?"

Let us return to Oxford professor Tom Fletcher and the importance of asking questions:

> If we fail to ask ourselves these tough questions, higher education will watch aghast as the next wave of disruption washes over it. It is not hard to envisage: Google qualifications quickly replace many classic university degrees. Accreditation becomes a free for all. Disillusioned and poorly rewarded academics drop out as the challenge of combining meaningful research with quality teaching becomes harder and harder to pull off.[8]

Fletcher predicts a fork in the road for higher education: we can choose either revolutionary change or obsolescence. He is part of a growing chorus of people warning us that paradigmatic shifts are afoot in the post-secondary sector.[9] The alarmists are not offering us new news. Pundits have been forecasting doom-and-gloom scenarios for years. Indeed, it is a recurring and ubiquitous narrative about the future of the humanities for the past forty years.

The "sky is falling" narrative is neither helpful nor particularly original in conversations around higher education. One might recall the anxiety MOOCS caused in the early 2000s as futurists claimed this new open-access platform would render universities irrelevant. Was this much ado about nothing or an early warning shot across the bow of the Titanic?

We are still waiting to see how this story unfolds.

What we do know, however, is that we are in an extraordinary time of reconfiguration. We must pay attention to stories as they unfold and are not-yet-told. In that spirit, let us return to Shakespeare and the old story of *Hamlet*.

The play is not *just* about what is rotten in the state of Denmark. That might be a beginning – and a critical first step in acknowledging the role systems play in shaping human choices – and yet that it is not how the story ends.

Yes: There are consequences to living in broken systems.

And: there is also renewal and emergence amid destruction.

As Shakespeare scholar Lisa Dickson reminds me, "Tragedy is, at its heart, about creation, not just destruction."

Hamlet defers hope until after the end of the play. We miss the hope lesson if the only thing we take from the final scene is the dead bodies littering the floor and forget that the future is, as yet, unwritten. Hamlet's dying words to Horatio are "Tell my story." This is not just a command to relate what has happened; Hamlet is also underlining the power of telling stories that are yet untold.

Horatio can tell a story about how the system broke Hamlet.

Conversely, he could also tell a story about how Hamlet broke the system.

We do not know which story Horatio will choose to tell. Instead, we get to choose how to fill in the gaps as we leave the theatre and go into the world of our own making.

We have an opportunity to tell stories that are still unfolding: what stories will we choose to tell?

Frameworks for Hope

"Hope" is the thing with feathers –
That perches in the soul –
And sings the tune without the words –
And never stops – at all.
– Emily Dickinson[1]

If hope is a bird that perches on the edge of your soul, is it singing to you?

What song does it sing?

What does the song sound like?

When are you more likely to hear that song?

In this book, we will try to cut through the noise and humdrum of daily life and get quiet enough to hear this little bird. Moreover, we will explore ways that might help to make the song clearer, easier to hear, and more recognizable in our lives.

The curious thing about hope is that we find it everywhere when we look around us with intention. Countless books, essays, articles, op-eds, memes, GIFs, and tweets explore "hope" and its many variations. I have found hope in the most unlikely places, where I least expect it, and often when I most need it.

In the hundreds of interviews I conducted for Hope University, hope means many things to many different people. For some, it is too soft, too floppy, too overexposed. For others, it is soul-renewing, a mindset, a source of meaningful change. The concept can also be amorphous, emergent, or faith-based. With such divergent interpretations, a shared understanding helps ground ourselves in the work ahead.

So, let us start with a foundational statement:

Hope is a verb.[2]

Hope is an act, an occurrence, a recurrence, and a state of being. In *Pedagogy of Hope*, educator Paulo Freire reminds us, "Just to hope is to hope in vain." He insists that hope "demands anchoring in practice."[3]

Hope is deliberate and intentional: we embed hope in daily acts, in the small and mundane, in the conversations we have, the stories we tell, the books we read, and the people who surround us. Hope manifests when we intentionally perform incremental steps toward the solutions we imagine. Only then can hope move from a thought experiment – a theoretical concept we talk about – to a set of actions, a mindset, and a social movement.

In other words, we need tools to build hope circuits at the systems level to bring Hope University to life.

The thinkers who have inspired this book remind us that hope lives in both the smallest and grandest of actions. Below are a series of offerings from diverse thinkers about the nature of hope. Instead of tracing the history of hope or placing these authors in various traditions, these lessons on hope are placed side by side as a series of thought prompts.

Rather than reconciling them, I invite you to find resonance and reflect on why some of these concepts illuminate your experiences while others might not, or at least not yet, sing on the edges of your soul.

Why do we need hope?

- The Brazilian philosopher Paulo Freire speaks of hope as the "ethical quality of the struggle." He explains, "The idea that hope alone will transform the world, and action undertaken in that kind of naïveté, is an excellent route to hopelessness, pessimism, and fatalism. But the attempt to do without hope, in the struggle to improve the world, as if that struggle could be reduced to calculated acts alone, or a purely scientific approach, is a frivolous illusion."[4]
- Ira Shor, American professor of rhetoric, defines hope in education as a dissonance between multiple forces, "a clash between a restrictive present and a reinvented future – call it, if you like, the hopeful challenging the actual in the name of the possible."[5]

Where do you locate hope?

- Hope, for Mariame Kaba, American prison abolitionist and organizer, is a discipline: "I always tell people, for me, hope doesn't preclude feeling sadness or frustration or anger or any other emotion that makes total sense. Hope isn't an emotion, you know? Hope is not optimism ... The idea of hope being a discipline is something I heard from a nun many years ago who was talking about it in conjunction with making sure we were of the world and in the world."[6]
- For the Czech dissident and politician Václav Havel, "Hope is not prognostication. It is an orientation of the spirit, an orientation of the heart. It transcends the world that is immediately experienced, and is anchored somewhere beyond its horizons."[7]

Can you learn how to hope?

- The American author and social activist bell hooks reveals, "My hope emerges from those places of struggle where I witness individuals positively transforming their lives and the world around them. Educating is always a vocation rooted in hopefulness. As teachers we believe that learning is possible, that nothing can keep an open mind from seeking after knowledge and finding a way to know."[8]
- For American educator and author Kevin Gannon, "Radical hope eschews despair, but does so in a way that often relies upon the faith that our current thinking and actions will create a better future – even without specifically understanding what that future will look like." He adds, "Teaching is a radical act of hope ... It is a continuing pedagogical practice rather than a set of static characteristics. Simply put, we teach because we believe it matters."[9]

How do we ensure hope is robust enough for the hard work ahead?

- Canadian education scholar Kari Grain proposes that hope lives in contradiction: "Critical hope is a type of hope that grapples with its own political, emotional, relational, and experiential dimensions in order to enact change ...To engage with critical hope is to uphold multiple conflicting truths simultaneously."[10]

- Maria Popova, creator of *The Marginalian*, argues that "Critical thinking without hope is cynicism. Hope without critical thinking is naïveté … But in order to survive – both as individuals and as a civilization – and especially in order to thrive, we need the right balance of critical thinking and hope."[11]

In our pursuit of hope, we must also be mindful there is room for hopelessness in our journeys.

- Buddhist teacher and author Pema Chödrön urges us "to stay with that shakiness – to stay with a broken heart, with a rumbling stomach, with the feeling of hopelessness and wanting to get revenge – that is the path of true awakening. Sticking with that uncertainty, getting the knack of relaxing in the midst of chaos, learning not to panic – this is the spiritual path."[12]
- Nigerian scholar and poet Bayo Akomolafe warns us that hope can be used as a colonial construct that perpetuates dominant systems and urges us instead to think about "theorizing the end of hope not as an absolute pristine hopelessness but as a querying of the binary that premises hope and hopelessness as twin or as enemies to each other."[13]

I revisit many of these quotations when I am working through a tricky encounter or sticky issue. These words resonate for me differently at different times and often help illuminate something otherwise difficult to name. Together they offer a constellation of perspectives that shed light in diverse contexts.

Hope, as we read above, is intertwined with learning and flourishing. And yet, as I conducted interviews, I encountered horror stories associated with learning environments – of graduate school, the trauma of job interviews, the palpable anxiety of promotion and evaluation, and the toxicity of workplaces.

What do we do when we encounter the contradictions between the values of learning and the lived experiences of higher education?

An early career professor reflected on the effect this tension has on individuals: "When I work on projects and committees that reflect the university's values, I am energized and refreshed. When I work on projects and committees dedicated to the functions of systems and structures of the university, I am depleted and disheartened."[14]

Therefore, this begs the question as we attempt to build hope circuits within university structures, "Is the academy hopeful?" If so, where does hope live?

In *Shakespeare's Guide to Hope, Life, and Learning,* a book I co-wrote with colleagues Lisa Dickson and Shannon Murray, we argue that hope lies at the core of higher education: "Learning is embodied hope. It happens in time. It happens in bodies. Each act of learning is unique and can never be reproduced on a factory line. It cannot be abstracted from the bodies and the lives of learners who embody it, any more than a verb can function grammatically without an agent. Hope is a verb."[15]

Hope lives in classrooms and in places where we learn. Many faculty I interviewed see the classroom as a refuge, a place to observe hope unfolding in real time, and an escape from soul-draining work associated with other aspects of the academy.

Where does the critical live?

In *Shakespeare's Guide to Hope,* my co-authors and I proposed a triad of virtues that mutually inform one another: critical hope, critical empathy, critical love.[16]

We added "critical" as a prefix to insulate hope and love and empathy from the critics who might dismiss these qualities as too soft, too feminized, too pink. I worried that love, empathy, and hope would evoke images of hippie-dippies sitting around in a circle braiding friendship bracelets. We thought the intervention of "critical" might make these concepts more robust, sturdy, insulated against the slings and arrows of outrageously critical detractors.

And yet, I am holding the critical lightly.

I am no longer interested in apologizing for these qualities. As academics, we are trained to engage exclusively in the realm of cognition; as such, critical analysis, deconstruction, and the dismantling of others' ideas or theories is at the core of a paradigm that no longer serves the work I want to do.

I am restless for something different – and am seeking out new ways of engaging in knowledge creation and sharing. And, I also wonder why I ever felt the need to disparage "hippie-dippies" when so many are working to make the world kinder, gentler, and more loving. Brené Brown explains my ungenerous thinking in this way: "People fear being ridiculed or belittled. In an armoured leadership environment, where you shame and blame, people are afraid. Fear is the currency. In daring leadership, empathy and self-compassion are taught, modelled, and expected. Not only do we treat each other with empathy and compassion, people watch us model it."[17]

When we stop being afraid, love, empathy, and hope are powerful enough without an academic alibi. They are worthy of our attention, our respect, our consideration. They are worthy of our commitment.

They are enough. We are enough.

The lost and found of hope

Hope lives in narratives of abundance and helps to combat narratives of deficit. And yet hope is also not without its complexities. There are dark sides to hope. Hope can be a masquerade for cruel optimism, toxic positivity, or gaslighting.[18] We can point to historical and contemporary moments where hope was weaponized, manipulated, or deployed for unjust purposes and enacted real harm.

Moreover, there are debates about what constitutes the opposite of hope: is it despair, grief, stagnation, passivity, cynicism, disengagement, apathy, compliance, conformity?

We should also remember that hope does not possess an inherently positive or negative value; similarly, we should not think of hope in binaries. If we do, we fall into traps that value the critical over the illuminating, privilege deficit over abundance, favour deconstructing over building.

When we move away from binary thinking, we can imagine differently. In *Staying with the Trouble*, philosopher Donna Haraway counsels us to be "truly present, not as a vanishing pivot between awful and Edenic pasts and apocalyptic or salvific futures, but as mortal citizens entwined in myriad un-finished configurations of places, times, matters, meanings."[19]

The relationship between despair and hope

Trying to change systems can be soul eroding. We can experience hopeless-ness in a myriad of ways: in difficult meetings with an un-collegial colleague, encounters with gatekeepers or confrontations with naysayers, watching a provocative project flounder or a progressive policy mired in the pettiness of politics, experiencing microaggressions fuelled by racial injustices, wit-nessing systemic misogyny – and the list goes on and on.

What appears as small, seemingly isolated encounters add up, compound, and lead to deeper, systemic burnout.

Moreover, there are consequences when you try to change a policy, struc-ture, or system that no longer serves – or never served – diverse com-munities. We have inherited resilient systems designed to return to their resting state: the status quo, the default position, the norm. In Newtonian terms – his third law – the force required to accelerate something will evoke an equal and opposite reactional force. If we pull a system in a particular di-rection, it will snap back with equal force.

Sara Ahmed writes, "A system is working when an attempt to transform that system is blocked."[20]

No wonder we are exhausted: it is a sign that the systems are resilient.

When we are engaged in culture change, we are often caught when the system recoils. However, the experience is often coded as human error or personal failure. I have often caught myself lamenting, "If I were only more [insert: strategic, consultative, etc.]" or "If only I had [insert: slowed down, seen that coming, sped up, talked to this person before that one]." Often, though, feelings of shame and self-recrimination are less about human errors and instead evidence that the systems are built to withstand attempts at change.

When daring leaders come up against armoured systems, there are real consequences: armoured systems deploy, according to Brené Brown, "sham-ing and blaming to manage ourselves and others, [which] drives a culture where we try to look, work, and deliver perfectly so we can self-protect against the pain of blame and judgment and shame."[21]

What are we supposed to do if we want to change systems for the better?

Despair is an option.

Howling into the abyss is a viable – and very human – response.

When I am in my most frustrated state, I often initiate wishful thinking with select thought partners:

- Let us start a brand-new university.
- What would it look like?
- What would we teach and learn?
- Whom would we hire?
- How would we govern?
- How would we research?

This thought exercise helps alleviate indignities in the short term. A foray into a golden world of imaginative possibilities is usually sufficient to restore depleted spirits and re-engage with courage and integrity.

However, escapism without change is self-indulgent. Furthermore, despair is a luxury many cannot afford.

Living in an imaginative realm without mobilizing these values into action can keep us from changing the systems within which we live. Even as we look to new and shiny institutions, we must recognize that they are still constrained by flawed funding models, vulnerable to governmental meddling, and subject to death-by-a-thousand-papercuts bureaucracy from internal and external accrediting bodies populated by people who have internalized older, antiquated systems.

The only option is to look to our systems and be brave enough to rewire them.

"We must," as an old maritimer once told me, "dance with the girl that brung us."

This is not an easy ask.

Hope is all the rage

Hard hope must make space for grief and rage. Building hope circuits sometimes means giving a voice to big feelings. In a system that favours the cognitive over the affective, the rational over the emotional, we must find ways to express the built-up emotional and spiritual energy that is a by-product of living within imperfect systems made up of flawed humans with good intentions.

In a moment of hopelessness, I sometimes send a text message that merely reads "[screams into the abyss]." Sent to a beloved thought partner, they know it is code for honouring a moment of emotive energy that does not ask them to skip immediately to the solution. It is always less daunting and more meaningful when we solve problems in communion with loving humans. A first step is to bring it forth into language, even if that language is jumbled and includes a few choice expletives.

Moreover, hope is not the absence of heartbreak.

Parker Palmer says there are two kinds of brokenheartedness. The first kind is to be "broken by unbearable tension into a thousand shards." However, the second kind is to be "broken open into a largeness of life, into greater capacity to hold one's own and the world's pain and joy."[22]

There is a place for rage as a tool for social change in conversations around hope. Rage ignites movements and people and can connect us to purpose.

- In *Good and Mad: The Revolutionary Power of Women's Anger*, Rebecca Traister talks about the galvanizing power of anger.[23]
- Soraya Chemaly, in *Rage Becomes Her: The Power of Women's Anger*, argues that rage is the best way for women to protect themselves against danger and injustice.[24]
- In "Refusal to Forgive: Indigenous Women's Love and Rage," Rachel Flowers advocates for the importance of indigenous women's rage as resistance to the regulative norms of colonial dispossession.[25]
- Willie Jennings, professor at Yale, delivered a speech in 2021 titled "Anger is the Engine of Hope Now."[26]

If you give yourself space to scream into the void, you might find something you are not looking for: hope. Sometimes the experiences of grief, rage, or despair are not antithetical states to hope; instead, they are part of a more complex hope circuit.

Thus, we can hone rage into hope.

TOM GAULD for NEW SCIENTIST

Why is hope hard?

Hope University is not built on relentless optimism. When we erase discomfort and despair, it leads to burnout, disengagement, and significant health implications. Hope requires us to face uncomfortable truths and sit in that discomfort with grace and a willingness to transform. We forge this brand of hard hope in challenging truths, radical compassion, clear-eyed assessment, and creative design.

Hope was never easy. Hope is not easy. Hope will never be easy.

There is horror in our daily news feeds, projected onto the backdrop of hatred, of anti-black racism, Islamophobia, sexual and gender violence, transphobia, and other expressions of intolerance, and further complicated by wicked social problems: the global climate crisis; the thousands of murdered and missing Indigenous women, children, two-spirit, LGBTQ+; a mass poisoning crisis; housing insecurity; income inequality; and food scarcity.

The CryptoNaturalist
@CryptoNature

We seldom admit the seductive comfort of hopelessness.
It saves us from ambiguity.
It has an answer for every question: "There's just no point."
Hope, on the other hand, is messy.
If it might all work out, then we have things to do.
We must weather the possibility of happiness.

3:09 PM · 7/22/22 · Twitter Web App

Many despair in the face of overwhelming human suffering and wonder how they can ever intervene to make a difference.

And yet, hopelessness lets us off the hook.

Some have adopted a model of criticism that imagines cynicism as rational, analytical, and even edgy. However, cynicism is lazy. Unnuanced. Filled with apathy. It is an expression of learned helplessness, a default setting, a recoiling to status quo.

Hope circuits that allow us to feel the range of feelings that arise from complexity can help aim us toward social and collective action.

Unfortunately, hope is under siege. It is often denied and disowned.

When I was conducting interviews for Hope University, more than one of the interviewees said defensively, "Well, I am not a Pollyanna!" Pollyanna has become a proxy for wide-eyed idealism, a foil for distinguishing more robust perspectives of the "real world."

A close reading, however, exposes anxiety at the centre: hope is purposefully gendered and infantilized so it will not be taken seriously. Hope is contrasted to the so-called rigour of Western patriarchal Reason and Rationality – capital R. We use statements such as "the way it is" and "the way it has always been" to bludgeon hope, idealism, and curiosity into submission.

Matthew
@CrowsFault

People speak of hope as if it is this delicate, ephemeral thing made of whispers and spider's webs. It's not. Hope has dirt on her face, blood on her knuckles, the grit of the cobblestones in her hair, and just spat out a tooth as she rises for another go.

However, the underlying anxiety embedded in the denial or dismissal of hope exposes the disruptive power to propose new ways of being.

Hope is a skill to hone through practice and repetition – another go, another brick wall, another valiant effort. So, let us not forget that hope is badass: dynamic, unruly, audacious, and fierce.

Consider the point made by Mariame Kaba, who discusses the difficulty of maintaining hope. She says, "When I would feel overwhelmed by what was going on in the world, I would just say to myself, 'hope is a discipline.' It's less about how you feel and more about the practice of making a decision every day, that you're going to put one foot in front of the other and you're still going to get up in the morning."[27]

Hope is not the absence of despair. Hope requires us to sit in the shit of uncomfortable truths with grace and a willingness to break open, not break apart. It is a lot to ask.

We started our discussion of hope with a poem by nineteenth-century American poet Emily Dickinson. Hope, for her, is a bird who perches on the edge of your soul and sings. As we move into discussions about the tools necessary to build hope circuits, I offer another poem, "I Worried," written more than a century and a half later by American poet Mary Oliver.

I worried a lot. Will the garden grow, will the rivers
flow in the right direction, will the earth turn
as it was taught, and if not how shall
I correct it?

Was I right, was I wrong, will I be forgiven,
can I do better?

Will I ever be able to sing, even the sparrows
can do it and I am, well,
hopeless.

Is my eyesight fading or am I just imagining it,
am I going to get rheumatism,
lockjaw, dementia?

Finally, I saw that worrying had come to nothing.
And gave it up. And took my old body
and went out into the morning,
and sang.[28]

This book has an earnest wish to unlock people's ability to hear hope sing
and to carry the song out into the world.

In the following chapters we will explore the conceptual tools that might
help to build towards a future hitherto unimagined. Let us imagine together
what systems we have to design so that our universities are places where our
hearts sing and humans flourish.

Conceptual Tools to Build Hope Circuits

It is a fundamentally life-affirming task to build institutions that are
not dependent on the diminishment of the life-capacities of others.
– Sara Ahmed[1]

This book is based on the concept of hope circuits. As we move toward a
new paradigm of higher education, we need the conceptual tools necessary
to rewire the circuitry of our systems and our selves. These tools can help us
transform mindsets, perspectives, and behaviours so that we can, in turn,
rewire and renew the systems within which we learn, live, and work.

I first came across the concept of hope circuits in a memoir entitled *The
Hope Circuit: A Psychologist's Journey from Helplessness to Optimism* by psychologist Martin E.P. Seligman. Thirty years ago, Seligman and fellow American Steven Maier presented the notion of "learned helplessness." When
conducting experiments where an organism is given negative or uncomfortable stimuli, they discovered that if that organism does not have control
over its situation, it cannot escape the negative stimuli even if there is a clear
exit available.

After they became famous for this work, Maier pursued a career in neuroscience with a particular focus on neurobiology. He started to map the
brain to understand how those circuits and wires are formed and communicate within the brain, while Seligman enjoyed an illustrious career as the
"father" of positive psychology.

When they reunited after three decades, Seligman and Maier came to a stunning new realization: "the arrow of our causality was wrong and that it was not helplessness but control and mastery that were learned."[2] In other words, helplessness is the thing we revert to if we have *not* created new pathways. Instead of learned helplessness, the mechanism we can actually learn is hope. They discovered the processes within our complex neuroanatomy that build a "hope circuit" in our brains through practice and intention.

Despair is the default.

Hope, on the other hand, can be built.

Seligman and Maier give us novel approaches to understand our brains while also offering us a case study for building hope circuits in ourselves and our organizations. Willing to rethink fundamental assumptions they had previously developed and promoted, Seligman and Maier admitted they were wrong; moreover, instead of presenting their new evidence as failure or apology, they shared their findings as something extraordinary to be celebrated. Most notably, they embraced the importance of unlearning. Seligman writes, "It is gratifying to have lived long enough and to be able to be in a vibrant enough science to find out you were wrong."[3]

Seligman's wonder in the face of new knowledge – and his palpable delight in unlearning – is a lesson to us all: we must hold our opinions and assumptions lightly. When we are confronted with ideas or data that contradict what we hold as fundamental, impervious, or unshakeable knowledge, we have a choice: Hope circuits help us choose wonder and delight over shame and despair.

Ten conceptual tools to build hope circuits

We can borrow the concept of hope circuits from neuroscience to understand other kinds of plasticity in systemic thinking. If we can create new pathways and connectors in the neuroanatomical structures of our brains, then we must be able to expand this notion to rewire other kinds of complex systems – institutions, cultures, communities, sectors – to be more hopeful so that individuals and communities flourish.

What conceptual tools are necessary to build hope circuits?

The following list emerged from interviews with people who navigate complex systems and have learned to metabolize the disorientation, discomfort, and despair that often accompany complex systems change:

- Slow down and pause
- Surface the systems
- Practise divergent thinking
- Commit to unlearning and relearning
- Live in the questions
- Stay with the trouble
- Reimagine authority and expertise
- Take a systems-level approach
- Change your language, change the world
- Build intentional community

These conceptual tools do not have hierarchical or sequential order; instead, they appear here side by side to encourage us to explore how ideas inform other ideas. These conceptual tools play a pivotal role in every chapter. Some come into and out of focus, emerge as a dominant tool, or step back as a subordinate one depending on the topic or challenge. Some of them might resonate more in a particular nexus or context; they are designed as an invitation rather than a prescription.

Below is an overview of each conceptual tool.

1. Slow down and pause

One of the side effects of living in a chronic state of crisis is that everyone is BUSY. Work is unrelenting. Time is of the essence. And yet, as Hamlet remarks, time is "out of joint." In crisis mode, our relationship to time expands and contracts in ways that seem to bend the space–time continuum. Days feel like weeks, while hours sometimes stretch with an elasticity that has us asking, "What day is it?"

There seems to be no time for reflection, much less strategic visioning.

If the question at the top of mind is "what does the future look like for higher education?," we must pause first and ask, "what reflection do we need to do before looking forward?"

In the humanities, we train students to go back to the past to illuminate the present and innovate the future. This skill set is particularly urgent at this moment in time.

In *Paradise Lost*, John Milton helps frame our present experience in the context of the past. In grappling with the complexities of past, present, and future, seventeenth-century poet Milton counters linear time with the concept of the "eternal present."

For Milton, a divine presence exists beyond earthly constraints, occupying a spiritual dimension that embraces and contains all expressions of time. He anticipates we might feel disoriented by this in *Paradise Lost*. The angel Raphael reassures Adam (first man) that our limited human brains will find it hard to grapple with such overwhelming metaphysical concepts because we are tied to the construct of linear time.

While most of us do not have the luxury to sit, "dove-like … brooding on the vast Abyss" as Milton's heavenly Muse likes to do, we can still step outside of our present moment to pause.[4] Slowing down and stepping outside the whirligig of daily lives helps us see more clearly – to take stock of what has happened and prepare for what is yet to come.

Our first instincts in the face of crisis are often to speed up. To take flight or fight. What happens if we pause instead, stepping out of time and into Milton's eternal present?

Nigerian scholar and public intellectual Bayo Akomolafe offers us this advice: "The times are urgent; let us slow down."[5]

Pausing to reflect on the context within which we find ourselves helps to locate and centre the discomfort we must process before aiming it in future-facing ways. Buddhist monk Pema Chödrön shares her own realization that "impermanence becomes vivid in the present moment; so do compassion and wonder and courage."[6] We need all these qualities to build robust hope circuits for humane systems.

Feeling an adrenaline rush in a moment of conflict makes us human. Martin Seligman argues that evolution wired our "ancient ancestors" with first responses whereby "threats engaged defensive reflexes, and these reflexes cost energy."

However (and this is another lesson the universe keeps asking me to learn), we can develop new responses which can shift "the balance of the flow of energy."[7] We can relearn our responses when we pause, take a beat, and then lead with YES/AND. Hope circuits help us move from default reactions into spaces that are wired with intention; this helps with energy conservation while at the same time creating pathways for new, learned responses.

If we slow down for a minute, we can develop a blueprint for a future university that harnesses our knowledge of failed past experiences and accounts for pressing future needs.

2. Surface the systems

Once we slow down, things start to come into focus. David Foster Wallace, American essayist, illustrates the importance of surfacing systems with the following parable:

> There are these two young fish swimming along and they happen to meet an older fish swimming the other way, who nods at them and says "Morning, boys. How's the water?" And the two young fish swim on for a bit, and then eventually one of them looks over at the other and goes, "What the hell is water?"[8]

Wallace explains the parable's message in the following way: "The point of the fish story is merely that the most obvious, important realities are often the ones that are hardest to see and talk about." In other words, we are all immersed in water even though the systems that shape our experiences are often invisible.

We can make the water visible by asking fundamental questions, going back to first principles, and rumbling our assumptions. Only then can we appreciate how water shapes our existence.

A fan of the liberal arts, Wallace argues that "the real value of a real education ... has almost nothing to do with knowledge, and everything to do with simple awareness; awareness of what is so real and essential, so hidden in plain sight all around us, all the time, that we have to keep reminding ourselves over and over:

"'This is water.'

"'This is water.'"[9]

Acknowledging David Foster Wallace's "this is water" is a starting point for any meaningful change. Effacing the systems and structures at work does not make them go away. Avoidance, deferral, or disavowal does not render the systems less potent. It only reduces the power and potential of change agents. Inviting "the most obvious, important realities" into the conversation is essential if we seek to dismantle, renovate, and renew systems, structures, and policies.

3. Practise divergent thinking

Once these systems become visible, the next step is to grasp their complexity and find a point of intervention. Systems can seem impervious, intractable, and therefore intimidating if we try to address them straight on.

To build hope circuits within institutional contexts, divergent thinking helps us conceptualize a problem from a different angle. Eric Ravenscraft, writing for *Scientific American*, offers this neuroscientific explanation of what happens in your brain when you have epiphanies or inspiration. He says, "When you make a new connection between two ideas, it's not just a metaphor. Your brain is literally restructuring itself to accommodate new processes. The more plastic your brain is, the more you're able to form creative or inspirational thoughts."[10]

To rewire our brains for hope circuits, we can use metaphors to increase neuroplasticity and see connections that were not there before.

> Poet Jane Hirshfield says, "A metaphor is language that simultaneously creates and solves its own riddle; within that minute explosion of mind is both expansion and release ... It is how the mind instructs itself in a more complex seeing."[11]

I want to share a story of how a metaphor made me see (and do) differently.

Several years ago, I delivered a workshop with my colleague Heather Smith, a Canadian political science scholar. At the time, we were working through a social change model that challenged traditional definitions of leadership through a grassroots social movement approach.

Using the framework of Paulo Freire's work in the *Pedagogy of the Oppressed* alongside Che Guevara – who encourages change makers to seek out allies in "wild places of small population"[12] – we asked delegates to think through the resources and strategies needed to dismantle oppressive structures.

To our horror, groups identified enemy combatants in ways we had not anticipated: faculty members identified enemy combatants as students, and educational developers identified enemy combatants as faculty.

I left the session in despair. This notion of guerilla leadership we had plucked from social justice movements was a failed metaphor. What we thought was a clever lens to explore contestation and social justice was flawed (and, in retrospect, irresponsible).

When I shared this failure with my friend Lisa Dickson, she looked at me and said, "What did you expect? Do you blame the salmon, or do you blame the dam?" In other words, the participants followed our (misguided) guidelines.

We were trying to encourage participants to surface the source of conflict and contestation at the systems level; however, we did not provide enough framing – so the salmon blamed each other, not the dam.

Once I saw the dam, I could not unsee it: salmon pool in places where they are guided.

Once we see the dam, the salmon take on a new dimension via critical empathy.

We often think of dams as part of the natural environment, and yet they are artificial, human-made, constructed. The salmon's actions are a direct response to the structures and architecture of a built environment; they will behave counter to their nature (even working against their survival) if the structures are poorly designed (or not designed with them in mind).

Once we see salmon behaving strangely, we need to pause and surface the systems. To extend this metaphor: in order to save the salmon, we have to go upstream to dismantle the dam while at the same time building salmon ladders for those fish pooling in places that do not serve them.

Inviting "the most obvious, important realities" into conversation is essential if we are to dismantle, renovate, and renew the systems we have inherited. This realization means going back to basic principles and seeing everything that we have taken for granted with fresh eyes.

4. Commit to unlearning and relearning

Familiar things inevitably become strange when we engage divergent thinking.

Once we see something in a new light, we cannot unsee it. What becomes visible can no longer remain invisible.[13]

The impetus behind transformative social movements comes from the impossibility of unseeing injustice once it is made conspicuous. Consider the Black Lives Matter movement, the #metoo movement, the Stonewall riots. While discrimination and violence have been palpable to many for many years, a moment in time (a tweet, a viral video, a picture) brings these deep injustices to the surface of social consciousness – and even the most privileged cannot look away.

Seeing – whether it is through post-structuralist, Lacanian, or sociological frameworks – is not a physical exercise; instead, it is a metaphysical experience of perception, insight, and recognition. We must, in other words, de-centre our ways of knowing to account for new ways of thinking and being.

When we occupy learner positions and are willing to sit in the discomfort of transformation, we encounter the world differently. Although we are wired to learn, when curiosity and wonder are not valued, they can become dormant. As I will explore in later chapters, the current systems and structures value and reward impervious knowledge and punish (or, at the very least, dismiss) fluid states of knowing. When we become "experts" – in disciplinary knowledge or forged through experience navigating professional and institutional organizations – we risk treating authority, expertise, and mastery as fixed notions.

Students are experts in states of becoming and self-actualization. However, many of us who identify as authority figures, experts, and masters of a discipline or body of knowledge have forgotten the very thing that called us to the academy.

Hope university is a means of remembering ourselves and building from what we value – and by doing so embracing unlearning.

5. Take a systems-level approach

Once we understand "this is water" and surface the systems, we must acknowledge, as American filmmaker Ava DuVernay says, "The system's not broken; the system was built this way. It was built to oppress. It lives off of our ignorance and we can no longer be ignorant."[14]

There is tremendous cognitive dissonance when we surface the discomfort that has been palpable for excluded groups and pernicious for the privileged for a long time – and it is now coming to a head.

- The systems are broken.
- The systems are working exactly as designed.

We have to sit in the discomfort of these two statements.

When asked about systems change, a few interviewees invoked Audre Lorde's maxim, "the master's tools will never dismantle the master's house."[15]

I think that, in many cases, this is true.

American activist and poet Audre Lorde's statement of resistance and refusal is powerful; taken out of context, however, this statement does not make room for "yes, and." Her insights are more complex – and more potent – within their original context. Speaking about feminism and intersectionality, Audre Lorde offers us a way forward:

> For difference must be not merely tolerated, but seen as a fund of necessary polarities between which our creativity can spark like a dialectic. Only then does the necessity for interdependency become unthreatening. Only within that interdependency of different strengths, acknowledged and equal, can the power to seek new ways to actively "be" in the world generate, as well as the courage and sustenance to act where there are no charters.[16]

In other words, our differences should not turn into barriers for cooperation or excuses for entrenched views; instead, they must precisely be invitations that nourish the urgent action and solutions we must imagine and build together – today.

Sara Ahmed, author of *Feminist Killjoy*, uses Audre Lorde to understand the complexities of working within university systems. She argues that reimagining systems from within is nothing short of revolutionary:

> Formal complaints can sound just like the master's tools – bureaucratic, dry, tedious – but they're also where you actually come to hear and learn about institutional mechanics, how institutions reproduce themselves. To use the Lordeian formulation, the effort to rebuild the master's house so that it can accommodate those for whom it was not intended cannot be understood purely as a reformist project. It is, potentially, revolutionary. Much of the work of revolution comes from what you learn by trying to build more just worlds alongside other people.[17]

The revolutionary change, Ahmed suggests, comes from taking the tools and systems we have inherited and using them to renovate spaces for those who were never invited – or have been purposefully excluded – in the original conception of these organizations.

While it is meaningful to protest loudly (there is a real and urgent place for this kind of advocacy on the streets, in public places, and at decision-making tables), there is also tremendous power in familiarizing ourselves with the "bureaucratic" and "dry" infrastructure of governance; these "tedious" policies, terms of reference, Roberts rules of order, might seem mind-numbingly dull, and yet they are the agents of material change as we design new blueprints for existing systems.

6. Stay with the trouble

The hundreds of conversations about Hope University – whether these are focus groups, summits, one-on-one interviews, workshops, or classroom practice – started with hope and, in the rumbling process, often surfaced unprocessed grief, despair, and rage.

Discomfort is a feature, not a flaw in building hope circuits. As I discuss in the "How Do We Learn" chapter, transformative learning, whereby you move from one state of being into a new one, is troublesome. It feels counterintuitive, alien, incoherent, and uncomfortable. The discomfort is not an indicator that things are going wrong: it is, in fact, a sign that change is happening.

Many innovators I interviewed have figured out how to metabolize their discomfort because the thing that keeps them up at night also gets them out of bed in the morning. They are willing to stay with the trouble, understanding that this decentring enables them to tap into purpose more fully or with more clarity.

As David Foster Wallace's metaphor reminds us, understanding that we inhabit water also requires that we make the currents and shoals visible and surface assumptions as the first step toward challenging the dominant paradigm. To extend the metaphor one more step, dredging the bottom can muddy the waters, which can be (especially at first) disorienting.

In the opening lines of *Staying with the Trouble*, American philosopher Donna Haraway writes, "Trouble is an interesting word. It derives from a thirteenth-century French verb meaning 'to stir up,' 'to make cloudy,' 'to disturb.'" She argues that we all "live in disturbing times, mixed-up times, troubling and turbid times. The task is to become capable, with each other in all of our bumptious kinds, of response."[18]

The consensus across the disciplines – educational development, scholarship of teaching and learning, neuropsychology, or philosophy – is that we need to sit in the shit if we wish to grow as humans and in relationship with one another. That requires a brand of hard hope – and a commitment to perseverance.

James Baldwin gives voice to the iterability of hope: "Hope is invented every day."[19]

Stoic philosopher Dory, from Pixar's *Finding Nemo*, advises us to "just keep swimming" with the hope that together, and over time, things will become clearer.[20]

The classical philosopher Epictetus's advice to "resist and persist" also frames hope work as ongoing.

It is in these spaces of iteration – repeated performances grounded in daily actions – that we build hope circuits.

7. Reimagine authority and expertise

James Baldwin, Dory, and Epictetus are a trio of strange bedfellows.

An American author-activist, a cartoon fish, and a Stoic philosopher do not usually co-exist in Very Serious Books characterized by Scholarly Rigour. However, rethinking our relationships with authority and expertise lies at the heart of hope circuits.

In *Decolonizing Education*, Canadian educator and Mi'kmaq scholar Marie Battiste asserts that "the ultimate struggle is a regeneration of new relationships among and between knowledge systems, as scholars competent in both knowledge systems seek to unite and reconcile them."[21]

She adds, "we need to centre educational commitment to, and our responsibilities for, the enhancement of humanity and its infinite capacities. Each strategy taken to rebuild human capacity is a decolonizing activity that turns collective hope into insights, voices, and partnerships, not resistance, resignation, or despair."[22]

In the process of building hope circuits, the eclectic, mixed use of sources is itself a tactic to foster divergent thinking by presenting novel connective threads to make room for the possibility of collision between and amongst powerful ideas.

For Marie Battiste, bringing together different forms of knowledge "is not a merge or a clash, but a space that is new, electrifying, and even contentious, but ultimately has the potential for an interchange or dialogue of the assumptions, values, and interests each holds."[23]

When authority and expertise are decentred and reframed, we open up new spaces – new horizons – to pursue shared human values, which makes room for playfulness.

At the core of this project is a delightful irreverence that conjoins the heart and mind inextricably in the pursuit of new knowledge(s) – both in its acquisition and creation and its sharing and reimagining.

8. Change your language, change the world

Reimagining systems starts with attention to language. We create experiences in language, through stories, with words. Narrative shapes our reality and relationships to others and orients our place in the world.

Take, for example, Satan, the hero of John Milton's *Paradise Lost*, who uses language to mediate his own experience. Finding himself cast into hell, he rouses himself from a lake of burning fire with these first words: "The mind is its own place, and in itself / Can make a Heav'n of Hell, a Hell of Heav'n."[24] Satan uses language as an act of defiance, creating his reality within which he locates himself via intentional storytelling.

We can find more prosaic examples beyond fallen angels.

Consider, for example, a Monday morning when a frazzled academic mother might find herself in a perfect storm of forgetfulness: she forgot to pack lunches, sent tiny humans to school without gym clothes, and overlooked the permission slip deadline for a much-anticipated field trip. After racing home, dropping off forgotten items with the school secretary, and racing to gather herself, she is therefore late for her first meeting of the day.

In this scenario, different stories are possible.

One narrative might go, "Oh, my goodness! Everything has gone wrong! What a Monday!" The scattered scholar might then carry that energy into every meeting for the rest of the day. Yet another version is conceivable: "Well, all the things that could go wrong happened in the first hour of my Monday morning, so we are in for smooth sailing for the rest of the week."

I have told both these stories. Neither story is true and neither story is false.

How we tell these stories has a tremendous impact on the tone and tenor of our everyday lives. The future is a space of our making, and our chosen language will shape it concretely. I can reify a lousy week or an auspicious day through the sheer power of my words.

I want to live in the second story because it issues forth a life of abundance, generosity, and hope.

Earlier in this chapter, we explored the power of "yes/and" as a way forward. It is the necessary phrase to keep improvisation – the co-production of meaning that unfolds spontaneously in the present moment – alive. Consider too how "no/but" kills the possibility of co-creation.

What happens when we tell the wrong stories?

American podcaster and host of *On Being* Krista Tippett argues that we, as a society, are telling the wrong stories, which is affecting critical outcomes in our lives:

We are fluent in the story of our time marked by catastrophe and dysfunction. That is real, and it is grave – but it's not the whole story of us. Here's what this phrase – the generative story, the generative narrative of our time – is insisting on: that there is also an ordinary and abundant reality of learning and growth that is happening, of dignity and care and social creativity and evolution … Calling out this reality, naming that there is a generative story of our time, is in fact a way to begin.[25]

We have the option to tell stories of abundance in a culture addicted to stories of crisis. Moreover, we need to be attentive to the language – words, metaphors, analogies, idioms – that shape our everyday existence.

When I interviewed Susie Andrews, an eminent Buddhist scholar, she startled me into a new awareness of language. In one of our wide-ranging conversations, she replaced the colloquial "killing two birds with one stone" with "feeding two birds with one seed." Her subtle yet significant upcycling of this phrase disrupted my relationship with figurative language and I have been trying to reframe violent idioms ever since.

Now I stumble upon phrases I use (unreflectively) that are embedded in violent imagery. Once we are attentive to the contours/contexts of the language we use (embedded, internalized, unreflective) in new ways, we cannot "unsee" them.

While I cannot excise figurative language from my writing (a turn of phrase, a metaphor, and a stylistic trope are all deep sources of delight for me), I strive to be more intentional in the unlearning and rewiring processes. Tiny tweaks are powerful in themselves.

For example, I have expelled the word "busy" from my lexicon because it signals deficit (I do not have enough time) and choose to move towards abundance (I am enough, we are enough).

I have unlearned the word "guys" because when someone pointed out that it is gender-exclusive, I could not unsee it. Now I awkwardly flail between "y'all," "folks," and "lovely humans," and I am open to more permutations of plural address because that is the beauty of language: it keeps evolving.

I have tried to excise "crazy" and other slang that invokes mental illness from my vocabulary because it is just as easy – and much kinder – to swap these with "wild" or "ridiculous." It costs me nothing *and* might mitigate harm to others.

Again, language is in constant flux because so are we. As American poet Maya Angelou notes, "I did then what I knew how to do. Now that I know better, I do better."[26] So let us ask crucial questions about the language we use every day.

- What stories are you telling and what words do you use to create the reality within which you live?
- What stories have you internalized and do you reproduce without reflection?
- What reality do you wish to create, and does your language match it?

Being cognizant of language not only changes the spaces we inhabit. It creates them. The act is crucial and revolutionary in how we shape systems. Likewise, it can be a pleasure when done with kindness and intention.

9. Live in the questions

From language, we move to the penultimate conceptual tool for hope circuits – questions – and perhaps my favourite because it frees us from the tyranny of being right and moves us into spaces where we can get it right – whatever right might resemble.

German poet Rainer Maria Rilke urges us to live in the questions for which we do not have the answers:

I would like to beg you, dear Sir, as well as I can, to have patience with everything unresolved in your heart and to try to love the questions themselves as if they were locked rooms or books written in a very foreign language. Don't search for the answers, which could not be given to you now, because you would not be able to live them. And the point is, to live everything. Live the questions now. Perhaps then, someday far in the future, you will gradually, without even noticing it, live your way into the answer.[27]

Krista Tippett, building on Rilke, says, "Our world is defined by raw, aching, open questions – personal, and civilizational – that we must live now if we hope to live our way eventually into new answers together."[28]

So, what questions do you want to "live into" when discussing building the systems-level architecture for future universities?

We must allow questions to decant to appreciate their quality and effect on us. As such, I have intentionally kept this section short and elliptical … because sometimes questions can just hang in the air for a while as our brains and hearts catch up.

10. Build intentional community

We cannot live into answers alone.

Community is essential in the building of hope circuits. In relational work, connecting to different ecosystems allows us to flourish as humans. Taking a page from bell hooks's *All About Love*, she proposes, "Rarely, if ever, are any of us healed in isolation. Healing is an act of communion."[29]

I agree.

A recurring theme that has emerged throughout my conversations with thought partners is that people frame hope as occurring between and amongst communities where individuals can connect to other people – whether that is to howl into the abyss, to imagine the possible, to seek out guidance, or to belly laugh.

As a Shakespearean, I believe that the theatre can teach us some valuable lessons about how to produce meaning in communion with each other. In Shakespeare's plays, there is no poet persona or omniscient narrator to guide – or misguide – us. Instead, the world is created in real time over the course of roughly three hours of exchanges amongst the players onstage. As spectators, witnesses, and participants we are inextricably bound up in creating an ephemeral moment produced by bodies in space encountering one another and animated by the force of our creative energies.

This model maps onto the classroom, organizations, and society more generally.

Indeed, this collaborative engagement model is essential to maintaining a civil and just society.

Nothing is created alone. And the work is never done.

We hear this idea echoed by public figures and current-day pedagogical thinkers. Canadian educational leader Joy Mighty, paraphrasing Archbishop Desmond Tutu, proposes a model for how we might build the foundations of hope university: "My humanity is bound up in yours, for we can only be human together. This is a way of thinking, of living our lives, where the focus is not on the intellectual and the physical dimensions of our humanity, but also on the emotional and the spiritual levels."[30]

Intentional community must be front of mind as we move from the individual level to the systems level to build the hope circuits necessary for human flourishing.

Concluding thoughts

These ten conceptual tools will appear in the following chapters in different order and magnitude depending on the topic and the wicked problem before us. Surfacing the systems, for example, will look one way when we look at governance and appear in a reconfigured form for mentorship.

Earlier I talked about the iterability of hope via James Baldwin and the notion that hope is a repetition of acts in everyday practice.

If hope is a verb – a continuous performance – then it builds meaning through each repeated performance. Rather than being fixed or static, institutions are provisional, shifting, contingent, and performed. There is power in iterability because every new performance offers opportunity for variation, disruption, and incremental change.

As these conceptual tools appear and reappear in subsequent chapters, building upon one another and illuminating concepts in different lights, we might see a blueprint emerge for a future paradigm of higher education.

If repetition is the key to pedagogy, as I often tell students, then repetition with variation is the key to creating something different – of working from the actual to the possible.[31]

Chapter 2

How Do We Value at Hope University?

I am still learning –
how to take joy in all the people I am,
how to use all my selves in the service of what I believe,
how to accept when I fail and rejoice when I succeed.
– Audre Lorde[1]

This is a statement of human flourishing, a celebration of constant emergence, and a testament to the grace of imperfection.

This is a hope circuit in poetic form. It values learning, joy, alignment, service, multiplicity, messiness, and wholeness.

And yet.

Just as Audre Lorde's poem invites us to embrace wholeness, it indicts systems that do not value the messiness of human experience.

In researching, interviewing, rumbling, and reflecting on how value circulates in the academy, it became increasingly clear that the current systems and structures in higher education do not reflect the values Audre Lorde's poem evokes.

Instead, the paradox between what our values *are* and *how* we value things has generated a tremendous amount of unprocessed rage that requires our immediate attention. Most of this rage is directed at the inequitable systems that do not value, compensate, or recognize impact in its diverse forms.

What will become a familiar refrain in this book – and bears repeating with emphasis – is that we have inherited outdated systems built on exclusion, mystification, and gatekeeping that do not recognize whole humans in all their states of becoming and evolution; nor do the current valuing systems have the capacity to appreciate diverse kinds of contributions and impact.

And yet.

While this project is committed to a systems-level approach to rewiring institutions, we are allowed to reserve a little rage for the gatekeepers and guardians of these systems. We can blame the dam, and yet we cannot let the salmon off the hook.

In social institutions that espouse the value of insatiable curiosity around the knowability of the world, many of us have internalized value systems that reproduce impervious knowledge without interrogation; many of us within the academy wield rigour like a blunt object, bludgeoning anything too soft, too different, too disruptive to Western-centric knowledge.

In some ways, a critically unreflective approach to value and evaluation is understandable: Sara Ahmed argues that those closest to the centres of power are the least likely to change how value is defined and circulates. She argues, "When people become more secure and better resourced institutionally, they also tend to become more conservative and more willing to do, as I call it, the work of institutional polishing – play by the rules, make the institution look good – because there are benefits attached."[2] This explains why so many of us in positions of power perpetuate systems that harm ourselves and so many others.

Shame on us.

And yet, shame is precisely what keeps us locked into these systems.

We are taught to be ashamed.

The academy perpetuates imposter syndrome at individual, cultural, and institutional levels. We spend much of our time talking about how imposter syndrome affects individuals, whether they are students and professors or staff, administrators, or other knowledge creators. There is a lot of research on "imposturous attitudes," with alarming data about the uneven effects on members of equity-deserving and historically excluded groups.

As Canadian psychologist Cara MacInnis's work reveals, "Students who are underrepresented in postsecondary education experience imposturous feelings more intensely, including ethnic minority students, women in STEM fields, and students from lower socioeconomic status (SES) backgrounds."[3]

For faculty and staff, imposturous attitudes are often exacerbated in systems that value and evaluate individual worth where there is a considerable risk of being deemed unworthy. Think about the myriad ways shame can flourish for professors: faculty are rejected on the job market, dejected after an unsuccessful grant application, and crestfallen when Reviewer 2 destroys a central argument.

Moreover, ideas are sometimes attacked during a conference session or at a departmental meeting, criticized over social media or via book reviews. Meanwhile, a class can spectacularly self-implode despite careful preparation, or a student might fail to thrive despite the best efforts of the instructor. We can just as easily map high-risk/high-failure situations onto staff and administrators, contract faculty and graduate students.

And yet, imposter syndrome is not limited to individuals: it also happens as a sector.

Universities themselves demonstrate imposter syndrome when we fail to make a case for the social mission of the university to government and industry, when we fail to tell the right stories to maintain and build public trust, and when we lack the confidence to convey a bold vision necessary to contribute to a healthy democracy.

Imposter syndrome is ubiquitous at every level. It is the air we breathe. It animates the system within which we are so often complicit and from which we just as often feel alienated. As a result, shame is baked into the walls.[4]

Consequently, there are so many layers to excavate and thus expose the rot – too many for this humble little chapter.

Since we must begin somewhere, let us start with the (in)famous *publish or perish* maxim, which haunts the dreams of graduate students, keeps job seekers awake at night, consumes early career researchers, and preoccupies even the most senior faculty. It informs how we teach, research, connect, lead, and work within institutions and disciplines, which likewise profoundly affects non-academic spheres of university life.

What kind of conundrum have we created for ourselves?

We have created a false binary between life (publish) or death (perish) that, in turn, exposes other binaries in higher education that we explore in subsequent chapters:

- Abundance versus scarcity.
- Wholeness versus silos.
- Vulnerability versus shame.
- Generativity versus stagnation.

- Worth versus unworthiness.
- Generosity versus gatekeeping.
- Messiness versus mastery.
- Wonder versus the status quo.
- Building/illuminating versus criticizing/deconstructing.

We create and maintain systems that reproduce binaries rather than making room for yes/and thinking. Indeed, we are so un-collegial as a collegium[5] that there are widely circulating jokes normalizing the systemic lack of generosity. Take, for example, the running jokes about the devastating critiques of Reviewer 2 in blind peer review.

We are our own gatekeepers.

We get in the way of each other. We block, exclude, criticize, demoralize, and deflate one another. We choose belittling over belonging. Generosity is eschewed in favour of gatekeeping.

And sometimes we do it for sport.

Furthermore, it is almost always unnecessary: most of the time, we are not directly competing with one another.

Let us stop and consider the following metaphor: the humble and yet mighty pie. In the academy, for the most part, getting a piece of pie does not result in someone else going hungry. Often, there are few or no limits to the pieces of pie available. And yet, our appetites are insatiable.

In academic spheres, we often envision lack where we could see love:

- If we apply for a teaching award, it does not mean that someone else is a lousy teacher (especially if they never applied for this particular award).
- If we get a research grant, it does not mean that other research is not fundable.
- If someone gets promoted, it does not mean someone else will not advance in rank.

There are many, many pies. Often there is enough for everyone to have their pie and to share with others. If we do not have one, we can find people to help us bake new pies.

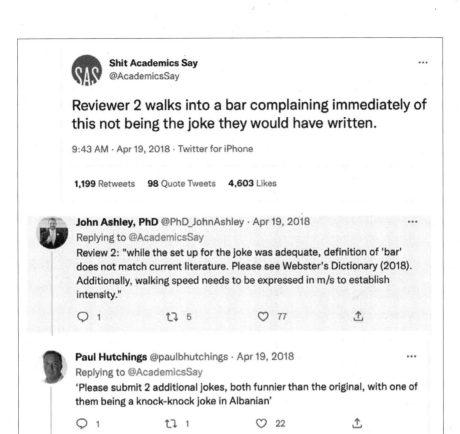

Shit Academics Say
@AcademicsSay

Reviewer 2 walks into a bar complaining immediately of this not being the joke they would have written.

9:43 AM · Apr 19, 2018 · Twitter for iPhone

1,199 Retweets   **98** Quote Tweets   **4,603** Likes

John Ashley, PhD @PhD_JohnAshley · Apr 19, 2018
Replying to @AcademicsSay
Review 2: "while the set up for the joke was adequate, definition of 'bar' does not match current literature. Please see Webster's Dictionary (2018). Additionally, walking speed needs to be expressed in m/s to establish intensity."

○ 1   ⟲ 5   ♡ 77   ↥

Paul Hutchings @paulbhutchings · Apr 19, 2018
Replying to @AcademicsSay
'Please submit 2 additional jokes, both funnier than the original, with one of them being a knock-knock joke in Albanian'

○ 1   ⟲ 1   ♡ 22   ↥

Jon Pierre @JonPierre2 · Apr 19, 2018
Replying to @paulbhutchings and @AcademicsSay
You all may be laughing now but sooner or later you will have to get past me again. I'll be waiting. Regards, Reviewer Two

○   ⟲   ♡ 3   ↥

The health of an organization can be quickly assessed when we pause to ask ourselves the following thought prompt: how do we feel when we see a colleague getting a piece of pie (insert award, grant, promotion, publication, spotlight, shout out)? If we feel more envy than jubilation, that is a sure sign that we are working and living in a culture of scarcity and shame.

We need to move from famine to feast, from scarcity to abundance, from *schadenfreude* to *freudenfreude* (a German word that means "the joy of someone else's happiness and flourishing").[6]

A mid-career faculty member recalled receiving a teaching award chosen by the students; while many of their colleagues emailed their congratulations, a few senior faculty members shared comments like, "I am not going to congratulate you because I would be ashamed of receiving a popularity award. It means you are too easy/not rigorous enough/too accessible."

During an interview, a faculty member recounted a particularly fractious faculty council meeting where they discussed external teaching awards (and whether the university should support applications). One faculty member declared, "I wouldn't dream of applying for this national external award. The people who apply are all about self-promotion. My classroom is a closed space that I don't need to share with anyone."

Something is rotten in the state of Denmark – and it has to do with *value*.

Slow down and pause

How do we find an entry point into a system that presents itself as a meritocracy and yet often feels rigged, exclusive, and impenetrable?

And how do we address the injustices, indignities, and aggressions that are of a staggering magnitude worse for historically excluded groups?

Rage is an option.

If we agree with Willie Jennings, when he asserts that "anger is the engine of hope now,"[7] how do we harness it in generous and generative ways?

In the final chapter of *The Courage to Teach*, Parker Palmer gives us a toolbox "to name, claim and aim" emotional information – difficulty and dissonance – in order to move toward transformative action and insight.[8] For Palmer, the first step is to name the emotions or issues that plague us and then "claim" them by understanding the context where various forces converge around us. Once we have identified what is in our sphere of control, only then can we get unstuck, moving past the otherwise debilitating despair to action – towards the "aim."

For Parker Palmer, the binary of cognitive and affective, of head and heart, is reinforced by the university systems themselves, which value objective knowledge that "distrusts and devalues inner reality."[9] He says, "In this culture, the pathology of speech disconnected from the self is regarded, and rewarded, as a virtue."[10] Parker Palmer invites us instead to imagine a system that takes "emotional intelligence as seriously as we take … cognitive intelligence."[11]

When I pause to name my rage, I realize that how we value things – and the lack of integrity between what we say and what we do – inspired the earliest germinations of this book.

In fall 2021 I experienced a stretch of wicked insomnia. The "wide-awake at 3 a.m. and angry about it" kind, where I refused to get up and my brain refused to shut off. I had just finished a five-year book project with Lisa Dickson and Shannon Murray, *Shakespeare's Guide to Hope, Life, and Learning*, so I had hope on the brain. I was still ruminating on my defence of Hamlet, long maligned as a moody, melancholic university student, and I kept returning to an idea in my *Hamlet* chapter:

> This play isn't about Hamlet's failure to act, or his inability to make up his mind: he isn't some whiny, spotted teenager in the midst of a self-indulgent existential crisis (although I have been there and it is a MOOD). Hamlet doesn't lack resilience or grit when faced with a changing world. The world is flawed. The system is rigged. He never stood a chance because something is rotten in the state of Denmark.[12]

I could not shake the conviction that Denmark could be superimposed onto some of our institutions and, moreover, we have overlooked one of Shakespeare's more pointed pieces of advice: look to the systems.

I wondered, what would it look like if we could build Hope University where the systems were designed for resilience so individuals could focus on thriving rather than surviving? So, one night, instead of counting sheep, I wrote the table of contents for an imaginary book.

The titles for cheeky chapters flowed:

- "Help! I'm a 19th-century body trapped in a 21st-century context!"

- "Universities won't love you back, and other lessons from the universe."
- "No one gives a Fuck about Teaching."

Eventually I fell asleep, and in the morning I could not shake off the idea. So, I shuffled a few meetings and spent the morning writing down the fictional table of contents. It felt indulgent, a few hours where I could play "hooky" from the relentless emails and countless meetings.

When I looked at the list of imaginary chapters taking shape, it struck me that I had been rumbling many of these concepts before – as a columnist with *University Affairs Magazine* and through other public scholarship contributions to the *Conversation*, the *Globe and Mail* – while also percolating these ideas in more informal writing spaces (blog posts, monthly reports, and even tweets).

I realized that I had been unintentionally writing towards Hope University for many years and had not connected the dots.

I needed to slow down. Pause. And see the pattern.

Surface the systems

After a cursory scan of my past writing, I realized that there was both method and madness to Hope University. For five years, my wonderful *University Affairs* editor, Leo Charbonneau, gave me one writing prompt – write about "Adventures in Academe" from your perspective. The rest was up to me.

It was, in so many ways, a formative experience. The series of articles traces the maturation of my professional identity from early career bravado towards a deeper appreciation of complexity. I found myself through the writing process – and most of the topics I gravitated towards were about how value circulates in post-secondary systems.

Returning to those imaginary, insomnia-fuelled chapters exposed a preoccupation with value.

"Help! I'm a 19th-century body trapped in a 21st-century context!" makes a joke about the old value systems we have inherited that are no longer adequate for managing new social realities.

"Universities won't love you back, and other lessons from the universe" speaks to the uncomfortable realization many of us have had that the things we love – the things we create, the energy we expend, the emotional labour we spend – don't always count (or, more precisely, don't have *value*) in existing evaluation systems.

"No one gives a Fuck about Teaching" is a howl into the abyss – a raw expression of the profound cognitive dissonance between what we say and what we value.

This final one hurts the most. We are truants to teaching.

Stay with the trouble

In our current value system, teaching is the thing we set aside to do other things. We get teaching releases to do research. We get teaching releases to take on administrative duties. And yet it is almost unheard of to get service releases to do teaching or released from research output so we can develop an innovative course. In fact, very few paths to full professorship include teaching as a primary or sole criterion in Canadian collective agreements.

The language we use tells us everything we need to know about what is valued: we have teaching loads (burdens) and research projects (boons); we have teaching releases (deficit) and research grants (abundance). We see this in the contradictions exposed by the publish or perish maxim: in this binary system, we are asked to choose between life or death even when – in my experience anyway – teaching is one of the most life-affirming, soul-sustaining endeavours we undertake.

We also outsource teaching in ways we would never imagine doing for research, service, governance, or non-academic expertise. Precarity is perpetuated when we outsource teaching to graduate students and contingent contract faculty who are making a pittance per course. We do not outsource research or service.

Let us sit with a provocative statement: in the current post-secondary education system, we do not value teaching – nor do we adequately evaluate or compensate it.

This is not new in conversations about post-secondary education. In 2011, higher education scholar Pamela Gravestock defended a doctoral dissertation titled "Does Teaching Matter? The Role of Teaching Evaluation in Tenure Policies at Selected Canadian Universities."

Her premise:

Teaching has always been and remains a core function of universities. However, there is a pervasive assumption that research activity is privileged over teaching contributions, particularly when hiring, tenure, and promotion decisions are being made. Where do such beliefs come from? Are these assumptions based on policy, practice, or a combination? Is research privileged, and if so, does teaching matter?[13]

Spoiler alert: the answer is a resounding NO.

How do we square this with the assumption outside the academy, and indeed for the 1.4 million students who attend Canadian universities annually, that teaching is foundational to higher education institutions (it is, after all, right there in the *name*)?

The gap between what we say we do and what we value (reward, incentivize, promote) is significant – and widening.

We need to mind the gap.

Take a systems-level approach

If you want to understand how value circulates in the collegium, read the collective agreement(s) (CA). If you want to understand the difference between individual value and institutional values, read the CA next to the university strategic plan. The strategic plan and collective agreement are the two most important systems-level documents that determine the academic life of a university or college. Reading these two documents together exposes the gap between what we say we do and what we value. The size of the gap depends on the institution and even differs by the division, unit, or department.[14]

If you want to gauge the appetite for change, creativity, or innovation in any given organization, look specifically to the articles on promotion, evaluation, and review for the incentive structures. Equally important, look for what is missing, i.e., the disincentives to academic work.

Evaluation committees, selection committees, and other bodies tasked with evaluation processes inevitably have a high volume of dossiers to review, and so they almost always start with counting the number of lines on the CV for peer-reviewed publications. And then a cursory look at teaching scores. A quick count of senate committees. Then a review of the cover letter, a perusal of letters, and that is it. You are worthy or unworthy.[15]

> In an interview, one faculty member confessed that he caught himself counting lines on a cv in a recent job selection committee. He was horrified: "I knew better! I have been working on decolonizing my classrooms, rethinking authority and expertise, designing more inclusive spaces for my students, and yet I still counted the lines of the cv as if that was an indicator of someone's worth. I had to catch myself only after I did it – and I am still amazed at how much I have to unlearn that is invisible to me."

I paint a stark (and purposefully unnuanced) picture to make a point, and it is important to acknowledge the many diligent, thorough, generous humans doing the challenging work of assessing, evaluating, and documenting impact of their colleagues.

That is not the point I am making: we can, individually, be as good-willed and fair-minded as possible and still be stuck with broken systems and flawed metrics that do not value wholeness, messiness, and evolution. We need to figure out how we can make the evaluation structures amplify the capacities of the individual rather than making the individual conform to outmoded evaluation criteria.

Live in the questions

Value is a topic that begets many questions:

- What are the criteria for assessing value?
- Is value fixed (intrinsic, based on merit, determined by concrete criteria), or is it variable (dynamic, contextual, comparative)?
- If value is not fixed, static, or merit-based, how is it assigned?
- How does value circulate within various systems?
- What are the formal and informal mechanisms that determine value?
- What happens when our perceptions of value systems (tried, true,

trustworthy, rigorous, standardized) are shaken (i.e., when the goal-posts keep moving or there is preferential treatment or inconsistency)?

In discussions of value and its relationship to metrics, we ask comparable questions: do we measure up or fall short? Value must be distinguished from metrics, which is a measurement – an instrument or tool – that seeks to quantify contribution, impact, worth.
Value, on the other hand, has an ontological and existential dimension:
Do we belong?
Does our contribution matter?
At the heart of any discussion of value and its expressions – evaluation, assessment, appraisal, review – is the following set of questions:

- Are we worthy?
- Are we enough?
- Do we add value?
- Are we valued?
- Do we matter?

If value is an assessment of something's worth, why do we often feel unworthy?
Until we value whole selves – messy, curious, emergent, daring, brave – we will not see those qualities reflected in our students, our research, and our contribution to a broader society.

Prototype for hopeful systems

When I was five years into my academic career, I had a realization that changed how I understand value and worth. I found myself coming home every night complaining that the projects I had built with colleagues and students were not institutionally supported. I was increasingly frustrated that creativity happened despite, not because of, the conditions within the academy. My (non-academic) husband, tired of my whining over wine, challenged me to move from despair to action.

He asked, *are you being paid for this work?*

In some cases, I was compensated for messy, frustrating work.

"Okay, then: no whining," he said.

Next up: if you are not being paid for it, *does your work count?*

In other words, does work count towards promotion, tenure, and periodic review? Does it help with external grants and awards? In many cases, the answer was yes.

"Okay, then: no whining," he said.

Still looking for sympathy, I wailed, "Some of this is neither compensated nor valued!"

Well, he asked, *do you love what you are doing?*

The underlying question was, would you do it for free?

In this context, I had to ask, is this work aligned to my purpose? Does this make me and others feel good? Does this contribute to making the world better, more just, more inclusive? And, more often than not, the answer is yes.

"Okay, then: no whining," he said.

I came out of the conversation with something much more valuable than sympathy: a three-branch decision-making tree that I have relied on ever since to make informed choices about where I put my energy. Ideally, my work has all three elements: *compensation, value,* and *purpose.* When I stop to reflect on my work, sometimes I can only identify one or two branches. If there are zero out of three, walking away from the project is necessary.

Indeed, from the hundreds of interviews I conducted, many individuals shared their own frameworks for determining where they invest their time, energy, and resources, often in tension with the policies and structures of the systems we have inherited. These stories, interviews, reflections help name the current disconnections in the existing systems, which enables us to rewire the systems and institutional cultures within which we are immersed.

The question at the front of mind must be: how do you prototype hopeful systems whereby value is clearly defined, that are dynamic enough to capture diverse kinds of contributions and that are supportive of human flourishing, and that advance the social mission of universities?

Stay with the trouble

One of the elements of labour we must attend to is the oft overlooked and yet ever-present emotional dimension of academic work. In many ways, hope circuits are about rewiring our affective circuitry. And yet, we tend to gloss over the emotional labour expended in scholarly evaluation processes.

Without naming and claiming our "inner reality," with all its dissonance and discomfort, we might carry on with a stiff upper lip, though with a cumulative effect that can manifest itself in different ways. Without careful management (and sometimes despite it), this can lead to burnout, elevated levels of psychological distress, physical health problems, substance abuse, and higher rates of depression.

If we hope to serve our communities, our discipline, and learners with integrity and wholeness, Parker Palmer urges us to engage in self-reflection: "Integrity requires that I discern what is integral to my selfhood, what fits and what does not – and that I choose life-giving ways of relating to the forces that converge within me."[16]

That means staying with the trouble, sitting in the discomfort, and trusting ourselves to break open.

Otherwise, when we render emotional labour invisible, we privilege perfection over process.

And that costs us something.

Erasing our vulnerability runs counter to true learning, which requires us to make mistakes as a precondition for generating new insights about our discipline, our classrooms, and ourselves. We often lose sight of our own roles as learners. Our students and our colleagues expect us to be experts in our field and the classroom, and any crack in the veneer is met with disbelief or mistrust.

No wonder we are so exhausted.

So, what do we need to name, claim, and aim around value?

The current formula for evaluating faculty performance fails to incentivize diverse approaches to higher education and creates barriers to creative and collaborative design.

When it comes to evaluating faculty performance, the one-size-fits-all model we use in many universities – roughly 40 per cent research, 40 per cent teaching, and 20 per cent service – must be reimagined if Canadian universities are to "support and sustain an innovative, resilient and diverse society" of global learners in the twenty-first century.[17]

The scenarios are familiar across institutions: ask colleagues to join a new committee only to be told that if it is not a senate committee it "does not count" towards service; invite colleagues to create new interdisciplinary initiatives only to be told that, until they get promoted to full professor, any free time or energy must be directed to research; urge colleagues to participate in professional development opportunities related to enhancing student learning only to be told that their efforts are best spent elsewhere.

We certainly cannot blame faculty for the state of affairs: they operate within the parameters established and enforced by their collective agreements. Failing to conform comes with consequences, including the inability to secure a job, stalling at the associate professor rank, and other financial and reputational deterrents.

The cycle is further reinforced when the individuals responsible for evaluating faculty performance are those who have successfully navigated the system themselves. In order to disrupt this system, we must change the concrete ways we acknowledge, legitimize, and reward scholarly activity.

Creating separate teaching and research streams does not fix the problem: it only reinforces the siloed systems. The pervasive assumption is that these three spheres of scholarly activity are compartmentalized and mutually exclusive rather than cross-fertilizing and mutually enriching. Furthermore, the division inevitably creates hierarchies that privilege research over teaching and service.

Let me be clear: I am not advocating for easier pathways to promotion. If we change how we think about the way work is valued within the academy – or at the very least expand the current definitions of what constitutes scholarly activity – we can design assessment to encourage individuals to reach their optimal capacities for the most significant impact on diverse communities.

We can set the bar to excellence. And then we can help everyone tap into their individual and collective purpose through capacity-building, mentorship, and equity-focused design.

With all this in mind, my most recent sabbatical report sought to disrupt, ever so slightly, the paradigm of value in my own university context. Instead of merely listing my peer-reviewed publications and conference presentations, I included activities such as public scholarship and community outreach, fellowships and awards for educational leadership, editing and publishing undergraduate research, new course proposals and senate reports, website and social media design, fundraising, non-peer-reviewed articles, and a whole range of otherwise invisible activities that do not currently count in the definition of scholarly activity.

I named the things that have little or no value, and then I claimed the messiness and emergence of this work:

Dear members of the Evaluation Committee,

Please accept my sabbatical report for Winter 2020. As you are all aware, March 13, 2020 marked the premature end of my planned six-month sabbatical as the global pandemic shut down schools and universities across the province and around the world. COVID-19 meant the abrupt cancellation of conference and travel plans, writing retreats, and other collaborative in-person activities planned for my research leave.

The personal toll of the pandemic has been heavy. My small children – then 4 and 6 – were home, and it became impossible to work consistently while managing full-time childcare. Furthermore, my husband was diagnosed with cancer in March 2020 and underwent invasive surgery to remove two lobes of his right lung on June 1: he was hospitalized and then quarantined in our home for many weeks.

Cancer, COVID-19, and caring for small children as the sole parent has been a traumatizing experience and it has been taken a tremendous effort to manage without family or friends to support us due to physical distancing requirements.

Nevertheless, in the 10 weeks of my sabbatical (instead of the planned 30 week research leave), I did accomplish a number of things, including submitting and/or seeing the publication of X peer-reviewed publications, contributing to Y peer-reviewed book chapters, presenting Z peer-reviewed conference papers at international conferences, A Op-eds for *University Affairs Magazine*, delivering B invited talks for national and international audiences, and C other professional activities.

… [insert an exhaustive and exhausting list of things] …

However, this report must come with a disclaimer. We often think that people who are productive are thriving. This summer, as my husband recovered from invasive cancer surgery, one of my colleagues started an email to me with "It seems, from a distance, as though you're having a fine and productive summer." I was most certainly not fine. In fact, I was going through hell. What I realized upon reflection was that my coping mechanism (for dealing with cancer in the time of COVID with small children) was to work. Work was the only thing that made me feel normal in the middle of very abnormal circumstances.

This is neither healthy nor sustainable behaviour, and it sets a terrible example, especially for the young people with whom I have the privilege to work. While I tell them regularly that working until exhaustion is not a badge of honour and that we need to practise an ethics of care, my words and my actions are "out of joint." Not only is it essential to pause often, write more, and listen better to support our own individual wellness, together we can shift the narrative away from manic productivity and towards a more humane mode of living and working in post-COVID times.

I hope that you review my report alongside all the others submitted from Winter 2020 with compassion and understanding. We are all experiencing trauma and respond in different ways. Thank you for reviewing my report, and for the essential work you are doing in valuing and making visible the many forms of scholarly engagement in the midst of a global pandemic.

Sincerely,

[insert sign off]

You know what the response from the Evaluation Committee was?

CRICKETS.

FUCKING CRICKETS.

And yet, I did not write the report to solicit a response from the evaluation committee, mostly because my expectations of humane and trauma-informed leadership were already well managed. I wrote the report instead as a response to Audre Lorde's invitation to reimagine how we reproduce and reflect on value.

Paradigm shifts happen slowly. By changing each repetition ever so slightly, we can disrupt the "regulatory fiction" of assessment, an approach inspired by Judith Butler's work on disrupting traditional and limiting norms through repetition. Every slight variation, resistance, or counternarrative can – over time – change the people and the systems in profound ways.

In conversations with so many around Hope University, a recurring theme emerged about how we need to value contributions that have otherwise been invisible or erased. Higher education institutions must renew efforts to focus on people and purpose to foster work environments that increase individual and community flourishing.

Moreover, if we model caring and supportive work environments, students will encounter better possibility models on their pathways towards purpose.

We must be better for ourselves and in community with others.

We cannot continue to perpetuate systems where working to the point of exhaustion is valorized; we cannot continue to burn out humans whose work has impact beyond traditional systems of evaluation. If we cannot do this for ourselves, let us do it for our colleagues and students, the precariat and the outliers, as we reimagine the ways we value.

And maybe, just maybe, by sharing the possibility of divergence – of ways we can value things differently – we can collectively slow down, reflect, and rewire the systems for hope and human flourishing.

Let's reset the bar to excellence by starting from a place where people matter.

Chapter 3

How Do We Learn at Hope University?

To contact happiness of any kind is "to be dissolved into something complete and great," something beyond the bruising boundaries of the ego. The attainment of happiness is then less a matter
of pursuit than of surrender – to the world's wonder, ready as
it comes.
– Maria Popova[1]

We are all learners.

We are all – at various points in our lives and in many spheres – crossing
thresholds of understanding, embarking on messy and circuitous journeys,
and striving towards the fulfillment of purpose.

Rewiring systems for human flourishing requires us to unlearn and relearn ways of being – as individuals and within systems, organizations, and
communities. This is not easy – especially for those of us who have built
identities as experts, knowledge holders, authority figures, and masters of
content.

And yet, learning is not as much something *fixed* (title, position, role) as
something we *do*.

Returning to an excerpt from *Shakespeare's Guide*:

Learning is embodied hope. It happens in time. It happens in bodies.
Each act of learning is unique and can never be reproduced on a factory
line. It cannot be abstracted from the bodies and the lives of learners

who embody it, any more than a verb can function grammatically without an agent. Hope is a verb.[2]

Learning is also a precondition for flourishing.

First introduced by Aristotle in *Nicomachean Ethics*, human flourishing is defined simply as "the way we are *supposed to be* as human beings."[3] Flourishing is the journey towards our full potential, fulfilling our best capacities, tapping into our life's purpose.

The only path to human flourishing – according to Aristotle – is by learning.[4]

Eudaimonia, often interpreted as "flourishing," translates as "good demons" or "good spirit." The literal translation captures something of the sublime: tapping into our purpose – some call it "flow" while others characterize it as being in the "zone" – has a quality of energy that elevates us beyond our day-to-day existence into something more expansive.

While a standard translation from the Greek *Eudaimonia* is "happiness," that does not quite embody the kinetic nature of the concept: happiness is a state of mind – something you feel – while flourishing is something we do over time.

Happiness is a moment. Flourishing is a mindset.[5]

(Which is why "I am happy" works in a sentence and "I am flourish" does not.)

Flourishing is the full expression of our human capacities; according to the Greeks, we are already wired with virtues: we must cultivate them through habit and practice – of "living well and doing well." Flourishing is a learned mindset that we practise over time: our virtues – such as courage, generosity, benevolence, wittiness, even righteous indignation – must be exercised like a muscle, with intention and deliberative attention so these virtues become habits and dispositions.

We can continuously improve – through practice and intention, education and in community – so that virtues that are internal become external and become part of our daily practice. When we cultivate a flourishing mindset, we can respond better to situations as they arise, react better to ambiguous encounters as they present themselves, and resolve ethical dilemmas as they evolve.

In other words, we are pre-wired with virtues: it is up to us to build the circuitry that best illuminates our purpose.

One of the first people I interviewed for this book was my friend Joy Mighty, a titan of teaching and learning in Canada and beyond. I wanted to know what she did when she lost hope. Instead, she told me a story about her earliest learning experience: when she was growing up in Guyana in the 1960s, her father was a public servant during a ninety-day strike when the whole country shut down. Protesters surrounded their family home, shouting and threatening violence. A man of steadfast integrity, her father waded through a sea of protesters outside their family home every morning on his way to work. Transportation was disrupted, so he needed to ride his bicycle. The problem was, the crowds were too thick to wheel his bicycle through the masses outside his house. His solution: he carried the bicycle above his head, and as he passed by the people demonstrating, he said good morning cordially and with dignity to all.

Joy recounts how that image of her father, gentle and firm, anchoring his integrity in every step, inspired her to manage the difficulty of being a change-maker in her own leadership journey. She experienced systemic and structural racism throughout her career, from promotion and review processes to being targeted by white supremacists for her work on equity, diversity, and inclusion. Joy Mighty lifted her metaphorical bicycle – her purpose – over her head and waded daily through a sea of hatred. She learned the tools she needed to transform institutions – to build more inclusive and just spaces for all – by watching her father.

Joy Mighty could have told me a story about trauma. Or a story about triumph. Or a story of rage. Or a story of grief. Instead, she told me a story about learning. She chose a story about a formative moment in her childhood where she learned that virtues – courage, generosity, benevolence, righteous indignation – were verbs that you can learn, conjugate, and integrate into your own rhetoric of hope.

As we move towards a paradigm shift in higher education, we must be attentive to the tools we use, the mindset we adopt, and the stories we tell.

We need tools to sit as learners.

We need mindsets to metabolize disorientation, rage, and despair.

We need stories to rewire our mindsets towards abundance and wholeness.

Surface the systems

My favourite toolbox – that combines tools, mindset, and storytelling – comes from Jan Meyer and Ray Land's theory of transformative learning, which offers us a framework for understanding the processes of transformation from the micro to the metaphysical levels.[6]

Although this theoretical framework has been used to understand the process learners undergo in the context of disciplinary knowledge, it has broad applications as we imagine paradigm shifts in PSE institutions.

Threshold concepts are core ideas that are hard to grasp. A challenging concept within a discipline or field will feel almost impossible to comprehend when you first encounter it; once you do understand it, it radically transforms your relationship to the field of study – and yourself in the process.

Crossing a threshold from one state of being to another is a powerful image that illuminates how change happens in microcosms (individuals), in ecosystems (classrooms, communities), in macrocosms (institutions, organizations), and in mega-systems (a sector, society).

David Foster Wallace's parable of the fish that I introduced in chapter 1 is a perfect example of a threshold concept. As I outlined earlier, the older fish swims by and asks the younger fish, "How's the water?" At first, the younger fish are perplexed: what the hell is water? What is that old fish talking about? They have not yet crossed the threshold. It is difficult for the younger fish to see the water at first; once they do, it changes everything. You cannot unsee the water.[7]

If this project can be distilled to one core threshold concept, it is seeing the water. This book on hope circuits is an invitation to see the water within which we are immersed and offer tools to understand the shape and boundaries of our ecosystems.

The seven features of transformative learning help us see the water:

1. Transformative learning is likened to crossing a threshold.

As we transform, we move through a liminal space from one state of being into a new one. As a literature scholar, I always imagine a knight heading off on a quest through a perilous landscape, travelling into unknown spaces – forests, plains, caves – where they are not sure where they are going or when they will arrive.

In crossing thresholds, so much effort is expended without knowing what lessons will help lead to the ultimate destination. There are many wrong turns and dead ends, which is part of the process of crossing unfamiliar terrain. Most of the invisible work that happens is only recognizable over time and in retrospect.

As we experience paradigm shifts in higher education, things are messy, disorienting, and we do not yet have a clear view of what is on the other side of the expanse we are traversing. Anything is possible, and there are lots of paths and competing articulations, with a healthy dash of discontent.

2. Transformative learning is troublesome.
Crossing thresholds feels counterintuitive, alien, incoherent, and uncomfortable. When the normative structures, policies, attitudes, tools come into focus, we can often experience deep disorientation. What we thought we knew might no longer hold and we do not immediately have a new framework to put in its place.

Poet and scholar Bayo Akomolafe's writings on rupture in the Anthropocene capture a quality of this discomfort:

> We live in strange times. Times of transgression and upheaval. Boundaries are porous, and once resolute lines dividing the world up into neat categories are faltering. The furniture in the room has moved, and things are no longer the same. If you tried to be still for a lingering second, you might notice just how dizzying the world's irreverent spin is.[8]

"What the hell is water?" the fish exclaim. Discomfort is a feature, not a flaw, of transformation.

3. Transformative learning is irreversible.
Once you cross that threshold and transform, you cannot go back.

Once you have seen the water, you cannot unsee it.

Once the butterfly turns into the caterpillar, there is no return.

As a society and a sector, we have seen many things that we cannot unsee, and there is an increasing awareness that there is no going back to "normal." This can happen at the individual and institutional level while also happening at a societal level. In many thresholds, as we move through the difficulty of learning, we have to sit in grief and rage. We need ways to metabolize this discomfort. Once we grasp the concept, everything changes – and we start to see the water everywhere.

4. Transformative learning is integrative.

Knowledge itself is reconstituted in this transformative process. In the integrative process of reconfiguring, we combine all the different bits of knowledge in an integrative, synthesized way so that the collection of distinct experiences or concepts starts to make sense as part of a larger whole.

Once the fish sees the water, they will start to see the currents and eddies, the whirlpools and the tide; what has previously been a collection of isolated moments or encounters is now part of a much larger and interconnected ecosystem.

"What is knowledge?" and "how do we know things?" are now up for discussion; fixed and impervious knowing gives way to questions. Answers are not readily available; however, we can start to piece together fragments that might not have been related before and are now interconnected or reconfigured in new ways to form an emerging picture.

5. Transformative learning is discursive.

The relationship between learning and language is my favorite design principle in this theory of change.

Jan Meyer and Ray Land demonstrate that transformation leads to an enhanced and extended use of language.[9] In other words, we can tell if someone has transformed because we can see it reflected in their language. Our grammar shifts. Our rhetorical strategies transform. How we tell stories mirrors our shift in perspectives. The words we use change as we change. Our origin stories might even start from a new place or focus on a different experience.

One of the conceptual tools of this book – change your language, change the world – can be inverted: when you change your experience in the world, your language changes.

6. Transformative learning is reconstitutive.

When we cross a threshold and grasp a new concept, we experience an epistemological shift (how we know things) and, more importantly, we experience an ontological shift (who we are).

As an undergraduate I remember walking out of a class with fireworks going off in my brain and thinking, I will never be the same again. Although

I felt electrified, I did not have the language yet to understand that I was in the process of being rewired.

Since change takes place over time, the shift in identity is more likely to be recognized initially by others. Learners might require a mirror, reflection, or a mentor to illuminate and make sense of their transformation.

We need intentional community to manage the disorientation of being remade.

7. Transformative learning is circuitous.

Finally, the concept of liminality is critical. Mastering a threshold concept often involves messy journeys back and forth across conceptual terrains. Jan Meyer and Ray Land assert that there is no simple passage in learning from easy to difficult. There is no straight line. There is no map. Moreover, when one first embarks on the journey across a threshold, we cannot know what is on the other side. This is why transformative learning is messy – and requires hard hope.

Bayo Akomolafe's reflections on the end times helps us think through this moment:

> Hope is beautiful, especially when it does the work we wanted it to do. The trick is noticing what comes with costs? What are the costs of all the things that are left by the wayside? the generativity of failure? the other orientations? [Leaving the linear progress of hope, we] move to the side to dance; [it] feels to me like a shifting of us [out] of our centrality; that's the call that I hear as the call of hopelessness ... maybe it's awkward, maybe there are ways of moving to the side that invites a shifting of our positions.[10]

Failure, disorientation, and circuitousness are all part of the transformative learning theory.

These are awkward times. As institutions of higher learning, we have not yet shed our outdated paradigm and emerged into a new form; and yet, restlessness and discontent (and even strife) are signs that the new paradigm is emerging.

The shit is actually manure.

Stay with the trouble

As individuals, institutions, and communities, we are crossing thresholds of various kinds – in the liminal, in-between spaces – where we have had to sit in our discomfort without a clear sense of when this process will end and what we will look like on the other side.

What threshold concepts do we need to grasp?

I recently grappled with a challenging concept: the fundamental difference between student and learner.

One is a unit, and the other is a person.

You can count students on spreadsheets.

- You can scale, massify, add, subtract, and cut.
- You can assess what they cost and how much revenue they generate.
- You can say, without risk of dismemberment, that the average class size is 26.7 students.
- You can track the number of courses taken, completion rates, retention statistics, and grades.

You cannot count learners on spreadsheets.

- People are indivisible.
- They add abundance and richness to learning environments.
- They are whole beings with diverse lived experiences.
- They each contribute something unique to the ecosystem that is better than the sum of its parts.
- They embark on messy, circuitous, and life-long learning journeys.

Students can be learners. Learners do not have to be students.

We make room for learners. We operationalize students.[11]

The process of operationalizing students is the desire to measure an abstract concept – learning – by creating variables, extracting indicators, and then designing instruments to observe, measure, and manipulate the data.

I just threw up a little in my mouth.

Do not get me wrong:

- I believe in valuing, evaluating, and reflecting on all work.
- I believe in transparency and accountability.
- I believe in data-informed decision-making and policy creation.
- I believe in clear and compounding (scaffolded) feedback loops.
- I believe in alignment and critical reflection as essential tools to understand who we are and what we are doing.
- I believe in frequent and ongoing assessment so that we can adjust and accommodate if a project is flailing, a student is failing, or we discover unintended consequences.

Yes.
And.

- I believe in treating students as learners.
- I believe in designing systems for learners.
- I believe learning can happen because of, not despite, the systems.

Take a systems-level approach

Why are we fixated on students and not learners?

James Vincent, in *Beyond Measure*, observes that "the underlying principle that any human endeavor can be usefully reduced to a set of statistics has become one of the dominant paradigms of the 21st century."[12]

What happens, though, if the tools are inadequate?

In Thomas Kuhn's theory of culture change, if the tools we use no longer resolve problems or contradictions as they arise, "anomalies" start to accumulate. In time, the inadequate tools expose the inadequacy of one or more fundamental principles. In response, we try desperately to tweak the current model, which merely precipitates crisis. The result? Revolutionary change from which a new paradigm emerges, one that offers improved explanations for the time we are in and provides a better guide for future problems.

What happens, then, if an underlying principle is exposed as flawed?

This is happening in higher education in real time. There is a systems-wide realization that some tools no longer serve us – and many never have.

Take, for example, the highly publicized case at Toronto Metropolitan University (formerly Ryerson) in 2018 when an arbitrator ruled that student evaluations of teaching (SETS) were inadequate to assess teaching performance.[13] In the decision, the arbitrator noted that "numerous factors, especially personal characteristics – and this is just a partial list – such as race, gender, accent, age and 'attractiveness' skew SET results. It is almost impossible to adjust for bias and stereotypes."[14] Since the landmark ruling, several Canadian universities have either revisited policies or suspended the use of SETS in performance reviews.

In 2021, the American varsity athletic organization National Collegiate Athletic Association[15] recommended dropping the standardized test score requirement for eligibility. David Wilson, president at Morgan State University in the United States, led the Standardized Test Score Task Force: "This work reflects the NCAA's commitment to continually reviewing our academic standards based on the best available data and other relevant information."[16] The best available data, in this case, is that standardized tests are racist and discriminatory: according to Ibram X. Kendi, author of *How to Be an Antiracist*, "standardized tests have become the most effective racist weapon ever devised to objectively degrade Black and Brown minds and legally exclude their bodies from prestigious schools."[17]

Both cases expose tools that are not merely flawed; they are deeply harmful and discriminatory to members of equity-deserving and historically excluded groups – which harms everyone.[18]

The inadequacy of the tools, in turn, exposes flaws in the underlying principles. In what now might be a familiar refrain, something is rotten in the state of Denmark. In the case of Canadian universities, our institutions are founded upon "deeper, systemic colonial and ideological structures of administration we all take for granted."[19]

Once we see the water, though, we can no longer unsee it.

Reimagine authority and expertise

Once we see the tension between student and learner, we can better articulate the gap between *what we say we do* in higher education and *what we actually* do.

At the heart of this tension is our obsession with measuring, which Jerry Ż. Muller, in *The Tyranny of Metrics*, argues threatens the quality of our lives and our most important institutions. The irony for Muller is that "not everything that is important is measurable, and much that is measurable is unimportant."[20]

The Richardson Effect is a paradox whereby "the more accurately you try to measure some things, the more complex they become."[21] The more you try to measure the coast of Britain, for example, the longer it gets. Or, as British physicist James Bridle reflects, "instead of resolving into order and clarity, ever-closer examination reveals only more, and more splendid, detail and variation."[22]

These are not new concepts. In *Prometheus Unbound*, romantic poet Percy Bysshe Shelley writes, "the deep truth is imageless." For Shelley, acknowledging that something is unknowable does not make the pursuit of it futile; rather, it is the struggle for knowledge that makes us "good, great and joyous, beautiful and free."[23]

Psychologists, physicists, and poets are fascinated with the principle that "the truth is always stranger, more lively and more expansive than anything we can compute."[24]

And yet, others – including some presidents, politicians, policy-makers, and pundits – believe that anything worthwhile must, by definition, be measurable.

The former makes room for the wonder of learners. The latter seeks to measure students as units.

Which approach we choose has far-reaching consequences for the future of universities.

Take a systems-level approach

If we are to excavate what is rotten in the state of metrics, we must go back to the roots: what gives rise to a fixation on metrics in the first place?

Metrics are a product of the trust gap.

In a scarcity culture, the less control we have (over projects, people, outcomes), the greater the tendency to grasp more control through measuring, surveilling, and policing.

Staying with the trouble, I am ashamed to admit that my default setting is to deploy metrics when I lose trust: if I feel I have lost class engagement, I will survey them, start taking attendance, or look at their engagement with the course management platform to see who is showing up and how. If I sense one of my working groups has gone off track, I compile reports, attend more meetings, check the meeting notes, add action items, and assign more duties. If I have lost trust in a team member, I ask them to account for their time, what they have been doing, report on their deliverables, and communicate more.

In a scarcity culture, metrics become a form of surveillance that increases as trust decreases.

In a culture of abundance, learners show up in spaces of trust because that is where the messiness of co-creation and emergence lives. Trust fosters creativity, innovation, and joy.

If trust is threatened, default mechanisms kick in, and we can revert to a scarcity mindset, which makes it hard to stay in the hope circuits. The default in our current systems includes micromanagement, calls for accountability, and more reporting. No one wins in cultures of policing and surveillance. For one thing, it is exhausting and depleting. It is also a colossal waste of time.

We can trace metrics mindsets from the macrocosm of bureaucracy to the microcosm of the classroom. Governments ask universities for more quality assurance and accountability frameworks when they have lost trust in the institutions. Evaluation committees ask faculty members for more information in their sabbatical reports when they have lost trust in individual performance. Faculty accuse the university administration of corporate overreaching when they have lost trust in collegial governance. Students cheat when they have lost trust in the process of learning.

> A senior faculty member notes, "we model [impervious knowledge] for students and wonder why they cheat on exams. We punish students for behaviours that we taught them. We taught them that the grade is what matters, not the way our learning changes us, or how to value what we learn."

So, the question is, will we blame the salmon or the dam?

Or are we willing to change our mindsets to move beyond binaries into new possibilities?

Commit to unlearning and relearning

What do we have to unlearn around students and learners?

American psychologist Carol Dweck's *Mindset: The New Psychology of Success* explores how different mindsets shape our daily actions and behaviours. She asks, "what are the consequences of thinking that your intelligence or personality is something you can develop, as opposed to something that is a fixed, deep-seated trait?"[25]

When we take a growth mindset for learning (we can always get better with effort) and a fixed mindset for students (intelligence or talent are fixed and can be measured), we end up with bifurcated systems – one mindset for learners and one mindset for students.

These are two distinct ways of being in the academy.

We ask learners to traverse unfamiliar conceptual terrains, sit in the discomfort of not knowing, trust the process, try hard, risk failing, and incorporate feedback while being curious and courageous.

We evaluate students on how well they incorporate knowledge based on specific criteria, then assign a grade that is supposed to reflect their effort and performance.

We need to be attentive to the difference between students and learners.

- There are contexts where instructors need people to be students.
- There are contexts where learners are disruptive to the lesson plan.
- There are contexts where wonder can only happen when everyone takes a learner position.

We need to be clear with ourselves – and then design accordingly.

> One mid-career faculty member reflects, "I used to treat students as if they were all off to graduate school. There is so much to cover … and I want them to succeed but also want to make sure my classes are rigorous … When my students perform well, I feel great but I am frustrated that many are failing to meet the standards."

The word "rigour" is often used in metrics and quality assurance mindsets. University of North Carolina professors Jordynn Jack and Viji Sathy argue that "rigour" is an exclusionary practice that promotes preferential practices: "it is a code for 'some students deserve to be here, and some don't.'"[26]

Full disclosure: rigour is one of my top five loathsome words, inextricably linked in my mind with *rigor mortis*.

And yet, many professors wield rigour as a badge of honour: "I want my class to be the hardest in the university!" one faculty member boasted during an interview. "I want it to be so challenging that a bunch of people fail, but for those who actually pass feel like they have really accomplished something."

In this approach, learners are an inconvenience.

To be fair, we perpetuate fixed, metrics-based mindsets when we ask professors to operate in a dominant paradigm that privileges perfection over messy states of becoming; professors become metonymic extensions of impervious knowledge – all-knowing, invulnerable, unassailable. We evaluate faculty members based on what they produce (articles, books, patents, papers, grant applications), and there are few or no incentives for other kinds of contributions.

> "[As a first-generation student] I was unprepared for the invisible codes and unspoken rules that differentiated insiders from outsiders; even the pronunciation of words ... was disorienting. I had to run out of seminars and scramble to look up [all the names and concepts] my peers dropped ... I didn't want them [to] know I had no idea what was going on."

Carol Dweck's research reveals how fixed mindsets are reinforced when we incentivize product over process. She notes,

I've seen so many people with this one consuming goal of proving themselves – in the classroom, in their careers, and in their relationships. Every situation calls for a confirmation of their intelligence, personality, or character. Every situation is evaluated: Will I succeed or fail? Will I look smart or dumb? Will I be accepted or rejected? Will I feel like a winner or a loser?[27]

In a scarcity culture, no one is immune from the tyranny of metrics. The non-stop hustle that comes with a metrics mindset permeates a university's academic and non-academic realms – from students to staff, faculty to administrators and beyond.

> A seasoned student success professional confessed the following: "I [had] a realization that in all my earlier roles … you could keep score. So [in my recruitment roles], there's not enough students. We need to have more applications, more acceptances, more enrollment, more retention. We know at the end of the cycle whether that happened or that did not happen. I liked knowing that I could say, 'hey, look, this was done. And it's 17% better than last year!' And I can just hang my hat on that and go 'I've done good work.' The role I'm in now is much more difficult to measure because it's about shifting people's minds, culture, systems. But we're still very much in a system that rewards the metrics, right? Thankfully I am doing these performance review conversations with smart people who say there's real value in this other thing."

We are caught in a trap of our own making.

> As Canadian Shakespeare scholar Shannon Murray reflects on the predicament of metrics, "I'm highly critical of this idea that we can define ourselves – our own success and virtue in human life – by a set of statistics. Yet I'm wearing a watch that tells me how many steps I've taken today, and how much sleep I've gotten. I am myself caught up in that interest in metrics, in numbers as part of what defines now."[28]

The good news is that we have a set of conceptual tools to rewire mindsets. We can move from default settings into learned responses that shift us from scarcity into abundance. We can cross thresholds into new ways of thinking and being.

adrienne maree brown suggests that "abundance is immediate. it's not something you have to plant and wait for spring. that too of course, it grows now and in all your potential futures. but if you truly call it in, you must be ready for it, because it shows up right away, and you will want to have room for it."[29]

Metrics flourish in a culture of scarcity that treats students as units.

Learning, with all its rupture and emergence and messiness, flourishes in a culture of abundance.

Practise divergent thinking

Learning is also essential to a flourishing creative democracy. At a time when the public sphere is animated by questions about the value of higher education, this feels particularly urgent:

- Is higher education relevant?
- How do universities fulfill their social contract?
- Is post-secondary education "worth" it?
- Are students learning anything?[30]

There are many ways into this topic.

Shakespeare – and theatre more generally – has taught me everything I know about learning as an act of community building. If all the world's a stage, the stage can teach us to be better learners and citizens in the world.

Deep civic engagement – as spectators, learners, and citizens – has a common set of design principles.

We exercise the same cognitive and creative muscles.

Shakespeare frequently reminds us that each audience member is a key participant and collaborator in the play, not merely a passive consumer. In the prologue of *Henry V*, the Chorus demands that the audience harness their imaginations if the play has any chance of succeeding:

Can this cock-pit hold
The vasty fields of France? Or may we cram
Within this wooden O the very casques
That did affright the air at Agincourt?[31]

Urging the audience to compensate for the actors' "imperfections" by employing their own "imaginary forces," the Chorus emphasizes that spectators must actively fulfill the theatrical illusion.

In other words, Shakespeare leaves room for the "gappiness" I discuss in the prologue. The Chorus draws attention to the space left for us to fill in the blanks. We are invited to "breathe into the airholes" so that meaning is made and achieved together.[32]

Gappiness is critical to building (and sustaining) a creative democracy.

John Dewey, an American philosopher and educator, coined the term "creative democracy" in a speech he delivered in 1939 in response to the rise of fascism. He posits that democracy is a moral ideal continually constructed through an actual effort by people; he argues that "the present crisis is due in considerable part to the fact that for a long period we acted as if our democracy were something that perpetuated itself automatically."

Written in 1939, Dewey's insights are shockingly relevant to our current global climate.

Dewey concludes, "Since it is one that can have no end till experience itself comes to an end, the task of democracy is forever that of creation of a freer and more humane experience in which all share and to which all contribute."[33]

Whether it is the theatre or the classroom or democracy, nothing is created alone. These social institutions take shape only through individual effort and collaborative spirit. Just like a university without learners, or a society without civic engagement, the theatre is just an ordinary "wooden O" – stripped of its potential for transforming us all – without the animating presence of people.

There is no democracy without learners willing to do the imaginative work of co-creation.

Build intentional community

I want to return to one of my earliest interviews with educational thought leader Joy Mighty because our initial conversations shaped the direction of this project, especially around building intentional community. A leading thinker in pedagogy, equity, inclusion, and organizational change, Joy believes that Ubuntu should be a guiding concept for universities in the twenty-first century.

The African philosophy of Ubuntu is a concept of collective unity – "I am because we are, and because we are, therefore I am" – that helps us to understand and embrace our common humanity. At the same time, it challenges us to reimagine post-secondary institutions as critical ecosystems for achieving equity, diversity, and inclusion in a fractured world.

Learning is deeply embedded in ecosystems and is a critical element that determines if and how we flourish together. Common elements of trust, in-between-ness, and unknowing are built into the learning process. As such, being attentive to the power of ecosystems – in community or in the biotic realm or through interspecies symposia – is crucial for rewiring circuitry that makes room for all of us.

American scientist and Indigenous storyteller Robin Wall Kimmerer, in *Gathering Moss: A Natural and Cultural History of Mosses*, illustrates her own experience crossing a threshold that incorporates divergent thinking, unlearning, and seeing with fresh eyes:

> A Cheyenne elder of my acquaintance once told me that the best way to find something is not to go looking for it. This is a hard concept for a scientist. But he said to watch out of the corner of your eye, open to possibility, and what you seek will be revealed. The revelation of suddenly seeing what I was blind to only moments before is a sublime experience for me. I can revisit those moments and still feel the surge of expansion. The boundaries between my world and the world of another being get pushed back with sudden clarity, an experience both humbling and joyful.

For Robin Wall Kimmerer, learning, which happens by intention and by accident, is a process that enlarges our capacity for seeing by broadening our perspective, our grasp of the sublime, our appreciation of being decentred and reconfigured. This model of transformation is, for her, inextricably linked to language: "Having words for these forms makes the differences between them so much more obvious. With words at your disposal, you can see more clearly. Finding the words is another step in learning to see."[34]

We are wired for learning, and it lights us up at a cellular level when it happens.

Concluding thoughts

Full disclosure: I have not always been a good learner. In fact, I have toggled between student and learner positions on my own messy and circuitous educational journey. I did not have the language to articulate these two mindsets, and yet I could *feel* the difference. I remember vividly the moment my professor, Goran Stanivukovic, shared a quotation from the influential philosopher Michel Foucault:

> There are times in life when the question of knowing if one can think differently than one thinks, and perceive differently than one sees, is absolutely necessary if one is to go on looking and reflecting at all.[35]

This electrified my brain: Foucault – and, by extension, my professor – invited me to approach knowledge with intellectual flexibility and limitless curiosity without restricting us to correct answers or universal truths. This was a threshold concept in my own learning journey: Foucault launched me from a student into a learner position, where I started to challenge deeprooted assumptions in order to see and think differently.

I am increasingly attentive to moments of illumination where I can *feel* learning taking place. Since I was an undergraduate I have referred to them as light bulb moments. One such moment happened recently while I was listening to a keynote from American educational scholar Robin DeRosa.

They shared the following slide: "Counting beans is most notably about calling things that are not beans 'beans' so that they can be counted."[36]

At the time, I was struck by the metaphor, and it rattled around in my brain for several days. When I was rumbling with Canadian theatre artist and educator Neil Silcox about the constraints of performance-based metrics for an external grant, I wailed, "I don't want to count beans! I want to plant them!"

In that moment, the metaphor split the bean into two parts and brought into focus what I had been grappling with for a long time: the countable noun – the student – and the uncountable noun – the learner.

This was a threshold concept for me. As a result, I have had to reflect, with some discomfort, that even though I hope to invite learners, sometimes I design courses for students – and then wonder why these humans are unwilling to cross thresholds with me. I wonder too how we might invite colleagues to show up as learners – in research, service, governance – and design spaces that value wholeness and vulnerability over armoured leadership and imperviousness.

When we sit in generative and messy spaces as learners, we tap into experiences that remind me of Maria Popova's reflections on happiness: "To contact happiness of any kind is 'to be dissolved into something complete and great,' something beyond the bruising boundaries of the ego. The attainment of happiness is then less a matter of pursuit than of surrender – to the world's wonder, ready as it comes."[37]

Learning moves beyond the bruising boundaries of the ego and expands our capacities for wonder.

Understanding the design principles that invite whole, imperfect humans rather than countable units (students, staff, faculty) will help us spend more time planting beans, not counting them.

Chapter 4

How Do We Teach at Hope University?

Part of my welcome as we talk about hope and hopelessness is to invite us to notice hope as the engine of modern progress and that sometimes there is a lot of abundance in the fields that we've rudely called hopelessness: there's a lot of inquiry, there's a lot of dying, there's a lot of beauty, there's a lot of emergence, there's a lot of intelligence and interspecies symposia waiting to happen.
– Bayo Akomolafe[1]

Inextricably linked to both who we are and what we do in the academy, teaching is one of the hardest spheres to imagine rewiring.

As I write elsewhere with Lisa Dickson and Shannon Murray,

An academic vocation is among the most hopeful. We go into teaching and scholarly work because we believe, even if we haven't articulated it to ourselves fully, that development, improvement, and transformation are all possible when we are engaged in nurturing an insatiable intellectual curiosity in ourselves and in young people.[2]

We make the case that "teaching is an exercise in hope: you must live in a world where you cannot see the impact you might have in some distant future you might never access – and do it anyway."[3]

Yes.

And.

If we acknowledge that the systems in higher education are broken *and* the systems are working the way they are designed, then teaching (as a verb and as a value) is in dire need of rewiring; otherwise, we run the risk of reproducing the tools and mindsets of a flawed paradigm that no longer serves us and never served many.

The challenge becomes, how do we imagine new ways of teaching for human flourishing without using the same epistemological tools we use to conserve, preserve, share, and create knowledge within existing systems?[4]

Flourishing – the full expression of our human capacities – can be learned and taught. Classical philosopher Aristotle believed we can develop virtues – of courage, generosity, benevolence, wittiness, righteous indignation – through practice, and by doing so change our mindsets. This mindset – what he calls practical wisdom – enables us to live into our virtues as situations arise and encounters unfold.

And yet, Nigerian scholar and poet Bayo Akomolafe argues that current educational systems are woefully ill-equipped for wonder – and for reaching the full expression of our human capacities – because they are built on oppression and exclusion:

> The world is alive in stunningly beautiful ways, creative magical ways, that our systems of learning, our educational paradigms do not know how to approach. When a star burns, it burns with hope; it's part of this field of hope. When it splutters and dies and spits its goods into space, that's hopelessness; and yet that hopelessness is generated. It is the generativity that makes our bodies, that spits the matter, that makes us a life, that makes us human.[5]

Our current educational paradigms do not account for the wondrous fact that we are made of stardust.[6]

"But," I hear some of my business colleagues wondering, "what about the professional knowledge students need for professional designations? Industries could suffer."

"But," I hear some of my engineering colleagues wondering, "what about the crucial building blocks students need to advance their knowledge? Buildings could collapse."

"But," I hear some of my natural science colleagues wondering, "what about the foundational content students need for health sciences? People could die."

Yes.

And.

One of the limits of rewiring teaching is the entanglement of teaching as a concept: we only have one word for "teaching," and yet it can mean many things across a spectrum of attitudes, mindsets, and behaviours, such as:

1 Conveying skills in an instrumentalized sense
2 Creating contexts for growth

A conversation about how we teach at Hope University requires us to return to the fundamentals of what we mean by teaching. If we locate ourselves within American historian Thomas Kuhn's theory of paradigm shifts from his influential work in *The Structure of Scientific Revolutions*, now is the time of "extraordinary research" where we find "the recourse to philosophy and to debate over fundamentals."[7]

And so, we must ask ourselves, what does teaching mean?

In one model, conveying skills involves the transmission of expertise from teacher to student. Transactional in nature, the teacher produces and transfers knowledge, then assesses students' ability to master the information.

In another model, creating context for growth intermingles teaching and learning that moves towards something new and yet unarticulated, where knowledge is made and shared in transformational ways.

The first reproduces sameness while the second generates newness.

These are not in binary opposition with one another, and yet they are not interchangeable. In many cases, teachers will draw from both models to equip and activate students as learners at different times for various purposes.

> Early modern author Lisa Dickson, reflecting on the different definitions of teaching, notes, "we barely have language that can make visible a paradigm that does not sequentialize or hierarchize learning as a subordinate space."

So instead of an answer, I want to live into the following questions:

- What existing narratives do we need to surface about teaching within dominant paradigms?
- What assumptions do we have to let die to move into a new paradigm that makes room for flourishing?
- How do we recognize when we have internalized and reproduced systems that no longer serve us and others?
- What does it cost us to work within dominant teaching paradigms? How does it affect us as individuals and as communities?
- How do we rewire our understanding of teaching that encourages us to learn in creative, wondrous ways while also giving learners the tools to enter the world and make it better?
- What called us to this work, and what do we want to take with us as we build a new set of tools and mindsets around teaching?

Articulating teaching mindsets – what stories we tell, what tools we use, how we define value, and what relationships we nurture – is an important first step in rewiring our systems.

There is an abundance of work being done on educational development and teacherly identities in the fields of educational psychology, the scholarship of teaching and learning, STEM education, and elsewhere. As a learner in these disciplinary contexts, I encourage you to explore the richness of pedagogy in its many forms and diverse fields.[8]

For the purposes of this project – building hope circuits to rewire systems for human flourishing – it is helpful to interrogate the prevailing stories we tell about teaching and teachers, which are sometimes latent or unexamined.

We cannot keep telling the same stories in circular loops without pausing to reflect and ask if these narratives are still helpful. Bayo Akomolafe challenges us to think about when continuity is a colonial construct that enacts harm: "Hope is just a fear of failing expedition or a breaking enterprise; I could [keep] holding on tenuously and the system continuously encourages us to keep the hope alive keep, the faith alive ... I wonder if that is in part of the problem, if endless hope is in part of what the system wants us to do and if that isn't maybe something that needs to die?"[9]

So, we must ask, "what stories, assumptions, or mindsets need to die for an educational paradigm that supports human flourishing to emerge?"

What do we leave behind to make room for the messy journeys and contested conceptual terrains of wonder?

Surface the systems

Many of the stories we tell about teaching need to die.

First on my list is the myth of the naturally gifted teacher.

When I wrote an op-ed for *University Affairs* titled "There Is No Such Thing as a Naturally Gifted Teacher," the response from some readers was irate:

- How dare I discount that high school teacher who changed their path?
- How dare I erase the impact of that elementary school teacher that saw something in them?
- How dare I downplay that undergraduate professor who made them think differently?

There was something special, they insisted, a kind of genius, a magic, a gift.

Yes.

From Mr Doherty, who in Grade Seven had us reading *The Tempest* and listening to Joni Mitchell, to Goran Stanivukovic, who was the reason I pursued graduate studies, I too had transformative teachers. Many of us have cherished memories of mentors who profoundly shaped our development.

> Literary scholar and academic coach Bassam Chiblak reflects, "Teachers are often someone's first experience with unconditional love (or the like). That is healthy because we all need one adult to love us unconditionally to develop healthy brains. I read a psychology report on people who are happy well into their 80s, and the findings pointed to unconditional love, which often feels magical. I would conjecture

> that most of our issues in higher education have something to do with magical thinking, which have something to do with interpersonal dynamics beyond the university. Most people feel unloved from what I hear everyday."

And.

We do not wake up one day in graduate school and miraculously know how to be productive researchers, nor do we step into our first classroom and automatically know how to be an effective educator. In fact, the more I immerse myself in pedagogical fields around inclusion,[10] decolonization,[11] high-impact practices,[12] authentic learning,[13] relationship-rich education,[14] and values-based educational leadership,[15] the more I sit in a learner position – humbled, decentred, awed.

There is so much still to learn. And unlearn.

I had more confidence in the first five years of my teaching career than I have after twenty years in the classroom, where I now find myself in a state of radical reconfiguration. Starting out, I crammed my students with content. Now, I wonder, how do I create classrooms that make room for us all to breathe into, to think into, and to make something together that did not exist before – and that might change us for the better?

Now I am less concerned that students can parrot back a definition of epistemology and more concerned with what they might still be thinking about a decade from now.

When we fetishize being naturally good at teaching, we short-circuit hope and agency and possibility.

As Craig Wright argues, in *The Hidden Habits of Genius: Beyond Talent, IQ, and Grit*, "often the genius assumes the qualities of a savior and thus gives humanity hope for a better world. At the same time, the genius provides solace – an explanation, even an excuse, for our own shortcomings. 'Oh, well, no wonder, she's a genius!'"[16]

This is a lose-lose situation: geniuses are expected to find solutions to the world's most wicked problems so we can relax; and, being a genius is unattainable, so we do not have to bother. Both narratives encourage helplessness, stagnation, and disengagement.

In this model, genius is always somewhere other than here.

Someone else will do it.[17]

Change your language, change your world

The second myth that needs to die is that being an extrovert (insert: charismatic, gregarious, eloquent) makes you a good teacher.

When people describe someone as a naturally gifted teacher, what do they usually mean?

I have heard the term most often used to describe someone full of charisma and capable of holding an audience's attention in large lecture halls. This glorified "sage on the stage" also comes with undertones of monologia, narcissism, and self-indulgence.

The "guide on the side" model is often proposed as a countermeasure because it is more "learner-centred" – and yet it can still have pejorative connotations (the side of what? one might wonder).

When interrogating the myth of the naturally gifted extroverted teacher, what starts to emerge is how definitions of teaching excellence are both reductive and disparaging.

This myth does double damage.

First, it erases spaces for teachers who deploy different styles, demeanours, pedagogical philosophies, and approaches to learning and teaching.

Second, praise for performing well in the classroom can, in certain contexts, become a backhanded compliment. And sometimes a downright dig.

> One mid-career faculty member shared, "When I received a university-wide teaching award, the temperature in my department cooled a few degrees. A few of my colleagues made passing remarks about how they'd rather be rigorous than popular, and I just wanted to hide under the table."

Furthermore, when we perpetuate the myth of the naturally gifted teacher, we overestimate the value of innate talent and underestimate the value of discipline, energy, and effort. What appears to be effortless and "natural" to others is almost always the product of deliberate practice.

The performance of expertise – and erasing signs of effort – is a concept that has been around for centuries. Baldassare Castiglione, a sixteenth-century Italian courtier, theorizes this concept of naturalized performance – which he calls *sprezzatura* – in *The Book of the Courtier*. He urges courtiers to devote countless hours to study and practice and then "make whatever is done or said appear to be without effort and almost without any thought about it."[18]

Genius. Perfection. Natural. Innate. Fixed. Nonchalance. Polished. Product.

There is no invitation here for us to see ourselves in messy and emergent states of being. There is no entry point for us to pull back the curtain, see what is behind the performance, and understand the inner workings of creating or building something.

When we erase the effort behind the performance, we do ourselves and others a disservice. In doing so, we perpetuate systems that value impervious knowledge and perfection rather than emergence or unfurling. We unwittingly reproduce the conditions we might seek to upend.

Commit to unlearning and relearning

Another myth that needs to die: the assumption that old men with white beards wearing tweed jackets with elbow patches are the best teachers.

> A junior faculty member confessed, "I imagined my professors and colleagues exuded confidence and mastery, effortless access to knowledge, and a high degree of cultural capital that I struggled to emulate. They looked the part, while I felt like a square peg in a round hole. I just didn't fit, no matter which way I contorted myself. I didn't know how to navigate the systems, and I didn't have the awareness then to understand I wasn't supposed to navigate them well."

Teaching, unlike wine, does not always age well.

Professors teaching for thirty years are not necessarily better in the classroom because they have clocked thousands of hours. Anders Ericsson and Robert Pool, in *Peak: Secrets from the New Science of Expertise*, argue that "automated abilities gradually deteriorate in the absence of deliberate efforts to improve."[19]

Expert performers focus on specific, targeted goals, push themselves outside their comfort zones, are consistent and persistent, seek feedback, and take time to recover from the intensity of deliberate practice.

Teaching excellence is not merely a function of time. It needs deliberate practice, self-reflection, curiosity, and a commitment to transform continuously.

Reimagine authority and expertise

One myth that *really* needs to die: professors are experts in the classroom.

University instructors are experts in their disciplinary field. Their training is deep and extensive. They have mastery in a particular area, whether that is astrophysics or organizational behaviour. Indeed, the expertise is often so focused that they may well be the world's leading expert on a particular topic, like my friend Susie Andrews who is the foremost expert on the cult of Mount Wutai, or my friend Heather Lawford, who is a leading scholar in youth and generativity.

Yet we do not teach professors, who happen to be experts, how to teach.[20]

Professors in higher education have, for the most part, no formal training in pedagogy – that is, the methods, practices, and principles of teaching. Nor are they expected to reflect on, much less research, their pedagogical practices. Most promotion, evaluation, and review procedures look at quantitative student evaluations to determine competency, even though we know these instruments are flawed, racist, and sexist and do not adequately measure teaching effectiveness.[21]

It seems almost absurd to say it out loud.

University classrooms are run by people who have little or no formal instruction on how to teach.

Moreover, we overlook the expertise of students in their lived experiences as learners.

Faculty-student collaboration at both the classroom and institutional levels helps us reimagine ways of engaging in pedagogical and professional development through collaborative partnerships. I have written elsewhere about partnering with students as co-designers in twenty-first-century classrooms,[22] and will explore the role these partnerships play in systems-wide change in the next book in the hope circuits series.

In the interests of this project, which focuses on building tools and reconfiguring mindsets, we need to think about the value of designing systems that allow for more "gappiness" (a concept I propose in the prologue): how do we intentionally invite students to breathe into the spaces, think into them, find invitation into them?

Just as Shakespeare scholar Emma Smith suggests that Shakespeare's "plays only happen if we're there to complete them,"[23] hopeful systems are only complete when we are all there.

Stay with the trouble

We are not there yet.

Many of us are still reproducing tools from an increasingly inadequate paradigm.

In my own journey as an educator and a human, there are still so many things I have to unlearn. Below I share one experience that is embarrassing *and*, I hope, an illustration of how we might move beyond narrow and restrictive academic identities into more aligned practices.

When I was pregnant with my first child, I experienced the usual mix of delight and trepidation that comes with impending parenthood. However, I was also concerned with how my pregnancy might threaten the professional identity I had so assiduously constructed for myself as a young, female professor in the early stages of my career.

My pre-pregnancy approach was to focus exclusively on the cognitive realm and disciplinary knowledge. I felt that this approach insulated me against a variety of awkward social interactions, ranging from students sending me friend requests on social media channels to comments like "great shoes!" in my teaching evaluations.

If I set the rules of engagement in the realm of the purely cognitive – or so my reasoning went – then I would enjoy the same respect and authority my male colleagues were afforded.

Despite my best intentions, pregnancy compelled me to deconstruct and then reconfigure my professional identity.

My pregnancy unfolded over a full academic year, with a delivery date in early May. For several months, I clung to the knowledge-centric model of academic selfhood: intent on policing the boundaries between the public and the private spheres of my life, I did not announce my state to my students and ignored any overtures they made to discuss it.

I said nothing.

Second semester coincided with my third trimester, and I became, to borrow Shakespeare's phrase, "great with child." As my Jacobean Shakespeare course began, I refused to acknowledge the elephant in the room.

And still, I said nothing.

Shakespeare, though, had other plans.

Because I had designed the syllabus and ordered the plays before I was pregnant, I had unwittingly chosen two plays in his canon where pregnant women appear onstage – *Measure for Measure* and *The Winter's Tale.*

In both these plays, pregnancy cannot be denied, hidden, or erased. In Juliet's case, her pregnant body belies that she and her fiancé had premarital sex, while Hermione's heavily pregnant body prompts her husband to suspect her of having an extramarital affair.

Pregnancy makes public what would otherwise be private acts; the men in these plays read (or misread) female bodies as uncontrollable, uncontainable, and beyond their authority. Although both women are exonerated in the end, Shakespeare uses pregnancy to explore how bodies (female bodies in particular) are open to multiple interpretations (and that the actual destabilizing forces are male anxiety rather than female inconstancy – but that is a subject for a different book).

As my students and I examined Juliet's and Hermione's loss of control over how their bodies were interpreted, the disavowal of my pregnancy became increasingly untenable in the three-dimensional space of the classroom.

My intentions were good: I treated the classroom as a space for sharing knowledge, conveying content, and developing tools for students to undertake their transformative learning journeys.

My fears were founded: women, people of colour, members of the LGBTQ2S+ communities are punished in teaching evaluations and denied other career opportunities if they deviate from the norm, from the default – which is white, cis, straight, male.[24]

My decisions were dismembering: by compartmentalizing my personal experience, I was harming my students and myself when I failed to show up fully. Parker Palmer helps us think about how individual dismemberment short-circuits community: "Community cannot take root in a divided life. Long before community assumes external shape and form, it must be present as seed in the undivided self: only as we are in communion with ourselves can we find community with others. Community is an outward and visible sign of an inward and invisible grace, the flowing of personal identity and integrity into the world of relationships."[25]

> A mid-career faculty member reflected, "My graduate supervisor told me not to have kids until I got tenure. She waited until she was an associate professor and had a book out before even thinking about having a family. So, I was really ashamed when I had to tell her that I was expecting in the first year of my TT position."

By internalizing the conditions of the dominant paradigm, I missed opportunities to explore the emotional responses, embodied experiences, and identity shifts that Shakespeare's characters undergo – and, by extension, our own transformations. I did not have the tools to incorporate brains, hearts, bodies, spirits, and souls into my pedagogy. I did not yet have the language of relentless welcome and radical hospitality because I had not experienced that firsthand.

Despite my earnest wish to create transformative learning in my classrooms, I reinforced the parameters I sought to upend because I continued working with the same conditions and mindsets that upheld the status quo.

Slow down and pause

I sat in the discomfort of that dismemberment for a long time.

Critical reflection offered me a way to write through the discomfort of these experiences. Then I started sharing my disorientation with others. Together, we started to say the quiet parts out loud. And that has made all the difference.

In *The Courage to Teach: Exploring the Inner Landscape of a Teacher's Life*, Parker Palmer writes, "If we want to grow as teachers – we must do something alien to academic culture: we must talk to each other about our inner lives – risky stuff in a profession that fears the personal and seeks safety in the technical, the distant, the abstract."[26]

While I have been blessed with many dear friends willing to howl about the systems for many years, I have increasingly brought these "risky stuff" conversations into more formal institutional spaces. When I work with faculty who are developing teaching dossiers – for the job market, tenure and promotion, and external fellowships – we engage in the "risky stuff" that moves us into critically reflective spaces together.

One of the common worries when we first begin is either "I have no idea what to say" or "I don't know how to connect all the things I do together." And so, I ask them to write their origin story, answering the following prompt, "How did you get here?"

I leave up to them what "here" is and where this journey starts.

While this process can be undertaken alone, there is something special when we do this work in clusters and communities. I prefer a small constellation of five to six faculty so that after some time writing on their own, I bring them back to the group and ask them about their experience. They often share a metaphor – a quest, a rhizome, a quilt, a mushroom – to characterize their journeys, which are almost always messy, circuitous, and non-traditional. In their origin story, they often recall a moment when they felt awakened to the curiosity of the world: a class they took, a moment from their childhood, a lesson from the land, or an observation of a phenomenon.

Their origin stories might be grounded in family, a place, a classroom, or a socio-political context, and yet what they have in common is a wonder and a desire to know more. It is indeed palpable on their faces and voices when they talk about what they love.

And yet, this is often the first time they have been asked the question in academic spaces.

Excavating our core values and deep delights – as leaders, scholars, colleagues, and educators – is hard work for so many because we were not taught how to engage in critical reflective practice.[27] This means we also do not teach, model, value, or facilitate the deep work of critical reflection for our students or our colleagues.

> A junior faculty member going up for promotion reflected, "I'm a biologist. I grew up on Lake Michigan, loving nature – and that love and [fascination] for me – nature is a part of who I am. But at the

same time, as I write that I can just hear my PhD advisor over my shoulder ... he's reading loads [of] cover letters, where it's like, 'ever since I was ten years old, I wanted to be a marine biologist,' and he would just wad that up and like, throw it out. He just hated things that he saw ... [and that] seeped into me and [when] I think about the teaching philosophy, that is [what] I see."

For many of us, we need to unlearn the behaviours we absorbed in our educational journeys – as undergraduate students, graduate students, and early career researchers. Many of our mentors internalized and then reproduced the systems within which they had to survive; it is here that continuity without reflection can be damaging and take us to places of hopelessness and harm.

Even though we *know* from research that critical reflection helps us unlock fundamental values, aligns the many things we do, and better connects us to purpose,[28] there are very few formal spaces built into our systems for this work to happen.

While alignment might be encouraged in select circles (e.g. teaching and learning spheres), it is treated derisively in some decision-making spaces that uphold dominant systems (I do not recall hearing the word "heart" or "love" at senate or the board of governors, much less at a departmental meeting).

A junior faculty member from the natural sciences reflects, "[In promotion dossiers or job applications] if someone is not talking about what they do in their teaching, and is instead of talking about what they think, and what they believe in their worldview, I feel like [that] is a hit against you; [adjudicators and evaluators might say,] 'get down to brass tacks! Tell us what you *actually* do in the classroom! How do you prove your effectiveness?'"

Another faculty member, responding to them, offered this, "But I'm just wondering, you talked about 'let's get down to brass tacks': everything you do in the classroom is determined by what you believe and what you think ... What you *are* determines what you *do*. So, is there some kind of set-up so [your personal reflection] won't be discounted right away? So that you can have a little bit more of that narrative and then talk about how that informs specific strategies?"

The central premise in Parker Palmer's *The Courage to Teach* is "when I do not know myself, I cannot know my subject – not at the deepest levels of embodied, personal meaning."[29] My experience of working in small, interdisciplinary and inter-institutional groups is that we can be braver together. We can encourage one another to share – as Parker Palmer encourages us – "risky stuff in a profession that fears the personal."[30]

We often lose sight of our fundamental role as learners: our students and colleagues expect us to be experts in our field and the classroom, and any crack in the veneer is met with disbelief or mistrust. This is not the fault of individuals: the systems within which we learn and work are inhospitable to awkwardness, messiness, and emergence; furthermore, challenges to the dominant systems are often penalized.

> One junior faculty member shared, "I do actually know somebody who did try and push up against the old guard and didn't get their tenure. We are talking about real risks here. And what do we have the flexibility to do? As tenured faculty changing the academy like, do you need tenure before you can change it? What are the risks? I don't even have a job, let alone tenure. So yeah, those are questions that are kind of nagging at me when we talk about the resistance [of impervious systems]."

No wonder we are so exhausted.

If we hope to serve our students with integrity and wholeness, we must explore the complex forces and pressures that generate academic identities.

In many disciplinary fields, critical reflection is not valued – whether that is on the job market, in grant applications, or in tenure and promotion structures. What is valued and visible is the shiny packaging of perfection rather than the more candid, contested, and authentic narratives of constant and ongoing transformation.

This is why we need a new paradigm.

Change your language, change the world

"What do you love?"[31]

When I first had to compile a dossier that required critical reflection (for an external fellowship on educational leadership), I talked about what I love. I wrote, "When I was in graduate school, I used to joke that if academia didn't work out, I'd become a party planner."

My flippant remark elicited the expected response – laughter – primarily due to the apparent incongruity between academia's enduring, seemingly profound, cerebral world in contrast with the party's ephemeral, seemingly superficial, bodily pursuits.

And yet, as I reflect on my almost twenty years in the academy, I have come to realize not that we take academia too seriously, but we do not take party planning seriously enough.

First of all, I still believe this. I love party planning. It brings me deep joy to gather humans together in relentless welcome, fill peoples' cups, connect them in conversation, and offer an attentiveness that lies at the heart of hospitality.

Second of all, there is a place for irreverence. We can and should foster delight, joy, silliness, playfulness as we encounter and interrogate normative structures and dominant paradigms.

Delight is the gateway into learning, and I remember as an undergraduate the experience of walking out of a classroom viscerally aware that my world-view had tilted on its axis by a few degrees. It was as exhilarating as it was transformative.

I remember that feeling in my bones.

I light up now when I think about it.

And so, one of my guiding questions in teaching has been, how do I design for this feeling of illumination? In some ways this will always feel elusive; I can tell when we get close to this energy – in a classroom, seminar, workshop, talk, or meeting – and yet it is hard to capture and often harder to reproduce.

In the teaching dossier I wrote a decade ago, I outline the values that I try to practise: Higher education, in its ideal form, creates spaces for individuals – in solitude and together – to explore intersections between knowledge, experience, and imagination. We ask one another and ourselves how we know the world and how can we live creatively, courageously, and responsibly within it.

Yes.

And.

What tools do we need to anchor this in practice?

The answer might lie not so much in *why* or *how* and instead in *who* we live into the questions with.

Building intentional community

If we are to release old stories and stale epistemologies that no longer serve us, we need to tools to reconfigure mindsets that turn into movements. To do this work, we need intentional communities.

My own journey towards wholeness happened when I found communities of people willing to say the risky stuff out loud.

When I started my first sessional teaching job at a large, comprehensive university, the other junior faculty members made fun of my enthusiasm for teaching, mocked me for holding extra office hours, and shook their heads in disbelief when I took students on field trips to the theatre. They were, for the most part, male, pale, and Yale (+/- other elite universities).

I learned very quickly to stay quiet about the joys of teaching, even when I moved to a primarily undergraduate institution.

When I stumbled upon my first teaching and learning conference, it was a paradigm-shifting experience. The largest Canadian teaching and learning conference (STLHE – Society of Teaching and Learning in Higher Education) was in Montreal a few days before I was heading overseas for a disciplinary research trip, and my friend Corinne Haigh, a psychologist working within an education faculty, suggested I attend.

I spent the entire conference gripping her arm, regularly exclaiming, "Did you know about *this*? Have you heard about *them*? Did you know there was a name for *that*?"

Encountering fully developed frameworks for things I had been struggling to articulate – from transformative learning to threshold concepts to universal design to high-impact practices – was electrifying.

To her immense credit, Corinne was deeply patient; she kept repeating, "Yes, this is a field. This is research. This is a discipline. This is a community."

At that conference I remember one session in particular: a panel of 3M National Teaching Fellows shared their journeys in educational leadership. Each talked about the delight and despair involved in institutional culture change. These innovators from multiple disciplines and fields had one thing in common: they were creating generous and generative things despite – *not* because of – the conditions within which they were working.

First, I fan-girled. Encountering an entire group of daring, courageous, kick-ass educators building things for others in otherwise inhospitable spaces was overwhelming for someone who had been struggling alone and undercover. I remember thinking, "So *this* is where you have all been hiding."

Then I found mattering.[32] Teaching mattered. The work we did mattered. It was like someone turned on a light switch in my brain. I was electrified.

At the time, I did not realize how radical it is to imagine and make space for different notions of expertise and authority. This community normalizes sitting in learner positions, which means that outliers and innovators can rethink mastery, redefine excellence, and reimagine the rules of engagement. Accordingly, there is a strong social justice and inclusion focus embedded in this group's social norms and expectations.[33] Their factory presets come already wired for hope circuits.

Yes.

And.

Like many associations and collectives run on volunteer goodwill and unpaid labour, these communities struggle with contestation and dysfunction, in-fighting and bashing one another with by-laws. They are, in some ways, more vulnerable to despair and dysfunction because their work is often precarious, contingent, invisible, or undervalued. Teaching and learning communities often struggle to go mainstream and are relegated to the margins when the serious business of running a university happens.

> One administrator shared, "I had a conversation with a seasoned university president at conference once: he told me if I wanted to make meaningful change, that I should become a provost (vice president academic) and avoid senior teaching and learning positions because they have no power and no status. 'The real change happens at the provost or even the decanal level,' he advised."

This is why we cannot have nice things.

We gatekeep each other, reinforce silos, and fortify hierarchies. It is an ongoing struggle to work in academic and academic adjacent spaces without reproducing the conditions we seek to upend.

> One senior administrator shared, "I affirm again that universities are essential to civil society, that they transform lives, and that the knowledge they generate and transmit is irreplaceable. I would argue, however, that as they are presently constituted and governed, and with the exception of large, wealthy institutions of high reputation, universities are less and less sustainable. To remedy this, nearly every aspect of their operations needs to be rethought and restructured. And the starting point for this radical exercise is that simple question: what will this do to or for students? If we get behind the surface simplicity of that question, and really do the hard thinking, we will be on the right path."

We need to start asking more radical questions that traverse the multiple domains of the academy.

What would it look like if we took design principles and research-informed practices from teaching and learning spheres and brought them into the board rooms, senate, academic planning, financial decision-making?

What would it look like if we took insights from inclusive classrooms and use them to shape every sphere of university governance and administrative decision-making: curricula, timetables, grading and assessment, faculty and staff hiring, business office policies, admission and graduation requirements, budgets, tuition rates and student financial support, information and technology services, advancement and capital campaigns, building projects, government relations, and more?

What would it look like to partner with students and non-traditional collaborators to imagine every table, every encounter, as an opportunity for learning together towards something different and yet unarticulated, where knowledge is made and shared in transformational ways?

What would university policies look like if we had to begin every document that goes to senate with a statement of learning philosophy or set of learning objectives?

What would committees look like if we shared our educational leadership philosophies as criteria for membership?

I want to linger on this last idea for a moment. Philosophy statements – teaching, research, educational leadership, visioning – give us the origin stories of what we love. In remembering what we love, we re-member who we are and where we might locate hope for something different – in a discipline, classroom practice, and journey as a human.

If we ask every member of our community to meditate on their origin stories, what might we learn that could help us rewire mindsets and movements?

There is wonder and awe in genesis stories.

Apollo astronaut Edgar Mitchell meditates on the origin stories of our bodies, "I'd studied astronomy, and I'd studied cosmology, and I fully understood that the molecules in my body and the molecules in my partners' bodies and the molecules in the spacecraft had been prototyped in this amazing generation of stars – in other words, it was pretty obvious … we're stardust."[34]

The origin stories of many of our institutions are grounded on hope. I was struck by a conversation with president of Morgan State University David Kwabena Wilson, who shared his reflections on the foundation of the Historically Black Colleges and Universities (HBCUs) in the United States as a model of hope and resilience – and of love.[35] Wilson reminded me that the founding of most institutions was grounded in hope.

Hope – and good intentions – are not a sufficient reason alone to maintain a mindset, an institution, a paradigm in perpetuity. In conversations about higher education, we need to mind the difference between hope as persistence and hope as possible.

Bayo Akomolafe warns us about colonial hope as continuity, forged on the assumption that "if we continue to do the things we've been doing then we will arrive someday at the end of the rainbow, the universe, heaven … What happens when that is disrupted? what happens when the things we have attached ourselves to become poisonous? what happens when continuity is toxic?"[36]

We have a metaphysical journey ahead.

How are the stars aligning for higher education?

What do we have to let go of that no longer serves us so that energy can be reconfigured in ways that enable us to fulfill our social contract to society?

What do we need to let die to live into the possible?

Chapter 5

How Do We Mentor at Hope University?

I used to want to save the world. This beautiful place. But I knew
so little then ... What one does when faced with the truth is more
difficult than you'd think.
– Diana, *Wonder Woman*[1]

I used to believe that mentorship was a generative relationship that builds robust hope circuits for both mentor and protégé.

What could be more hopeful than a mentor guiding a mentee through an institution's disorienting and dismaying structures that might otherwise feel inhospitable or exclusive?

What could be more hopeful than a mentor making the otherwise mystifying systems, codes, and unspoken academy rules visible for mentees who otherwise have very little help wayfinding?

What could be more hopeful than a mentor amplifying and supporting the mentee on their often perilous and lonesome journey towards mastery in a disciplinary field?

When I sat down to write this chapter on mentorship at Hope University, I thought, "I'll write this quickly. This is an easy one." However, when I interviewed diverse thought partners and reflected on my own experiences, what emerged were stories of misalignment, misrecognition, and misunderstanding.

This process surfaced tremendous sadness, heartbreak, and unprocessed grief that took me a long time to unpick.

As Viola exclaims in *Twelfth Night*, finding herself at an impasse, "O time, thou must untangle this, not I. / It is too hard a knot for me t' untie."[2]

So I went back to the conceptual tools: I slowed down, surfaced the systems, and started to rumble in conversation with others. The knotty emotions are, I discovered through my research, a *feature* of the mentorship relationship rather than a *flaw*.

As Brené Brown shares, "When you ask someone about love, they tell you about heartbreak; when you ask people about belonging, they tell you the most excruciating examples of being excluded; and when you ask people about connection, the stories they told me were about disconnection."[3]

While I was writing this book, some of the most profound guidance I received on mentorship came from a class I team-taught called "Metaphors of Mentorship in the Marvel Cinematic Universe." Together with youth generativity expert Heather Lawford, we created a course that explores the intersections of generativity and mentorship to help people unlock superhero powers for themselves and others. Every week we explored the origin stories, identity work, mentorship, and intersections between agency and communion of Marvel superheroes.

The constellation of insights from students in this course helped to articulate the role of purpose to better understand how we mentor and are mentored as a fundamental principle of flourishing.

As we experience a paradigm shift in higher education, the question remains: how do we do this work with intention and agency – and in more human and humane ways – that focuses more on world-building than world-breaking? Since the question of who creates new worlds and who destroys them is explicit in the Marvel cinematic universe, the course allowed us to play with these concepts at arm's length while also superimposing them onto our own local contexts.

What worlds do we inherit?

What is our legacy?

How do we tap into our purpose?

How do we use our abilities to help others?

These are all generative questions.

Generativity comes from Erik Erikson's theory of psychosocial development in the 1950s. He defined it as "the establishment, the guidance, and the enrichment of the living generation and the world it inherits." Furthermore,

Erikson framed generativity as "a concern for establishing and guiding the next generation."[4]

Mentorship, then, is generativity-in-action. Indeed, looking at mentorship through a generative lens illuminates how this relationship is animated by the intention to shape legacy – whether that is individual, institutional, disciplinary, or pro-social.

It turns out that legacy is more fraught than I initially imagined – and it is tangled up with power, identity, hierarchy, and feelings. The messiness, discomfort, and big feelings are woven into the fabric of mentorship relationships. And so, mentoring relationships can come undone when we fail to make room for these emotions.

As we move towards a paradigm shift in higher education, some of the best-equipped mentors we can mobilize are the young people who will inherit the current systems and imperfect institutions. Without their help, we risk being mired in the status quo unless we reflect on our complicity in internalizing and reproducing the current structures. We need help imagining new paradigms – and young people help us tap into audacious thinking to move us all from stagnation to generativity.

> A learner in Marvel remarked, "I think the biggest hurdle one can face with these situations is closed-mindedness. There's often people put in place of power that do not have any intention of changing or listening to new ways of doing. Which makes sense when something has worked for you for so long; why would you change something that does not need fixing?"

Students read, rumbled, and shaped this chapter – more so than anywhere else in this book – and their guidance helped unlock the potential for purpose-driven, humane, inclusive systems by imagining new mentorship models – including reverse, clustered, and reflective alternatives to traditional mentoring relationships.

> Another undergraduate student shared, "It is crucial for these [people in] positions of power to be open to new ideas, as well as being aware of new goals. Maybe the best way to combat this is breaking down those existing structure of powers."

In reconfiguring mentorship, we might take a page from Antoni Gaudí's design of La Sagrada Família in Barcelona, Spain, which I discussed in the introduction; Gaudí's understanding of legacy leaves gaps for future cohorts to create in ways he could not have imagined. In doing so, he offers us a blueprint of a complex system made to be continuously undone and redone. What does intentional planning for new generations to think and gather differently look like?

Mentorship that is willing to produce something that is not itself requires the most generous version of generative thinking possible.

> Another student in the course reminds us, "Mentorship isn't about silent learning or shadowing anymore; I think it's about discussion, interaction, and experience. Mentors aren't just teaching and telling mentees what to do; they allow growth through freedom of creativity. It's more about guiding than imposing a way of thinking/growing."

Slow down and pause

As I embarked on this chapter, I was initially overwhelmed by the amount of research on mentorship – from fields as diverse as psychology, sociology, business leadership, self-help books, and so on.

Everywhere I looked, I found "how-to" guides – from professional schools, business programs, and formal mentor programs in STEM – that rhapsodize about mentorship as unequivocally positive:

Find a mentor! Seek out a sponsor! Build your networks! Get the inside track!

There is increasing pressure for young people to "network" (as a verb).

- Mentorship is a lucrative industry, a shiny new app, an apprenticeship for executives.[5]
- Mentorship is idealized, promised, sought after, and even fetishized.
- Mentorship is increasingly operationalized and monetized.

A deep dive into mentorship initially left me in despair: my first response was, "What could I possibly have to contribute to such an oversaturated sector?" After working through my initial imposter syndrome, what I did notice was that less attention is paid to the complexity of the relationships themselves.

Going back to literature – a space where I have always found illumination – gave me a way forward. The first use of *mentor* appears in the *Odyssey* (ca. the eighth–seventh century BCE). Homer's epic poem offers us a key to unlocking the design features of mentorship in our contemporary contexts that illuminate the complexity of the relationships.

Here is the story:

During the Trojan War, Odysseus leaves his son Telemachus under the watchful eye of Mentor. Homer reveals that "on leaving, Odysseus had entrusted his whole house to him: they to obey the old man, he to keep all things safe."[6] The original Mentor informs common assumptions we make in discussions about mentorship:

- A mentor has authority *in loco parentis* (in place of a parent).
- Mentorship is intergenerational (old to young).
- Mentoring develops over a long period (in this case, ten or more years).

Leaving aside notions of authority, power inequalities, and unidirectional dynamics for a minute, what is most stunning about this origin story is that Homer's Mentor is an utterly ineffective guide for Telemachus in his father's absence.

Suitors for Penelope overrun the palace, and Mentor is powerless to stop them nor can he adequately guide the increasingly anxious Telemachus. Despite Mentor's appeals for help, the men of Ithaca dismiss him, telling him that his "wits are wandering."

Only when Athena, Goddess of Wisdom, intervenes do things get back on track. Athena impersonates Mentor to advise Telemachus, setting in motion the events that precipitate the return of Odysseus to his throne, thereby securing Telemachus's succession.

Athena-as-Mentor (A/M) gives Telemachus the first mentorship advice on record:

There is every hope of you achieving your goal. So, forget the Suitors' plans and intentions, they are fools, neither sensible nor just, nor are they thinking of death and the dark fate that is truly near, and will one day strike them. Nor will the journey you set your heart on be delayed, since I, a true friend of your father's house, will ready a swift ship and sail with you. Go home now and join the crowd of Suitors: then assemble provisions: the wine in jars, the barley meal, that nourishes men's marrows, in tough skins. Meanwhile I will gather a volunteer crew in town. And there are plenty of ships, old and new, in sea-faring Ithaca. I will choose one of the best for you, and we will prepare her swiftly, and launch her in open water.[7]

A close reading reveals some of the guiding principles of mentorship:

- A/M **gives hope** ("there is every hope of achieving your goal").
- A/M reminds Telemachus to **focus on purpose** (don't think "of death and dark fate").
- A/M reinforces the foundational importance of **loyalty and trust** in the mentorship relationship (I am "a true friend").
- S[he] provides **clear instructions**, not merely vague guidance ("assemble provisions").
- And, finally, A/M is willing to **spend political and social capital** by helping with preparations for Telemachus's journey (gather volunteers and commandeer a ship).

Athena-as-Mentor does not merely provide armchair advice; she provides Telemachus with emotional support, a game plan, a timeline, a direction, and material help. She gives us the prototype of mentorship.

Mentorship here is not altruistic: Athena has skin in the game.

She is the patroness of Odysseus, who won special favour through reverence and loyalty. For Athena, Telemachus's success is Odysseus's succession, which also means that her brand of mentorship focuses on legacy-building. Moreover, in Book 13, Athena reveals a special kinship with Odysseus, remarking that they are "both well versed in craft, since thou art far the best of all men in counsel and in speech, and I among all the gods am famed for wisdom and craft."[8]

She sees herself in him.

She receives loyalty and tribute in return for her patronage.

Mentorship, Homer tells us, is never one-sided: it is mutually enriching, reciprocal, and transformative. As we see in the origin story, it is also fraught, precarious, and flawed.

Mentor is a failed mentor and requires divine intervention from a goddess to resolve an otherwise hopeless situation. (Mentor, as it happens, also benefits from Athena's interference because he is credited for wisdom he never imparts.)

Failure is a feature, not a flaw, in the origin story of mentorship.

Take a systems-level approach

How does this framework apply to post-secondary spaces, and can it help us to better understand who is mentoring and how these relationships are formed?

Elon University in the United States is one of the first universities to develop and implement a campus-wide framework for mentorship. This research-informed design project, led by educational and rhetoric scholar Jessie Moore and her colleagues, identifies who mentors are and how these relationships are formed in higher education contexts.

In one study, her research revealed that faculty/professors are the most prevalent group identified as "people who helped you in significant ways," followed by peers and then staff members. Participants in this study reported that most mentoring relationships "developed informally over time," with fewer relationships formed when they were "sought out" and even fewer meaningful relationships when they were "assigned."[9]

In light of how important faculty are, and how informal mentorship is, it is alarming that, for the most part, there is little to no intentional design, ethical training, or even language for professors or students to frame one of the most complex and ever-shifting relationships of mentor and mentee.

We do not learn about the design principles of mentorship in graduate school. We only see it modelled for us. Furthermore, our default is to reproduce the dynamics of our own experience. No wonder so many stories of mentorship include harm and hurt.

One interviewee, an expert on EDI, reflects, "What does it even mean to be a mentor? From the EDI perspective, I look at the power dyna-

mics and the intercultural differences in the role and how mentorship has often been used as gatekeeping, to do harm, or to reinforce
existing norms rather than breaking down barriers and walls."

Stay with the trouble

These are not new conversations. Scholars have warned us about the messiness of mentorship in peer-reviewed journals for decades; and yet these calls
to action are often hidden behind paywalls and read by scholars within a
particular disciplinary field.

Scholars such as Maria Lund Dahlberg and Angela Byars-Winston, for example, have long argued that there is a need to "frame a set of greater conversations by providing language, constructs, and theoretical underpinnings
that in turn can guide the creation of a culture of effective and inclusive
mentorship." They identify a need to "encourage and stimulate both more
theoretically informed and evidence-based mentorship practices and more
practitioner-informed research."[10]

What does this look like in everyday life?

What emerged in hundreds of interviews for the Hope University project
was that, for the most part, even the most generative relationships have included moments of disappointment, distancing, or disagreement.

> A senior faculty member reported, "I don't think I had mentors,
> really, as a grad student or junior faculty member. I think gender had
> a lot to do with that. When I was hired, there were no women in my
> department."

> Another interviewee, reflecting on their own lack of mentorship in
> graduate school, wondered, "if you are not being mentored and you
> see somebody being mentored who's in a position of power, there is
> the possibility of jealousy. Why not me? Why did they get chosen for
> special attention?"

> An administrative leader commented, "[Mentorship] is a one-on-one
> relationship that you can either really empower somebody and help
> them or you can fucking kill them without even knowing."

> A mid-career staff member queried, "How does somebody even do mentorship? Do you even have a paradigm for what that looks like? Or do you and your mentee go into the space already in conflict? This can be [an] adversarial type of positioning because you haven't talked about consent, or what a mentor is or does or doesn't do."

> An undergraduate student commented, "I've never had someone come up to me and take me under their wing, protect me no matter what, teach me things no matter what, no matter how difficult, no matter how hard the truth. I've never had that because I've never had the opportunity for that. Not only because I haven't been in situations where I couldn't have that, because you can find mentorship anywhere, because I've always been really busy … Is mentorship something I need to start worrying about on top of everything else?"

Oof. These stories are hard to read.

Build affective circuitry in mentorship

As I asked others to reflect on their mentorship experiences, I had to revisit my own.

I had two undergraduate professors – Goran Stanivukovic and Janet Hill – who inspired me to pursue graduate studies. They did so by spending extra time inviting me into conversations around early modern scholarship, and they did so beyond the paid labour and incentive structures of their academic work. Their extra supervision was neither valued nor compensated, and yet their unconditional professional love helped me flourish in ways I would not have reached on my own.

As I embarked on my graduate school adventure, Goran and Dr Hill told me stories of the wonderful supervision I could expect in graduate school and beyond – of supervisors who would guide, coach, advise, challenge, inspire, and stretch me in yet unimagined ways.

However, these highly anticipated mentors never materialized.

Instead, I found myself in a hyper-competitive culture with overworked and exhausted professors who did not have the bandwidth for far too many graduate students.

Reflecting on this chapter, I realized that my unrealized hopes for mentorship generated internalized sadness. If I did not have a grad school mentor, did that mean I was not worthy of professional love? Not rigorous enough for undivided attention? Not (insert novel, shiny, promising, precocious) enough for a special one-on-one relationship? Surfacing these latent feelings has been a decentring exercise, and I had to go back to my fundamental conceptual tools – like surfacing the systems and unlearning – to build more robust hope circuits.

Moreover, in doing so, I also realized that my mentors took on shapes different from the ones I was promised and yet they were nevertheless instrumental both in moments of distress (confusion, disorientation, and despair) and in times of celebration (victory, joy, and hilarity).

Mentors, like Athena, can be shape-shifters.

They can take many forms: mentor, coach, teacher, instructor, guide, guru, elder, master (apprentice), manager, boss, leader, role model, and possibility model.

Commit to unlearning and relearning

We have some unlearning to do around mentorship. When I first broached the topic of mentorship with Canadian university president Jeff Hennessy, his initial response was, "Well, I hire a good team that I can mentor." When I challenged him to think about the difference between *manager* (with designated titles, job description, performance assessment, or direct reports) and *mentor* (which can be informal or outside prescribed roles), he started to question his assumptions.[11]

Indeed, this is a common conflation to make.

In a *Harvard Business Review* article, "The Leader as Coach," Herminia Ibarra and Anne Scoular highlight the difference between management, coaching, and – by extension – mentoring. They discuss how present-day managers as leaders are, more than ever, asked to coach employees to produce greater engagement and innovation. Ibarra and Scoular warn that when we assume managers are mentors who "tell" their employees what to do, this conflates management and mentorship because it "assumes that the boss knows things that the recipient of the coaching does not – not always a safe assumption in a complex and constantly changing work environment."[12]

So, let us consider how mentorship is not always (or often?) paid work. What if we started from a different set of assumptions: namely, that mentorship is a reciprocal, interconnected relationship founded on "professional love." Charlene Marion, Work-Integrated Learning expert, first introduced me to this concept, which she explained as taking a deep interest and curiosity in someone combined with an enduring commitment to their flourishing.

This idea aligns with bell hooks and her work in *Teaching Communities*, where she talks about the fundamental first principle of love as "a combination of care, commitment, knowledge, responsibility, respect, and trust. All these factors work interdependently. They are a core function of love irrespective of the relational context."[13]

Teaching, and by extension mentorship, is founded on professional love, forged through trust and loyalty.

| One undergraduate student shared, "Our biggest concept [in mentorship] is that we learn from each other because we love each other."

Reimagine authority and expertise

One of the potential pitfalls in mentorship happens when professional love is conflated with familial or other forms of love.

Consider the Odyssean example in which mentorship occurs in lieu of/instead of a parental figure.[14] Family is a fraught metaphor for mentorship and often used to denote belonging in institutional and organizational spaces: "Welcome to the X university family!" is a familiar trope, often used to differentiate smaller communities like departments, sports teams, alumni circles, and other groups.

Yet there is increased risk of harm when different kinds of love elide.

In an influential *Harvard Business Review* article, "Your Company Is Not a Family," Reid Hoffman, Ben Casnocha, and Chris Yeh argue that the concept of family is misused in our efforts to articulate "a model that represents the kind of relationships [organizations] want to have with their employees – a lifetime relationship with a sense of belonging."

This slippage in our language is problematic because "the term family makes it easy for misunderstandings to arise."[15]

> An interviewee asked, "What are the boundaries around a family versus a community? And what are the ways that your family or family is going to hurt you if that's what you're expecting from this relationship? ... We can be loving and caring and intentional but [a university community] is not a family, and we can't start from there. So how do we shift that? How do we avoid referring to ourselves as the [university] family or the sports-team-as-family, or the [X or Y] department as family and rename it around belonging and mattering?

When I was a junior faculty member, a senior female colleague took me under her wing and declared, "I'm your big sister." I was delighted, honoured, and then harmed in ways I am still untangling.

When I had my first child, she came over for a visit. I had a brand-new baby in my arms while she chastised me for continuing to work on a few projects while I was on parental leave. From her perspective, the parental rights she had personally fought for – negotiated, sacrificed, demanded – were now in jeopardy. She reasoned that if people (men) saw me contributing while I was on maternity leave, they would assume future parents would not need accommodations. At the time, I was devastated. Where were choice and agency, empowerment, and possibility, I wondered?

This was a case study of classic(al) mentorship: intergenerational, unidirectional, and legacy-focused. However, I now see it more clearly through the lens of generativity: my behaviour jeopardized her legacy.

She was trying to protect me and protect her hard-won victories. This was the same colleague who rebuked senior administrators for inviting me to sit on committees when I was a junior faculty member because she wanted me to focus on my research (without informing or consulting me).

These actions were well-intentioned. They were even generative. But they were not grounded in generosity.

At the time, I did not have the framework to manage the tension between generosity and generativity, which might have helped me respond with empathy rather that confusion.

When we look at potential protégés, we might imagine they are following the same path as us. From genuine places of goodwill, we want to shield them from the obstacles, failures, and warn them of the brick walls or closed doors we encountered.

However, if we assume that mentees will follow the same path we did, we risk short-circuiting their unique trajectory – along with their imaginative and creative potential. Stripped of choice and lateral movement, they are left with the default, the status quo, and the existing systems. Sticking to the path can lead to stagnation, which is the opposite of generativity.

> A senior faculty member reflects, "A lot of my own thinking about mentorship in the academy is coloured by how convinced I am that the system is designed to run on sick people, so that mentorships reproduce that system. Hard to excavate the positive especially given that the grad student [and] new faculty systems [are] so tied up with labour exploitation."

Live in the questions

As we create new circuitry in post-secondary education, many of the old tools and past practices are no longer relevant to present-day mentorship. So, if we are committed to rewiring the systems, we might start by living into the following questions.

- What does mentorship look like if it makes space to produce new pathways towards purpose instead of reproducing old ones?
- How do we create systems and structures that do not make assumptions about other people's journeys?
- How do we create systems that are dynamic enough to respond to possibility rather than the past practices?

During an interview about mentorship, one of my interlocutors had a lightbulb moment about their mentoring experiences. They exclaimed, "When I was trying to protect, was I actually blocking?"

Honest questions like these are crucial. And hard. We may discover gaps between good intentions and unintended consequences.

Unfortunately, there are no clear instructions because the context is constantly changing. Nevertheless, there are conceptual tools that help us to live into questions in each mentorship encounter.

> Early modern scholar Shannon Murray articulates the importance of generosity in mentorship: "It suggests how important representation is too; to extend my experience [of no mentorship] to BIPOC, LGBTQ, disability [and other historically excluded groups], you have a whole bunch of people mentoring themselves … Which brings me to the big generosity question: because I think mentoring requires a generosity of spirit that universities do not always encourage. You have to be happy that someone else will flourish, even if you didn't. And you have to see junior faculty and students in your discipline as collaborators and not enemy combatants. We may not be good at this in the humanities, but the science labs are much worse: [there is] so much exploitation of junior colleagues' work. If we can inch towards seeing university life as NOT a zero-sum game, we will be a lot further along."

Practise divergent thinking

Metaphor is a useful conceptual tool for helping us make visible the systems we take for granted and pushes us out of the well-worn grooves into new ways of seeing and knowing. American biologist Beronda Montgomery wrote a piece for *Nature* titled "My Most Memorable Mentors? Plants." She reflects on how the academy fosters siloed thinking and emotional dismemberment: "Many scientists hesitate to apply the ideas that inspire their research and fuel their publications to their working lives and interactions. We've been trained not to. Instead, we're socialized to construct artificial barriers between scientific and personal insights."

Beronda Montgomery deploys metaphor to counter the critical culture of the academy with an approach that illuminates new possibilities:

> Some people tell me that I'm oversimplifying in thinking that plants can supply useful analogies for humans. They say such knowledge is simply not transferable. Others might counter that nature is about the survival of the fittest; that it, too, is a fierce contest for scarce resources,

in which the most competitive wins. I say, let's apply all the cognitive tools we have to solving important challenges. Even though prevailing scientific norms demand that we remain personally distant from our subjects of study, I've been deeply inspired by mine and the metaphors they offer.[16]

These insights recall Parker Palmer's "new professional," which he describes as a willingness to "stand where personal and public meet, dealing with the thundering flow of traffic at an intersection where 'weaving a web of connectedness' feels more like crossing a freeway on foot."[17]

Lisa Dickson, in *Shakespeare's Guide to Hope, Life, and Learning*, reflects, "Like Lear dividing his kingdom, a teacher who models a divided life can hardly be surprised to see division ramify across the land. Unless I model an undivided life, how can I convince my students to seek it? If I opt for a compartmentalization of feeling from 'real' thinking, my authority from the students' agency, how can I expect my students to do anything but recapitulate that division?"[18]

Beronda Montgomery uses plants. Parker Palmer uses traffic. Lisa Dickson uses Lear.

Each of them deploys divergent thinking in the pursuit of wholeness in the academy.

What metaphors, I wonder, help unlock your capacities to live an "undivided life?"

Stay with the trouble

The opening voiceover in *Wonder Woman* plays with the tension between assumptions and encounters: Diana, Princess of Themyscira, reflects, "I used to want to save the world. This beautiful place. But I knew so little then … What one does when faced with the truth is more difficult than you'd think."[19]

The film exposes the naïveté of this saviour trope and its underlying assumption that there are well-defined moral distinctions between the "good guys" and the "bad guys." We follow Diana's development as she confronts troublesome knowledge: her resilience, and eventual triumph, is only made possible through her capacity as a learner and a mentor.

There was one concept in particular from *Wonder Woman* that illuminated my understanding of mentorship that I have tried to make more explicit in my academic practice. Early in the film, soldiers invade the Amazonian island; in the midst of battle, the Amazonian general, Antiope, yells "shield!" and her compatriot angles her shield to propel Antiope high into the air in order to destroy their enemy's strategic position. Steve Trevor (self-styled "good guy") witnesses this display on the beaches of Themyscira. Later in the film, when Diana and her ragged band are under fire, Steve repurposes a tank door and yells "shield!" and three men launch Diana into the air so she can take out a sniper's nest and win the day.

The shield represents a mindset of generosity, solidarity, and humility that enables us to advance others so that they can reach new heights and exceed their individual capacities. The shield bearer is foundational to success but assumes none of the glory. They must be attentive to moments where their intervention can change the outcome.

How do we respond to changing contexts and circumstances and develop the agility to adapt as situations arise? And how do we do that together in mentoring relationships?

American essayist Rebecca Solnit describes hope as "the belief that what we do matters even though how and when it may matter, who and what it may impact, are not things we can know beforehand."[20] Put another way, mentorship is a reciprocal relationship that requires trust and the willingness to stand in solidarity with others, even when we do not know the outcome. James Bridle, in *Ways of Being*, defines solidarity as "a product of imagination as well as action, because a practice of care for one another in the present consists in resisting the desire to plan, produce and solve ... Active, practical care resists certitude and conclusions ... It is the result of encounters, not assumptions."[21]

How we respond to conflict or contestation, culture change, or clarity of purpose is informed by how robust our hope circuits are.

How we encounter others – and move beyond binaries into the multitude – is a learned response that requires intentional circuitry.

Build intentional community

As we move towards new models of mentorship, we need to challenge the assumptions inherited from Homer's origin story.

- A mentor does not have to occupy traditional positions of authority.
- Mentorship does not need to be intergenerational (old to young).
- Mentoring can have different timelines.

My mentors have lifted me up and propelled me farther than I could have achieved on my own. My collaborators and colleagues have performed countless acts of "shield bearing" at meetings and in classrooms, in online forums and research receptions. Some of my most cherished experiences being mentored have been forged through co-design with students, young people, and innovators more junior than me. Sometimes referred to as reverse mentorship, students-as-mentors have transformed how I understand hope at local and systems-wide levels.

Young people have tremendous capacities for generosity, generativity, and legacy-building in mentorship spaces, which upends the unidirectional intergenerational model (transmission of knowledge from expert to initiate) we see expressed in Homer's works.

British career coach and executive Patrice Gordon, in "How Reverse Mentorship Can Create Better Leaders," asks us to reimagine mentorship:

> We've always thought of mentoring as the older generation passing down wisdom to the young, but there's a huge benefit to flipping that around and allowing the novice to teach the master … There's a growing gap between leaders and their people in regards to their perspectives and experiences. Our organizations can fall right through that gap into the trap of stale thinking, blind spots and having policies that could alienate these underrepresented groups, not only in regards to age, race or gender, but all different kinds of viewpoints … Reverse mentoring [is] one of those tools that you can use to amplify the voices of underrepresented people.[22]

In higher education, students act as reverse mentors for faculty, staff, and administrative leaders in courageous, audacious ways because they can see possibility when more experienced humans are stuck in default mode. They inspire us to jump out of the well-worn grooves we have built through repetition over time and be brave enough to create new circuits that move us from conformity to creativity.

> An undergraduate student shares this insight: "For me, a totally new paradigm is a higher level of back and forth between youth and mentor. There is a lot that people forget as they age and I feel like it's important that the mentors themselves are able to learn about what it's like to think like the youth, or even just to be able to use different technologies. A back-and-forth system where the youth is able to teach the mentor a thing or two may solidify a greater connection."

Concluding thoughts

In *Old Masters and Young Geniuses: The Two Life Cycles of Artistic Creativity*, David Galenson traces the genealogy of the most innovative and creative endeavours through two groups: "Experimental innovators work by trial and error, and arrive at their major contributions gradually, late in life. In contrast, conceptual innovators make sudden breakthroughs by formulating new ideas, usually at an early age.

"Experimental innovators seek, and conceptual innovators find."[23]

Universities are such important social institutions because they bring together old masters (professors, staff, alumni) and young geniuses (students). Young geniuses are wired to build and illuminate; professors-as-old-masters can help young people navigate systems and structures. Together we can engage in deeper social and systemic change.

If we design for it and amplify (instead of squashing) the audacity and curiosity of novices and newcomers, we learn across generations.

> Another undergraduate student offers, "I believe that one way we could reframe the mentorship system could be to allow for it to go both ways ... the mentor/mentee roles should be interchangeable."

Moreover, mentorship does not need to be one on one.

American educational researcher Jessie Moore has theorized "constellation" mentoring whereby "mentoring relationships function within a broader set of relationships known as a constellation, and this disrupts the power because the students are actually contributing to that constellation as well." In this network approach, "multiple mentors fulfill meaningful roles for students." Jessie Moore reflects on the power of divergent thinking: "When we say 'constellation,' this possibility opens up and the students run with this metaphor right away … They are going to map out the people influencing them."

This model offers a high-impact intervention that supports mentorship access for historically excluded groups. Jessie Moore shares, "This came up over and over, particularly for students with minoritized identities: I want somebody who understands my multiple identities, and even if they can't understand all of me, they may understand part of my lived experience."[24]

We all have multiple identities and diverse lived experiences.

Parker Palmer in *The Courage to Teach* says, "I want to learn how to hold the paradoxical poles of my identity together, to embrace the profoundly opposite truths that my sense of self is deeply dependent on others dancing with me and that I still have a sense of self when no one wants to dance."[25]

There are echoes here of Bayo Akomolafe's invitation to move away from dominant paradigms so we can "move to the side to dance; [it] feels to me like a shifting of us [out] of our centrality … maybe it's awkward, maybe there are ways of moving to the side that invites a shifting of our positions."[26]

Athena, our original shape-shifting mentor, gives us one possible way forward: operating in the in-between spaces of the mortal and supernatural worlds, she works on the edges, taking many forms, and spends her own capital to help others find their purpose – for individuals and for a greater social good.

The goddess is a protector of heroes on epic quests and a mentor for those who are stagnating. If we channel Athena – with her wisdom and invention – we might meet together on the edges of new paradigms.

With our mentors and mentees, our proteges and learners, our elders and guides.

Together and alone.

And then we can dance.

Chapter 6

How Do We Lead at Hope University?

I stood at the border, stood at the edge and claimed it as central.
I claimed it as central, and let the rest of the world move over to
where I was.
– Toni Morrison[1]

As we experience a paradigm shift in higher education, we need leaders who
are wired to work on the edges and margins.

Leading in an "extraordinary" time (to deploy Thomas Kuhn's theory of
revolutionary change) requires a skill set we have not hitherto developed for
aspiring leaders.

Since there is a veritable mountain of literature on leadership, from self-
help books to scholarly tomes, this chapter takes a different approach that
asks us to reconsider the position from where we lead, with particular attention to in-between spaces.

In universities, leadership comes in many shapes and forms. We lead in
labs, classrooms, committees, communities, associations, disciplinary fields,
and disciplines. Indeed, we are not short on leadership opportunities and
leaders in the academy.

- We have formal leaders in administrative roles with titles and positional authority.
- We have informal leaders in educational, transformative, grassroots,
  entrepreneurial, and research spheres.

- We have students, scholars, and staff – all leaders in diverse contexts.
- We have leadership dyads, triads, partnerships, and clusters.
- We have countless theoretical leadership models: change leadership, authentic leadership, academic leadership, distributed leadership, transformative leadership – to name just a few.

For the most part, though, we don't train, recruit, hire, and support leaders to flourish on edges and margins.

The good news is that we already have leaders in higher education with these well-developed skill sets: they are most often informal leaders – outliers, innovators, and early adopters – that work between systems, engage in community partnerships, create integrated or grassroots hubs, and deploy social justice lenses for collaborative systems change.

And yet, in interviews, high-impact innovators reported that their work is either invisible, undervalued, or actively impeded.

More than one interviewee confessed that they stay away from the spotlight, purposefully avoiding institutional attention or accolades to continue to do the meaningful grassroots leadership tied to their purpose. They would rather ask for forgiveness than permission as they embed their teaching and research in non-traditional spaces.

Another, the lead of a research centre, joked that they tell everyone they spend their time knitting sweaters for baby goats. When asked a follow-up question from a probing administrator, they provide long-winded explanation until administrators' eyes glaze over: they want to fly under the radar so they can engage in creative research partnerships.

An award-winning scholar with a distinguished record of international leadership disclosed their strategy: they stay in the spotlight, drawing attention to the work they are doing at all times. If they stay in the spotlight, their logic goes, it is harder to get stabbed from the shadows.

- Forgiveness rather than permission.
- Nothing to see here.
- Beware of shadows.

These are well-honed strategies to survive in systems and cultures that punish the extraordinary.

The best these educational leaders can hope for is benevolent neglect. This is not okay.

Some level of discomfort in systems change is to be expected. Indeed, more than one person I interviewed argued that innovation happens in the friction between the change agents and change-resistant systems. They believe that the act of chafing against the system is a necessary element in the process of building new things.

Certainly, in transformation, discomfort is a feature, not a flaw – a concept we explore in depth in the "How Do We Learn" chapter. By extension, transformative leaders will encounter contestation, difficulty, and strife. If systems are resilient, challenging the status quo inevitably leads to systems recoiling.

And.

I want us to spend more time thinking about structures that accommodate wonder, curiosity, and new ways of knowing and being. It is worth revisiting Mi'kmaq scholar Marie Battiste's reminder to "centre educational commitment to, and our responsibilities for, the enhancement of humanity and its infinite capacities. Each strategy taken to rebuild human capacity is a decolonizing activity that turns collective hope into insights, voices, and partnerships, not resistance, resignation, or despair."[2]

We must be able to reconfigure systems that produce leaders able to build and illuminate new spaces rather than reproduce the status quo.

Practise divergent thinking

As a Shakespearean, when I think about educational and grassroots leaders, I look to the wyrd sisters in *Macbeth*.[3]

In Macbeth, the wyrd sisters occupy the margins and haunt the fens of Scotland – a treacherous, often flooded, and marshy landscape. These women are called "witches" in the stage directions and "weird sisters" in the text. The "weird sisters" moniker originates from "wyrd," the Anglo-Saxon word for fate. In *Macbeth*, the wyrd sisters appear at unexpected moments with prophetic utterances that can be interpreted in various ways. Macbeth's failure to heed their words, which contain troublesome and complex truths, leads him down a path of social and personal destruction.

Shakespeare's wyrd sisters live on the edges of the play world, removed from the centre of power characterized by the masculine, militarized, patriarchal world of king and court.[4] The wyrd sisters observe from a distance and encounter men only when they wander onto the edges. Despite – or because of – their liminal position, the witches comment on the goings-on of these men insistent on self-destruction and civil war.

The only power the wyrd sisters wield is words.

Words matter: these three outliers manage to disrupt the very centres of power through incantations and equivocal language and, by doing so, become the most powerful change agents in the world of this play. The wyrd sisters sit on the edges looking into the centres of power; without title, authority, or resources they manage to expose the rot and dismantle the systems foundational to political power in Scotland.

So, what can we learn from the wyrd sisters in our own leadership journeys?

As we experience a sector-wide paradigm shift, we need wyrd mindsets to lead from a place of complexity; we need wyrd leadership to metabolize discomfort that comes with traversing awkward and unfamiliar spaces; we need wyrd thinking when "fair is foul and foul is fair" – in other words, when what we thought we knew is no longer true and reversals and inversions become the new normal. We need wyrd tools – language, intentional community – to flourish in the otherwise inhospitable academic landscapes.

Live in the questions

Edges and margins can be powerful places for change. And yet, many people don't have the tools or the mindset to navigate this less traversed terrain. When I first did a deep dive into the literature on leadership several years ago, I struggled to find models that discussed contestation and conflict as part of the leadership journey. Plenty of models discussed conflict as a byproduct of bad leadership, and yet very few acknowledged difficulty as a design feature.

And then I stumbled upon Canadian political scientist Heather Smith at a conference where she delivered a provocative presentation on her emerging theory of "guerilla leadership," and we have been rumbling leadership theories ever since. We have wondered together,

- How do we imagine socially just change within our institutions of higher learning and the connections to broader society?
- How do we improve our universities by engaging in "leadership from the edges"?[5]
- What decisions do we need to make and who needs to make them at our universities?

Wonder itself is an act of decentring and reorientation.

Wonder invites us to unlearn and relearn when encountering the unknown and the uncertain.

We need to figure out how to rewire for wonder.

For Lisa Dickson, wonder came into focus during her experience tandem sky-diving. She describes diving out of the plane as "falling through wonder" and theorizes that "wonder is the space between who you are now and who you will become."

"Mapping the contours of wonder," Lisa Dickson tells us, "suspends us, it decentres us, and asks us to reconfigure our understanding."[6]

Wonder is itself an in-between space where we can imagine the possible.

If "wonder suspends our habitual ways of seeing and describing the world," then higher education, according to her, is a "wonder engine."

So, I wonder, what does leadership from the edges look like as we rewire our universities for human flourishing? How do we claim the edges' materiality, agency, and ethics? Furthermore, where can we find (and mobilize) the early adopters, pioneers, outliers, disrupters, and innovators who often occupy the edges of systems and institutions and move them into new centres? Or, at the very least, create dynamic systems willing to embrace the edges, embrace the edgy, embrace the extraordinary.

In our current paradigm shift, as we sit in a nexus between an old system and the emergence of a new model, we will increasingly need leaders who are wired to occupy in-between spaces of radical uncertainty and disruption – and still be able to wonder and imagine within the immediacy of crisis management.

Commit to unlearning and relearning

Let us return to the witches of *Macbeth* to discuss what leading from the edges requires: the ability to pivot.

The wyrd sisters both look into the play's action by being on the edges and turn around to look over the edges into the unknown (for them, the supernatural). This reorientation – a shift in perspective – can provide us with the experience of wonder.

As we look at the centres of power within our institutions, wyrd thinking encourages us to turn around and look over the edges of the current paradigm into the unknown with wonder and curiosity. Only then can we remember, as John D. Caputo reminds us, that "something different is always possible."[7]

We also must acknowledge that looking over the edge into the unknown is uncomfortable. Decentring our perspective requires that we look with fresh eyes at old habits and mindsets that may no longer serve us. Wonder, as Lisa Dickson tells us, "knocks us sideways out of our habitual frame and the new flows into the space left by the old." After we peer over the edge into the unknown, we engage in a reconfiguration process with an expanded understanding of our world anew.

This fresh perspective has the potential to transform us, our institutions, and the edges upon which we teeter.

Buddhist philosopher Pema Chödrön gives us another way of thinking about looking over the edges into the unknown. She urges us to sit in the discomfort of the present moment:

We can step into uncharted territory and relax with the groundlessness of our situation. When we resist change, it's called suffering. But when we can completely let go and not struggle against it, when we can embrace the groundlessness of our situation and relax into its dynamic quality, that's called enlightenment, or awakening to our true nature, to our fundamental goodness.[8]

This brand of leadership – of letting go, of relinquishing authority, of decentring expertise – is a difficult model for many.

When I was in the middle of a difficult encounter with a collaborator, I realized I was pushing up against a door and my colleague was pushing with equal force on the other side. When I decided (metaphorically) to stop push-ing and instead open the door, the swing in momentum changed everything. I had to let go of the struggle and embrace the groundlessness that led us from combative into new collaborative spaces. The ability to sit in conflict and allow for difficult conversations to unfold is something I have to learn and relearn regularly in my own rewiring process.

Reimagine authority and expertise

As we move between the edges and the centre, we must acknowledge that the academy does not train people to be bosses. Nor does it teach us the dis-tinction between leaders and bosses. When leadership, governance, and man-agement roles are blurry, people and systems suffer.

Moreover, when academics move into positions where they are expected to manage staff and build dynamic teams, the skills they have developed as researchers, teachers, and leaders do not translate easily into these new roles.

One Canadian university president remarked, "the only equation that matters is people."

Yes.

And.

We set ourselves up for failure if we assume that managing people is in-tuitive rather than intentional.

When successful scholars and award-winning educators manage human resource issues without the appropriate skill sets (including performance as-sessment, conflict management, and trust-building frameworks), a myriad of problems arise.

As I wrote earlier, there is no such thing as a naturally gifted teacher.

The same statement is true about leaders.

And bosses.

So how do we rewire our mindsets to get comfortable on the edges and in-between spaces that are increasingly becoming our lived reality?

Followership theory offers us one model of leadership that illuminates the sticky problem of edges and centres in higher education institutions. American entrepreneur Derek Sivers defines a leader as someone who "needs the guts to stand out and be ridiculed." The first follower, however, is crucial to "transform a lone nut into a leader."[9]

In this theory, the leader embraces the first follower as an equal when they begin a movement. As the movement is made public, new followers emulate the first follower, not the leader. Nurturing the first few followers as equals, Sivers argues, is essential to nurturing the movement. Furthermore, research on followership in higher education suggests that followers often see themselves as leaders, an identity that shifts depending on different contexts.

The instability of power dynamics, the shifting roles of leaders and followers, and a paucity of management training make for a complex relational terrain to navigate.

A lack of management training has caused countless challenges for academics who have thrived as scholar-leaders and are then thrust into positions where they need to design job descriptions, hire and train employees, build teams with diverse stakeholders, engage in staff and administrative performance assessments, and manage interpersonal relationships and conflict. Add unionized environments, multiple collective agreements, and entrenched politics, and this becomes downright disorienting.

Stay with (more) trouble

Staying with the trouble, I must confess my own failure as a boss with my first employee.

As Sivers points out about the first leader and the first follower, I treated my first employee as an equal. We co-designed their aspirational job description. I gave them *carte blanche* to dream and scheme and also put them in charge of a small team of volunteers. This first employee kept calling me "boss" in jest and at meetings with others, and I kept chafing against that term, preferring to reframe our relationship as collaborators and co-designers.

Only in hindsight do I realize how much harm I caused by erasing the boss-employee relationship. I thought I was creating a movement. In truth, I was building an organization – albeit with that same mission and foundational values. Organizations need structure, boundaries, and systems. I learned the hard way that we do not, as James Clear points out, "rise to the level of your goals. You fall to the level of your systems."[10]

I had an employee who needed boundaries, onboarding, ongoing training, clear expectations and deliverables, regular performance assessment, and, most importantly, regular and consistent access to me. However, I did not explicitly teach them to collaborate across complex organizations, act professionally, or upskill for difficult conversations, nor did I provide guidance on corporate stewardship and shared values – essential for the health of any organization. I was not taught that myself and had to figure it out along the way, so my method was intuitive, unexamined, and totally unhelpful to anyone else.

As a first boss and first employee, we started with a shared purpose and then lost alignment along the way. I believe now that I caused the misalignment by reproducing systems of scarcity that I internalized from working in and across chronically under-funded and under-resourced institutions.

Scarcity, according to Brené Brown, means "there's never enough blank, never enough time, never enough people, never enough clarity, never enough, never enough, never enough." In a scarcity-driven culture, "leaders use fear and uncertainty to drive productivity. We could lose the accounts, we could shut down, we could do this, we've got to do this. It is exhausting, it is unrelenting, and it does not drive productive, innovative, creative thinking."[11]

I was 100 per cent guilty of this mindset.

Because I worked for years within institutions with declining provincial funding, precarious enrollment, and multi-year structural deficits, the scarcity seeped into my bones. The "never enough" mantra drove me to work harder, sacrifice my research, compromise my health, and go the extra *pro bono* mile because I thought that if I tried my best, I could help the university.

Because I did not have the language to name or claim it, I reproduced scarcity in my leadership – especially when I inherited a fledging consortium with minimal grassroots buy-in and many people demanding metrics to justify "the bang for their buck."

This professional context accelerated the hustle and the harm.

For Brené Brown, "[In] scarcity-driven armored leadership cultures … our perceived value is often tied to our performance, [so] we tend to hustle for our worth. Now, one of I think the hardest relationships to manage is the person who is constantly hustling for their worth, constantly vying for validation that they're good enough, that their work is important, that they're a contributor. And you often see that in scarcity-based cultures."

I am 100 per cent guilty of this mindset, too. It is something I must unlearn regularly.

When organizations operate in a scarcity model, shame is "baked into the walls." As such, my refusal to boss (both as a verb and as an identity) and my insistence on co-design engendered behaviour from my first boss-employee relationship that perpetuated shame.

Surface the systems

Brené Brown's research shows us what shame-based behaviour looks like: "*Shame shows up at work [as] back-channeling.*"[12]

If you have ever shown up at a meeting only to realize the decision had already been taken, you have experienced back-channelling. New forms of back-channelling have become pernicious in virtual meetings where texting amongst people during meetings creates insiders and outsiders. Coordinating, whipping votes, caucusing can all be examples of back-channelling, which has the potential to significantly undermine trust and goodwill.

"*Favoritism is shame in action, because the people that are subjected to your favoritism and not part of the favorites feel smaller, diminished, less than, put down.*"

This behaviour also shows up in inside jokes, social media shares, and other micro-actions that demarcate insider and outsider status.

"*The invisible army. This is when I come to you and I say, 'We've all been talking and we really think you should reconsider,' my first question is: 'Who's we?'*"

When someone shares issues without naming the interlocutors and claiming the conversations, it puts the person receiving feedback on the defensive – which is never a good look.

"*Perfectionism … is absolutely a function of shame. Perfectionism is the 20-ton shield that we carry around, if I look perfect, work perfect, turn everything in perfectly, do it all perfectly, I can avoid or minimize shame, judgment, and blame. Any kind of management tool where we're tying people's self-worth to their productivity, you are as good as what you produce, shame in the walls.*"

This one resonates especially, I think, for academics who have been rewarded for producing (insert publications, grants, awards, prestige). When we work within conditions of scarcity, we are always asked to prove our worth and account for our place in the budget line. And it quickly moves from "we don't have enough [X]" to "I am not enough."

"Gossiping. Let me tell you, if you've got a gossiping issue, you got a shame behind the wall issue. Teasing, shame in the walls; passive-aggressive behavior, I would look for shame."

When schoolyard behaviours and spicy ripostes are pervasive in work cultures, they embed shame into the deep culture of the organization. While I saw this behaviour manifesting in my first employee, it felt yucky, and yet I did not have the framework to draw the connection between shame-based behaviour and the inevitable erosion of trust that followed.

Trust is the glue that bonds us together in healthy organizations where we have the goodwill necessary to operate in radical uncertainty. One of my favourite definitions of trust comes from the American author of the *Thin Book of Trust*, Charles Feltman, who describes trust as "choosing to risk making something you value vulnerable to another person's actions." Conversely, distrust is deciding that "what is important to me is not safe with this person in this situation (or any situation)."[13]

In my case, I reproduced a scarcity model that led to a shame-based culture; with no training to upskill for difficult conversations and an inability to call out or "call in" toxic behaviours, my benevolent neglect led to irresolvable tensions. To compound the issue, the team of volunteers under the first employee followed the first employee (as Sivers predicted) and reproduced the behaviours they saw modelled.

When trust is lost, things snowball. I struggled to recapture a shared purpose with weekly check-ins and alignment exercises too late in the process. The more I chased, the more elusive alignment became. The damage was done and trust was lost on both sides.

The first employee eventually left for a new job that was stable and well-funded, moving from precarity to security.

This should have been a happy ending – and yet it was not.

I thought of myself as a transformative educational leader – and my professional identity was inextricably bound up with this belief. However, it turns out I was a terrible first boss. I experienced grief for a relationship that I had valued. I had to sit in this discomfort and ask, "What do I do with this shame?"

As Brené Brown remarks, "We do not have the skills culturally in this country around accountability, we just shame the shit out of everyone, we have cancel culture, we literally do not know how to hold ourselves and others accountable."[14]

We need better systems so our leaders and followers can flourish in an extraordinary time of edges and margins.

Practise divergent thinking

First, though, we can stay with the discomfort. In the aftermath of my failed boss experience, my friend Shawna Garrett, herself an exceptional leader and manager, told me about the Buddhist practice of "inviting Mara to tea."

American psychologist and Buddhist teacher Tara Brach tells a story of the "Demon God Mara, who attacked the then bodhisattva Siddhartha Guatama with everything he had: lust, greed, anger, and doubt. Having failed, Mara left in disarray on the morning of the Buddha's enlightenment." However, Mara was not vanquished for long and had a bad habit of turning up at the most inopportune times.

"Instead of ignoring Mara or driving him away," Brach recounts, "the Buddha would calmly acknowledge his presence, saying, 'I see you, Mara.' He would then invite him for tea and serve him as an honored guest. Offering Mara a cushion so that he could sit comfortably, the Buddha would fill two earthen cups with tea, place them on the low table between them, and only then take his own seat. Mara would stay for a while and then go, but throughout the Buddha remained free and undisturbed."[15]

This story helps us to name our shame, claim it wholeheartedly as part of our human imperfections, and aim this knowledge into generous and generative spaces. This proposition is not an easy one, especially for those of us who are conflict averse.

Canadian author Ann Voskamp reminds us, "Shame dies when stories are told in safe spaces."[16]

Writing gives discomfort a narrative shape, and doing so helps me understand the contours of shame so I can learn from it.

Moreover, pausing to reflect on the context within which we find ourselves helps to locate and centre the discomfort. Then, and only then, can we aim this discomfort into new spaces to do better and be better. In my case, I had to grasp the concept of the scarcity model and recognize how I had unwittingly reproduced shame-based systems.

Let me tell you, that was a difficult guest to invite to tea.

Once I understood the shape of the problem, I could design systems that value the spirit of curiosity, critical reflection, and open-mindedness.

Take a systems-level approach

As a failed first boss, I have become an intentional and reflective second boss.

For one, I listened to Brené Brown when she said, "Leaders acknowledge the fear and uncertainty, they name it, they normalize it, with the goal of not leveraging it or using it, but de-escalating it."[17] Before, I named the messiness and disruption of building a movement without de-escalating or mitigating the emotional and cognitive labour of working in flux. Now that I know better, I can do better.

In subsequent leadership cycles, I have been careful about setting clear boundaries, spending more time onboarding, sharpening my focus on ongoing training, paying more attention to clear expectations and deliverables, and designing regular performance assessments. Onboarding now includes explicit discussions about collaborating across complex projects or departments, grounds professional behaviours in shared values and social norms, upskills for difficult conversations, and, most importantly, ensures regular and consistent access to me and to one another in trust-focused spaces.

When untrained bosses run organizations, toxic cultures thrive.

When the busy-ness of business takes us away from human relationships, scarcity prevails.

When the best we can hope for is benevolent neglect, shame gets baked into the walls.

I want to replace benevolent neglect with intentional attentiveness.

When we slow down, invest time in building and maintaining trust, listen to truth tellers, respect leadership as a practice, reward diverse thinkers, anchor values in daily practice, and reflect often, we create the conditions where all of us – leaders, managers, bosses, followers, employees, and staff – flourish.

Concluding thoughts

In an exchange between two literary luminaries, Toni Morrison first writes, "I stood at the border, stood at the edge and claimed it as central. I claimed it as central, and let the rest of the world move over to where I was."[18]

Akwaeke Emezi, in an open letter to Toni Morrison, responds, "You should see my centers, Ms. Morrison. They're glorious. They pull with the force of a planet and I'm patient; it's only a matter of time. I'm just waiting on the world. With all my love, Akwaeke."[19]

Here is to finding wyrd folks on the edges and in the margins.

Here is to brewing up recipes for change and making good mischief.

Here is to peering over the edge with wonder and a willingness to transform.

And here is to rewiring systems that make space for leadership from the edges and reconfigure the centres built on hope and human flourishing.

Chapter 7

How Do We Research at Hope University?

As imagination bodies forth
The forms of things unknown, the poet's pen
Turns them to shapes and gives to airy nothing
A local habitation and a name.
– Theseus, *A Midsummer Night's Dream*[1]

Research is the wonder engine that drives universities. We are wired to research because we are wired for wonder – to ask questions, seek answers, and think more deeply about ourselves and the world around us.

Research is, at its core, animated by the curiosity to *know* and the generosity to *share*.

Research takes us to the edges of known knowledge and asks us to peek over the edge to see, as Theseus says, the "forms of things unknown." As in Shakespeare's formulation of poetry, research is, likewise, a creative endeavour: it illuminates, builds, and generates new frameworks and paradigms for understanding ourselves and the world around us.

Research helps us fulfill the university's social contract with the broader society by conserving knowledge and expanding the limits of what we know while recognizing that we still have much to learn to make the world more just, humane, and healthy.

Research is an antidote to agnotology – the study of deliberately manufactured ignorance or doubt. Even ignorance is itself a research field.

Research, like hope, is a verb that happens in space and in time. The metaphors we use to talk about research – a research *field*, research *area*, research *frontiers*, *body* of research, a research *corpus* – capture the essence of embodiment.

Research, like hope circuits, can help us build new pathways, reorganize structures, reflect on functions, and build new connections that, in turn, help us rewire and reimagine what is possible.

Research is itself a hope circuit that engages in the ten conceptual tools animating this book.

We begin a research project by **living in the questions**:

- What is possible?
- What do we not yet know?
- What do we seek to understand more fully?

Then we **slow down** and look around with fresh eyes to understand how we might engage in research field(s) and gather as much information as possible.

What do we already know?

To figure out an entry point, we must **surface the systems**, looking for the theoretical or practical features in a body of research. Understanding the systems of known knowledge informs how we design the methodology – the systematic approach – to seek out data that can illuminate how we live into the research questions.

What is the bigger picture telling us?

Research **takes a systems-level approach** to a particular challenge or question, moving from individual or isolated information to more extensive data sets that enable us to see larger patterns.

What biases or assumptions must we avoid?

Uncomfortable truths and inconvenient detours are a feature rather than a flaw in any research journey. We must make space for the discomfort – and appreciate the work necessary to transform our thinking, adapt our approach, or manage unexpected findings. If we stay with the question long enough, we often discover data/evidence we could not anticipate. If we **stay with the trouble** (and, crucially, design for it), the answers are almost always more complex than our initial assumptions or expectations.

What did we assume we knew that is no longer helpful or true?

In many cases, researchers must **unlearn and relearn** fundamental assumptions of earlier research and eschew ego in favour of understanding.

How can we know better?

Practising divergent thinking can be a catalyst for identifying creative solutions or innovations. Using metaphor or approaching a question from a different angle or discipline can help us see and think differently. Trans- and inter-disciplinary thinking encourages novel connections and unlikely convergences that are illuminating and generative.

Who might help us in knowing more?

Research requires us to approach existing knowledge with an openness to **reimagine authority and expertise** – which sometimes means finding solutions in different disciplines or fields or discovering new knowledges from other contexts, regions, or worldviews. We look to research and clinical evidence while also valuing lived experience, land-based knowledges, intergenerational wisdom, intersectionality, and community-engaged insights.

Where might we look for more diverse understandings?

We never "master" research because there is always something new to learn. Favouring intellectual humility over mastery appreciates that while researchers work towards expertise, we are always in service to the questions, to curiosity, and to the social good.

How do we share what we learn with others?

Research gives us new frameworks to understand the world around us, enabling us to **change our language, which in turn changes the world**. In the creation of new knowledge, language adapts to reflect novel ways of understanding a concept or phenomenon that has hitherto been opaque. We are always adding new terms and redefining older ones in research inquiry and discovery.

Who do we share our insights with?

Finally, and perhaps most crucially for research, we build and maintain **intentional communities** – through peer review, ethics, adjudication, publication, and dissemination – so others can build upon foundational knowledge. Research is based on relationships, grounded in communities, attentive to diverse traditions and worldviews, and accountable to communities within which research is situated. And, increasingly, researchers are tasked with democratizing knowledge through knowledge mobilization and increasing accessibility through open educational resources.

Research is a hope circuit.

Paradoxically, though, research is the cause of much despair. In interviews for this book, research is one of the most fraught spaces: many interviewees shared stories of the dark sides of traditional research – as hierarchical, prestige-driven, shame-based, and built on mystification and exclusion.

Why does something so hopeful – curious, generous, generative – make so many of our colleagues feel like imposters, outsiders, misfits?

Live in the questions

If higher education is indeed an "engine of democracy," then we need to rumble on how research contributes to this social mission in the conservation of knowledge and the ongoing commitment to reconfiguring and re-constituting how we know things.[2]

We need to live into some difficult questions around research.

- What is the role of research in fulfilling the university's social mission?
- What conditions are necessary for good ideas and new knowledge to emerge?
- Why is there a distinction between "real" or "legitimate" research" and its perceived opposite?
- Why is research treated as something separate from teaching?
- And, perhaps most pressing for this project, what do we need to re-wire in our current research systems to enhance flourishing at the systems level?

As Kevin Gannon says in *Radical Hope*, "Make no mistake: higher education has both a role and a responsibility in creating and sustaining a free democratic society – whether we admit it or not, whether we are aware of it or not, whether we think it's our job or not, whether we like it or not. If we mean what we say about the intrinsic value and good in our collective enterprise, then we cannot abdicate that role or our responsibility for playing it."[3]

As a post-secondary sector, we are increasingly tasked with drawing a throughline from higher education to a civil, just society.

American cultural historian David Scobey, founder of the Bringing Theory to Practice Project, is one of many calling "for a national conversation about the purposes of higher education at a time when the dominant public understanding of those purposes has shrunk."[4]

From North America to Europe, from the Global South to Australasia and beyond, these calls are getting louder.

How do we best respond?

Research is, in many ways, our greatest asset in making a case for the democratic purpose of higher education.

Indeed, we witnessed first-hand the tremendous contributions research makes to the greater good in responding to the global pandemic: nationally funded science research at universities across Canada and around the world led the discovery and rapid mobilization efforts of life-saving vaccines in the battle against COVID-19.[5] Decades of research, failed experiments, and often unglamorous work in obscure labs led to the speedy development of tests, treatments, vaccines, and other health innovations that saved millions of lives.

These contributions have not been limited to the STEM (science, technology, engineering, mathematics) fields. Paul Davidson, long-time president of Universities Canada, reflects,

> If you think about what universities have done things that they thought they couldn't do, this is [also the case] on the research agenda. Again, universities have delivered and delivered well, not only on the medical side, but also on the social science side; Canada's more socially cohesive than in other parts of the world [and] the social science research has helped us adapt ... through the pandemic more successfully than some other societies. Research in liberal arts and humanities research has been critically important to the pandemic, and I'm really looking forward to the huge cultural production that's going to come out of the pandemic as people come out of their basements and reflect on their experiences.

Paul Davidson expands on the relevance of post-secondary institutions around dynamic and resilient institutions: "Universities have played a really important role across the country both as stabilizers, in a time of disruption and as catalysts. Stabilizers for the most part, as universities maintain [knowledge]. They maintain their supply chains. They help minimize the distress of the communities, [as an example] during the first phases of the pandemic. And then as a catalyst."[6]

Yes.

And.

Research is often also least understood in the public sphere.

Research is sometimes purposefully misunderstood in public discourse.

Once in a while a publicly funded research project is picked up by the mainstream news media as proof that universities are either out of touch or over-indulged (or both).

When I was an undergraduate in the mid-1990s, a SSHRC-funded doctoral project on the television series *Buffy the Vampire Slayer* hit CBC news; my practical, immigrant father exclaimed in disbelief, "Is this what they are teaching you these days?" It was a running joke at family parties for months. "Jessie is doing a degree in Buffy." The implication was: my education was fluffy, my professors flaky, and my future iffy (she'll never get a job and contribute to society, my aunts taunted).

At the time, I did not have the language to defend the importance of research in diverse fields as a life-affirming expression of the academic enterprise. I just felt unlocatable sadness and very locatable shame – of myself, of the humanities, and, by extension, the academy.

Indeed, one just has to look at how academics are represented in popular culture to see the misalignment between what we do and how we are perceived.

As American higher education leadership expert Jeffrey Buller notes,

If you look back at the way college professors were depicted from the 1950s and earlier, usually they are scientists who look pretty much like Einstein, brilliant, very respected, high positions. If you look at the way college professors are depicted from the 1960s on, they're usually literature professors – always male, bearded, sleeping with their students, taking drugs, and really disreputable. And I think that that environment both has been a *reflection* of a change of mindset in the wider culture, but it has also *intensified* that change [of public perception and perceived value of the academy] in a wider culture. So, when I hear a lot of people who don't have a background [in] higher education talk about colleges today, I hear them parroting back to me things that have happened in popular culture, not things that really happen at universities.[7]

When caricatures of ivory towers filled with absent-minded professors fixated on pet research projects are allowed to proliferate, it is not just harmless misrepresentation.[8] It jeopardizes the social mission of universities. Jeffrey Buller explains,

And where we have problems here in the [United] States is when we have governing boards, which usually consist solely of people from outside higher education. They come from the corporate world, they come from government, they're lawyers, they're this and that, but they're not in higher education. And they think they know how higher education should work because they went to college, which I always say that's sort of thinking like you can deliver a baby because you're young. It's not a good way of seeing how the system actually works.[9]

Compound this with the rise in misinformation,[10] growing suspicion in science,[11] the proliferation of conspiracy theories,[12] a notable increase in climate skepticism,[13] and widespread anti-intellectualism,[14] and it quickly becomes clear that the academy does not merely have an image problem: the lack of understanding and diminished value in research poses a real and present danger to the legitimacy of universities as publicly supported social institutions.

Surface the systems

How did we get here?

We could look to a multitude of wicked problems, sticky issues, and grand challenges for answers. Many reasons are enumerated in countless books, articles, op-eds, podcasts, vlogs, blogs, and tweets from experts, scholars, pundits, public academics, philosophers, journalists, and anyone with a social media account. The conversations are multiple, ongoing, exhaustive, and – frankly – exhausting.

We are losing ground in the debate about whether a university is a business.[15]

We are victims of toxic competition across a sector precipitated by league tables and ranking races.[16]

We embraced massification whereby funding models have turned students into "bums in seats."

We have failed to make a case for the value of publicly funded higher education to government, funding agencies, policymakers, and the public.

I could go on – and many have (in the endnotes, I gesture to much more qualified humans offering much more comprehensive overviews);[17] instead of overextending myself, I want to pause instead on this last point and draw attention to the stories we are telling (unintentionally or otherwise).

One key conceptual tool in this book is that language matters, and that stories both reflect and shape our reality. A pervasive narrative we need to surface is the perception that some of the greatest innovations and contributions to our society happen outside post-secondary institutions.

Steven Johnson, in *Where Good Ideas Come From*, traces the history of innovation and argues that creating fertile environments facilitates "collisions of creativity" where people from diverse fields of expertise "converge in some shared physical or intellectual space."[18] He almost never mentions universities.

If we consider the origin stories of the major shifts in Western-centric knowledge, the university's role is either erased or diminished in popular retellings and apocryphal tales of innovation.

Literary historians rhapsodize about the Mermaid Tavern in London, a pub that hosted a seventeenth-century drinking fraternity whose members included literary luminaries such as Ben Jonson, John Donne, and Walter Raleigh (and, tantalizingly, maybe even William Shakespeare). Over pints, these poets and adventurers gave birth to Metaphysical and Cavalier art and philosophy movements.

In the eighteenth century, the coffeehouse culture in England and France gave rise to the age of reason and the Enlightenment.

Parisian salons in the nineteenth century nurtured an informal academy that became a ground-breaking form of cultural innovation: salons fostered social networks fuelled by intellectual fervour, political debate, artistic creativity, and sexual liberation. Revolutions were conceived amid these gatherings of polite (and not-so-polite) society – or so the story goes.

Garages and suburban basements in the twentieth century are credited in the origin stories of some of the most transformative technologies – including Google, Apple, Hewlett-Packard, Microsoft, and Amazon – that have immeasurably shaped our everyday lives.[19] The story itself is so powerful that Jeff Bezos confessed to the *Wall Street Journal* that he bought the house where he planned to start Amazon specifically for the garage because he wanted the same origin story as Hewlett-Packard and other tech entrepreneurs.[20]

Perhaps most titillating for students is that *the symposium* (used now to denote a high-brow gathering of intellectuals at a conference or research exchange) is Greek for "to drink together"; in this Hellenic social institution, men drank wine while rigorously debating poetry, philosophy, music. Debauchery and debate animated these gatherings, which gave rise to the foundations of Western thought.[21]

To trace the origin story of innovation is to trace the history of the party – not the university.[22]

(Let us qualify what is often overlooked: the history of innovation is Western-centric, exclusively the realm of men, and reinforces whiteness, supremacy, and other normative systems.)

This narrative locates the origin of good ideas within the intentional creation of informal spaces – in taverns, coffeehouses, salons, garages, basements – where individuals from differing disciplinary backgrounds – scientists, philosophers, poets, musicians, politicians, artists – interacted and where these interactions sparked innovations that led to profound cultural transformations.

While the locations change and the libations differ, these social gatherings share a set of common values: namely, an emphasis placed on egalitarian spaces for conversation, conviviality, and deep delight in exchanges amongst diverse people leading to knowledge creation.

This set of values is often used to describe institutions of higher learning. Universities – in their ideal form – create spaces rich with opportunities for collisions of creativity where innovation and transformative learning flourish. Moreover, the university exalts itself as an egalitarian space grounded in collegial governance and the free exchange of ideas.

So why is the university absent from the story?

The harsh reality is that some structures and systems routinely block spaces of intellectual revels and make it harder to design for delight with people from diverse backgrounds and disciplinary lenses.

For example, it is difficult to teach across departments because of collective agreements and rigid workloads. The incentives are low and the disincentives are higher for collaborative research, and indeed "several studies have shown that [interdisciplinary research] often achieves lower impact compared to more specialized work, and is less likely to attract funding."[23] The Herculean efforts of de-siloing curriculum are well documented,[24] and the value of a liberal education – which is founded on the belief that an interdisciplinary approach to knowledge creation and sharing – is on the decline (reflected in enrollment numbers and other barometers of public perception).[25]

We can blame larger social and political forces external to the academy for the erosion of trust in publicly funded social institutions until we are blue in the face.

And yet, the call is coming from within the house.[26]

Take a systems-level approach

As G. Gabrielle Starr, president of Pomona College in the US, says, "I've long been concerned that we in higher education are cooperating in our own obsolescence, as opposed to engineering for [innovation] … I've been on stages like this [opening plenary at the AAC&U] … for many years [where] college presidents are perfectly willing to cede the ground."[27]

Oof. This one hurts.

Where do we begin unpacking our own complicity in the broken systems that are also working exactly the way they were designed?

In this book we have already done some of the heavy lifting. We have:

- reflected on the publish or perish maxim and how we move from binaries to yes/and;

RuPaul ✔
@RuPaul   •••

"Call's coming from inside the house" is metaphor for self-sabotage – get outta the house!

8:47 PM · Apr 12, 2011

- surfaced the complexity of mentorship and how we can pay more attention to generosity in generativity;
- explored the pervasiveness of imposter syndrome;
- identified the factors that lead to shame-based cultures and, by extension, behaviours that contribute to toxic workplaces;
- talked about the "dismemberment" and siloed thinking that lead to what Parker Palmer calls "living a divided life";[28]
- recognized that discomfort is a feature, not a flaw.

It is worth keeping these concepts close as we rumble on a particularly sore spot exposed by the interviews: namely, the power of gatekeepers and guardians, arbiters and arbitrators of knowledge who engage in the demarcation between "real" research and "illegitimate" research.

We see the binaries reassert and reconfigure themselves in conversations about research, lining up dichotomies of insider and outsider, worthy and unworthy, lauded and obscure. In some disciplinary fields, lines are drawn sharply between quantitative and qualitative, masculine and feminine, rigour and softness.

> Brené Brown tells the story of the first week of her PhD program: "I had tremendous self-doubt. And the kind of self-doubt that includes the fear of getting caught, the fear of being found out, the fear of being the mistake in [the] admissions office, which is all just actually functions of self-doubt. And it's hard because 'impostor' is a very seductive and fitting word. It's the syndrome that makes it harder, right, for me. But I remember sitting in this class and the professor came in, it was week one, and said ... 'I know you think you belong to the field of social work, which is a very progressive ... But now, you're a doctoral student and you no longer belong to social work.

> Now, you belong to the academy. And that is just shift in culture. Our culture in the academy is pale, male and Yale' … Becoming a qualitative researcher, they called it, 'Oh, you like the pink book,' because unfortunately, the qualitative book was pink and the quantitative book was blue."[29]

We must surface the binaries, rumble them, and move away from critique and compartmentalization towards building and illuminating,

Stay with the trouble

I had a very rumble-y series of interviews with one colleague about how we define and value research that had me yelping "yes/and" or "AND YET!" with an occasional "WHAT – !?" This interviewee defined "real research" in the following way: "Research is about answering questions. Yes, in a systematic, robust manner, not based on your opinion or anecdotal evidence. And not just because your friends say so."

Pushed further to explain what they meant by "robust," they expanded, "Robust for me starts with ethics. A lot of what people call research is unethical because it's not been properly peer reviewed as an idea. And I think people do research and they cause trauma and upset [when] people can see their lived experience being exploited."

This colleague works primarily with human subjects and has seen firsthand what happens when researchers do not design with equity lenses, or overlook the complexities of power and consent, or fail to share how the research will be used, or are inattentive to diverse cultural worldviews.

It is understandable, then, that this well-published, highly decorated, and incredibly generous academic has also developed deeply held beliefs that research must be applicable, practical, demonstrable, and ethical. They research within in the health-related and educational fields and, therefore, witness the urgent need for practical interventions within flawed systems.

When I pointed out to my interlocutor that I did not know what research ethics was until after I had my first full-time job at a university, our disciplinary differences expanded the tone and tenor of the conversation. I had to explain that, for the most part, the humanities do not go through research ethics boards because we do not study human or animal subjects; I, for example, work with texts written by old dead white guys. Since I didn't want to immediately engage in defensive manoeuvres in my own field of the humanities, I relocated their criteria in STEM: "What about astrophysics? What NEED do we have to know how many stars are out there?" I asked.

What were originally hard and fast definitions began to expand, to reconfigure, to be reconstituted in the generosity of exchange.

I offered the following propositions.

- Research does not need an immediate "use value" to illuminate the human condition.
- Research does not need to be immediately applicable to help make the world better.
- Research does not need to be instrumentalized, monetized, or corporatized to be valuable.

If these were the criteria, some of the most beautiful insights into humanity – including much humanities research and entire theoretical fields like physics, mathematics, astronomy – would have a hard time meeting the narrow definition of "real research."

Together we arrived at a place that was richer for our engagement; our interaction also revealed the importance of rumbling with people within higher education from different disciplines to negotiate shared definitions – and shared value. If we don't share consensus even within the academy, how are we supposed to make the case in the public sphere?

We cannot let the call come from within the house.

We need to stop getting in each other's way and focus our energy on forging new ways forward.

In short, when we take a YES/AND approach to research, we can also curb the censuring, judging, dismissing, and jockeying for position and prestige.

Yes: peer review is important.

And: exploratory research into farther-flung fields – whether that is astrophysics or metaphysical poetry – is soul-sustaining and contributes to the academic enterprise.

For many fields, like the study of human subjects, ethics is essential. And yet, it is not prescriptive for everyone.

It is important to acknowledge that many of the systems and structures are in place for a reason and serve crucial purposes. We need intentional communities of scholars to ensure (and sometimes reinforce) shared ethics, integrity, accountability, trust, and transparency. Research ethics boards, national funding agencies, and peer-review processes are crucial for quality, assessment, engagement, consent, confidentiality, and intellectual beneficence. We need well-governed and clearly bounded spaces to have candid and contested conversations that push the limits of our disciplinary knowledges.

Systems are themselves neither good nor bad. Rather, what matters is how we design the systems, how we use them, and how often we reflect on whether the architecture of systems (structures, policies, statutes, rules, regulations) still serves (or ever served) diverse communities. Moreover, we should always be in the process of reflecting on how we define, support, and evaluate research as we reconfigure what we know, how we know it, and what we can know better.

And we can be better.

Change your language, change the world

Countless interviews exposed a recurring theme: the qualities that called people to the academy – curiosity, delight, joy, love – are squeezed out of them as they advance through the ranks. Moreover, they are trained to adopt a scholarly voice that is "objective," "rational," "cerebral" while leaving their full selves at the door.

As Canadian Shakespeare scholar Lisa Dickson writes, "In the space of research, which is to varying degrees demarcated from the space of the classroom, notably as the space of 'real' intellectual work, I stand behind a podium of entrenched practices and values, where the architecture of authority is manifested in the tone of the academic voice: distant, aloof, disinterested."[30]

If research is storytelling, why have we created research voices that erase our imperfect curious selves in favour of a scholarly language that is opaque, obtuse, and out of touch with many communities? Sadly, this is not a new or even particularly fresh observation: Jacques Derrida, Gayatri Chakravorty Spivak, and many others have criticized academic prose as alienating, exclusionary, mystifying.[31]

One interviewee reflected, "[I] remember something from the early days of teaching: I went to a department colleague's talk and sat with a [senior colleague]. I started to get worried, because I wasn't sure what the colleague was talking about. Was I dumb? Could I not keep up? Afterwards, my [colleague] leaned over and said, 'what an idiot – even HE (meaning the talk-giver) doesn't know what he's talking about.' It made me realize that most of academia is just stringing together words that don't mean anything and hoping nobody is brave enough to poke the balloon."

Obscure and incomprehensible academic writing is such a commonplace that every year *Philosophy and Literature* (an academic journal) runs a bad-writing contest to celebrate "the most stylistically lamentable passages found in scholarly books and articles."[32] When Judith Butler, literary theorist and former president of the Modern Language Association (MLA), won the award in 1998, they were held up as a model by many, including Denis Dutton in the *Wall Street Journal*, of what is wrong with the ivory tower. Denis Dutton lambasts the "inept," "jargon-laden" prose as "typical of the obscurantist writing being admired and emulated in the most elite circles of today's academic humanities."[33]

Philosopher Martha Nussbaum also warns that the "lofty obscurity and disdainful abstractness" of scholarship harms our ability to work towards positive social action: the impenetrability of academic language, according to Martha Nussbaum, "instructs its members that there is little room for large-scale social change, and maybe no room at all. We are all, more or less, prisoners of the structures of power that have defined our identity."[34]

This is a damning indictment, especially given our social contract to the broader society.

When did we stop sounding like ourselves?

And, by extension, when did we stop bringing our whole selves to our research?

No one explicitly instructed me to dismember myself (in Palmer's formulation), and yet I did.

I can trace my own language shift from undergraduate (playful, irreverent, curious) to graduate student (tentative, nervous, defensive) to junior faculty (critical, impervious, even ungenerous). The changes were ever so slight, incremental, and therefore it is impossible to pinpoint a moment where the delight and curiosity that called me to the work was methodically stamped out and replaced with the academic jargon and impenetrable language that masquerades as rigour.

When did the academy tell me my whole self was no longer welcome? When did I short circuit my own creativity to survive in a system that privileges impervious, armoured, critical knowledge? And how many more people, more precarious, excluded, and overlooked, have had to do this at an order of magnitude that made academia untenable?

If we are dismembering ourselves at the linguistic level, we are – by extension – dividing ourselves from the multiple communities that would benefit from building meaning together. Furthermore, by dividing our work – between research and teaching, between departments and disciplines, between hard and soft skills, *ad infinitum* – we are complicit in the act of diminishment. It never takes us towards wholeness.[35]

> One faculty member (a mathematician), reflecting on silos in the academy, shared this: "Zeno's Paradox – the idea that we are trying to get to a destination and we first go halfway, and half of that, and so on. In the infinite limit, we get there, but we never get there in a finite amount of time. It is a very fitting way to describe how we are stretched so thin and can't fully give what is needed. I feel like we are all so burnt out and stretched that when it comes time for faculty meetings or places where the status quo could be challenged, we just don't have the energy."

And yet, we work within systems that treat research, teaching, and service spheres of scholarly activity as compartmentalized and distinct rather than cross-fertilizing and mutually enriching. Furthermore, the divisions and disciplines (think hard sciences versus soft or social sciences) ramify hierarchies that privilege certain kinds of research over others – above and beyond their superiority to teaching and service.

It's no wonder everyone is too exhausted to wonder.

The unequal value attributed to teaching versus research has been a thread we can trace across the chapters. It bears repeating, here through the research lens, that our incentive structures – how we value and measure scholarly activity – are misaligned if we want to encourage collaborative, inclusive, diverse modes of research necessary to generate new knowledges.

> As one mid-career faculty member notes, "We create incentive structures that actually promote mediocrity. Promote conformity. Promote just doing the basics: rocking up teaching a class, get an okay set of evaluation scores, publishing one paper a year and then disconnecting. We are not incentivizing institution building. We are not incentivizing, in very explicit ways, supporting student success. And we are not incentivizing taking a radical approach to our research. And then we're also certainly not incentivizing combining all of them together."

> As one colleague aptly stated, "To delegitimize investigation of classroom practice is to ignore the role that the classroom plays in shaping our culture and the values we espouse beyond the classroom."

It is also the case that many research offices do not understand or value teaching and learning as a scholarly activity. I had a conversation with a research officer who was trying to convince me to apply for a large research grant based on my profile and they warned, "You cannot mention teaching or suggest your research has any practical application in the classroom. It has to be *pure* research."

Pure research? Here we bump up again against the notion of "real" research – and by extension the suspicious whiff of fake or fluffy research or – even worse – *teaching*.

This, folks, is why we can't have nice things.

Research – as a wonder engine – encourages us to hold a lens up to all spheres of our professional lives – teaching, service, educational leadership, administration, research, community outreach – for exploration and analysis. We need new systems to value this work and commit to expanding the current definitions of what constitutes scholarly activity.

Concluding thoughts

Research forms the core of higher education: it is the wonder engine at the heart of universities that drives new knowledge through curiosity and inquiry. While other organizations engage in research, universities are the only social institution that does so as its core purpose, intimately tied to education as a way of building, expanding, and animating our disciplines and knowledge more broadly.

Research is at the core of who we are and what we do. Research is intentional storytelling, which means we are always in conversation with future generations who will adopt, question, and build in ways we cannot foresee and yet, nevertheless, we must design with an invitation for new and yet unimagined forms of engagement.

As theoretical physicist Karen Barad reminds us, drawing insights from both French philosopher Jacques Derrida and quantum theory, we inherit the future with the past. We sit, as researchers, in a dynamic simultaneity between what has been and what might be – and so our epistemological relationship to the world is always in the process of changing and being reconfigured.[36]

How do we do this with an ethics of care?

For Karen Barad, the answer lies in "diffractive reading," which engages in "close respectful responsive and response-able (enabling response) attention to the details of a text; that is, it is important to try to do *justice* to a text. It is about taking what you find inventive and trying to work carefully with the details of patterns of thinking (in their very materiality) that might take you somewhere interesting that you never would have predicted."

We need to engage generously: "It's about working reiteratively, reworking the spacetimemattering of thought patterns; not about leaving behind or turning away from. (And surely not about making a caricature of someone's work and knocking it down, which unfortunately has been a form of engagement [in the academy].)"[37]

We have become caricatures of critique: cruel, exclusionary, obfuscating, and out of touch.

French sociologist Bruno Latour frames the scholarly penchant for critique in metaphors of violence: "Should we be at war, too, we, the scholars, the intellectuals? Is it really our duty to add fresh ruins to fields of ruins? Is it really the task of the humanities to add deconstruction to destruction? More iconoclasm to iconoclasm? What has become of the critical spirit? Has it run out of steam?"[38]

Karen Barad, like Bruno Latour, is done with critique.

And so am I.

Or, to clarify, I am finished with critique as a weapon that destroys and dismantles without the courage or love to propose something new in its place.

We can encourage candid, contested, vibrant conversations.

We can rumble, build, illuminate the edges of known knowledge so we can peek over with wonder.

We can contribute to mattering in the world.[39]

Otherwise, we risk our own obsolescence.

Earlier I quoted President G. Gabrielle Starr, who named our complicity. In that same talk she also invited us in to think about how we might resist obsolescence: "So every opportunity that we can, not just to promote collaboration, but to promote one of the democratic ideals that we need to support which is multiple kinds of affiliation. We don't talk about that enough. It's what democracy needs is eight people working together. And the only way they're going to do that is if they feel they have something vital in common."

As individuals and institutions, disciplinary experts and interdisciplinary learners, we must, as Canadian sociologist Vicki Chartrand reminds me, favour dynamic and collaborative methodologies that give us possibilities rather than prescriptions.

We are in the middle of a paradigm shift that we can't see the full shape of and yet that is already unfurling. How we choose to engage and what commitments we make to renewal and rewiring will affect generations to come. We must live into the question about how research – our most compelling argument for social impact on the broader society – can lead the conversations with wonder, curiosity, and hope.

Chapter 8

How Do We Govern at Hope University?

There are no new ideas still waiting in the wings to save us ...
There are only old and forgotten ones, new combinations, extrapolations and recognitions from within ourselves – along with
the renewed courage to try them out. And we must constantly encourage ourselves and each other to attempt the heretical actions
that our dreams imply, and so many of our old ideas disparage.
– Audre Lorde[1]

Governance is an old idea with fresh urgency.

Governance is often invisible, overlooked, and taken for granted – until it stops working.[2]

In times of stability, governance is a nice thing to have in the background.

In times of high institutional trust, the rules are regarded as a benevolent guide, just as often indulged as overlooked, sometimes unevenly applied or bypassed in favour of expediency.

Over time, however, inconsistencies accumulate and compound until a crisis exposes the slow, longer-term erosion of an institution's underpinnings.

The integrity of governance systems is tested in times of crisis.

Broken governance can lead to the erosion of trust, a decline in coopera-tion, and the proliferation of toxic workplace culture.

These days, the term "toxic workplace culture" has become so overused that it has lost its potency. "Toxic" is often used to dismiss, destroy, or cancel something or someone, often without a commitment to meaningfully engage in systems change. It has outpaced "pivot," "unprecedented," and "rigour" on my list of top five loathsome phrases – surpassed only by "busy."

And yet, a toxic workplace culture by any other name is still as rotten.

Shakespeare is fascinated with bad governance – and not just in his indictment of Denmark. King Lear, reflecting on his own failed governing, exclaims, "Oh I have taken too little care of this." Amidst a storm, dispossessed of his land and soon to be dispossessed of his wits, he has a moment of revelation: neglecting good governance has left his people in a state of "houseless poverty" and led to "houseless heads and unfed sides."[3]

Impoverishment. Dislocation. Scarcity.

This – Shakespeare warns us – is what happens when we ignore governance. The consequences are real – and have a high human cost – when truthtellers are banished, when consent is unclear, when consensus is taken for granted, when community is unintentional, and when compliance is enforced.

As we imagine a new paradigm, governance is at the heart of this shift. Indeed, it is at the governance level where we can identify the tension that is both driving the change and inviting us to imagine new paradigms – or as Audre Lorde calls them, "extrapolations and recognitions" from older ideas – of being interconnected within a complex system.

In interviews I conducted for this book, almost every person acknowledged that change is afoot: what varied was the level of hope – and by extension agency – about how much influence we have in shaping what these new paradigms look like. As Canadian historian Michael Childs concedes, "I agree with you that there is a paradigm shift going on, [but] maybe sometimes I am a little bit more pessimistic about whether it is controllable."[4]

How are decisions being made?

And about whom?

It is here where the intentional design of our organizational architecture – the blueprint that comprises our systems – enables us to rewire for hope and human flourishing.

This rewiring is in progress. To come back to adrienne maree brown's observation, the seismic shift is already underway:

Everything is falling apart, but also, new things are possible. And Octavia [Butler] said that "[t]here's nothing new / under the sun, / but there are new suns." We are in a time of new suns. We're in a time of new suns. We have no idea what we could be, but everything that we have been is falling apart. So it's time to change. And we can be mindful about that.[5]

If we are going to have any hope of shaping the paradigm, our best chance lies in governance.

> American thought strategist David Scobey reminds us, "If the recent past has taught us anything, it's that the academy finds itself at an inflection-point. Change – big change – is coming. Higher education confronts crises of precarity, of legitimacy, and of purpose. The stakes of change are high, and so is the urgency of the moment. Twenty years from now, I believe, college education will be very different for most students – for students attending all but the wealthiest institutions. But the shape of that future is still up for grabs. There is no standing still; the options are to make change or be changed. The question that faculty, staff, students, and our public allies face is, what kind of change do we want? And what can we do about it?"[6]

Live in the questions

So, we must ask ourselves and our colleagues some difficult questions about governance.

- Are the rules being applied evenly, consistently, and judiciously?
- Are the policies and statutes favouring some and disadvantaging others?
- How adaptive are these systems when unintended consequences expose inequalities or injustices?
- Are we focused on ensuring the current governance systems are resilient, or are we committed to designing governance systems that improve conditions for human flourishing?
- Do we continue to ask people to cope in deteriorating conditions, or are we willing to do the work necessary to change the systems that make us unwell?

- How do we balance the world when we are in a state of constant disequilibrium?

> As Ross Paul, former Canadian university president, reflects, "'A corporate culture where everyone shares the same goals and benefits from the same outcomes is not only much more difficult to achieve in a university, but it is also often antithetical to its values of open dialogue and dissent in the search for truth.'[7] I have long been fascinated by the inherent contradictions in this which I have always likened to herding cats. How does one forge an institution where everyone works to common ends when an inherent part of that is not only tolerating but actually celebrating diversity and dissent?"

If we are paying attention, these questions are increasingly urgent and the stakes are increasingly high. Investing time in good governance is the only way we will rewire systems for human flourishing.

Stay with the trouble

As I mentioned in the opening chapters of this book, universities have a deferred maintenance problem, and not just in our physical infrastructure: when our policies, structures, and statutes are left unchecked, deferred maintenance poses one of the biggest risks to individual institutions and the sector more broadly.

Accusations of toxic workplace culture are, in fact, symptomatic of broken governance systems. Loss of trust, lack of boundaries, limited agency, enforced compliance and conformity, and blame/shame behaviour exposes something rotten at the decision-making levels.

In other words, when governance structures are not working to keep humans within the system safe, brave, healthy, and flourishing, harm is enacted at the systemic level. It does not matter if those policies and structures were initially drafted with a spirit of neutrality or benevolence: if we are not surfacing each one to ask if it still serves diverse communities, we are doing a disservice to all communities.

The challenge with governance is that we usually confront the limitations of systems and structures in moments of adversity or contestation. A policy or structure comes into focus when some change is proposed or a conflict arises. Only then do we encounter the system that has hitherto been invisible.

Returning to the parable David Foster Wallace offers us of the fish, the systems are "so hidden in plain sight all around us, all the time, that we have to keep reminding ourselves over and over: 'This is water.'"[8]

Governance is the lynchpin, the vital piece of the academic enterprise that administers every other aspect of the university. It is also one of the least understood elements in the academy because it is the very water within which we are immersed; the policies, procedures, and rules are – to stay with this metaphor – the invisible currents, shoals, and eddies controlling the tides of the institutional culture; the fish pool – and humans behave – in specific ways guided by the powerful yet invisible structures that govern any ecosystem.

Practise divergent thinking

So, how do we see the water?

Audre Lorde gives us a clue at the start of this chapter: she reminds us that there are no new ideas, only older ones that might have been forgotten or overlooked. If we can commit, with "renewed courage," to remember what we have lost, we can reconstitute meaning so that we can move forward.[9]

Theoretical and literary lenses help tease out the tensions of governance in the academic enterprise.[10] I propose two lenses – one drawn from the corporate sector and one drawn from sixteenth-century politics – to help us better understand governance with particular attention to the role of time.

Simon Sinek, American author and founder of the Optimism Company, uses gaming theory to develop the infinite versus the finite mindset concept. Influenced by American philosopher and theologian James Carse's theory that there are two types of games – finite games and infinite games – Sinek expands the concept to organizational behaviour.

If a finite game is "defined as known players, fixed rules, and an agreed-upon objective," then there is "always a beginning, middle, and end, and if there's a winner, then there has to be a loser." In contrast, infinite games are characterized by dynamic players, shifting rules, whereby the "objective is to perpetuate the game, to stay in the game as long as possible."

As Sinek points out, we almost always exist within an infinite game: "There's no such thing as winning global politics. No one's ever declared the winner of careers. Nobody wins health care or education. You can come in first for the finite time you're in high school or college, but you don't win education, and there's definitely no such thing as winning business."[11]

Higher education is an infinite game, yet we assess our performance as if there are winners and losers with endgames and timeframes, metrics and impact.

If we agree that higher education has a social mission to a broader society *and* acknowledge that society is constantly changing, then we must look to our systems and ask, "are we playing the wrong game?"

"The problem is," argues Sinek, "when we play in an infinite game with a finite mindset, when we play to win in a game that has no finish line, there are some predictable and consistent outcomes. The big ones include the decline of trust, the decline of cooperation, and the decline of innovation."[12]

While Sinek takes the business world as his subject of study, the finite versus infinite mindset can help other sectors like post-secondary education critically reflect on why and how we govern.

> In a report on "Pathways for University Presidents" (2017), researchers at Georgia Tech conducted a series of interviews that found "increasing pressure on presidents to look for quick wins. As a result, many are looking for the proverbial low-hanging fruit on their campuses where they can show fast results, not only for their own boards but also for search committees for their next job. 'Presidents approach their job with the expectation that they'll be judged on what they can finish,' said the president of a private university. 'They think, "I'll only be here five years, so I should only focus on what I can do in that time before I move on." They run their schools like pseudo-corporations. It's short-term thinking. You might satisfy the immediate issue of the day, but this is unsustainable as a model.'"[13]

This is not a new idea.

If we go back four hundred years to early modern England, we see the tension between finite and infinite roles embodied in political theory. The monarch was an extension of the body politic and had two legal bodies: the body corporeal (also called the body natural) and the body politic (animated by the divine right of kings). The body corporeal is mortal and finite, subject to illness, aging, and death. The body politic, however, is immortal:[14] monarchs reign by God's ordinance, and the divine essence is seamlessly passed onto the heir when they die.[15]

A monarch rules for a fixed period of time (usually their lifetime), whereas the body politic is infinite. As new leaders take the throne, the transition is seamless because the body politic is designed to endure finite (mortal) leadership shifts.

> Cheryl Foy, a Canadian governance expert, offers this comparison: "Universities are corporate entities meaning that they have recognized personhood under the law. As notional person[s], corporate entities have the possibility to be infinite."

A university president or provost leads the organization for a fixed term (usually a five-year term, renewable), whereas people responsible for governance must, by necessity and mandate, take a longer view. While academic leaders are hired to implement a strategic vision that is achievable, measurable, and moves the institution forward, members of the board of governors and senate are responsible for governance – not leadership – and must therefore adopt an infinite mindset.

These binaries – finite and infinite, fixed and eternal, leadership and governance – are always in dynamic interplay. The binaries are also helpful for exposing when and how governance roles might complement – and sometimes compete with – the finite game of administrative leaders.

Both Sinek's approach via gaming theory and the sixteenth-century body politic underscore how governance should not be confused with leadership even though they are interconnected. When we forget which game we are playing or lose touch with the role we are supposed to fulfill (leader versus governor versus manager), the health of the collective is compromised.

Take a systems-level approach

Governance looks different in practice and yet shares some common features, including the four major spheres of governance identified by Canadian governance experts Kelly Rowe and Zac Ashkanasy:

- Performance (future-orientated): The governing body's leadership role in policy-setting, rule approval and developing and monitoring the delivery of strategy.
- Conformance (present-orientated): The governing body's role in ensuring accountability through activities like monitoring finances and compliance with policies and codes.
- Internal focus: Ensure that the university is aligned and managing risk effectively.
- External focus: Prepare for the future and maintain accountability to stakeholders.[16]

Moreover, the people who animate the bicameral governance bodies – the board of governors and the academic senate – must share some common values, such as

- a generative and generous commitment to legacy building[17]
- clarity about fiduciary duty
- an appreciation of corporate stewardship
- a focus on the long-term sustainability of the organization

We can use gaming theory and early modern monarchs to determine who makes what decisions in university governance. It becomes increasingly clear that undertakings like strategic visioning or succession planning are not under the sole purview of the president or provost. In the case of succession planning, for example, the board of governors is the body responsible for a scaffolded succession plan that includes finding, recruiting, and onboarding new leaders to ensure smooth and seamless leadership transitions.[18]

That is not to say presidents and provosts are exempt from thinking about, and designing for, longer-term or infinite-thinking portfolios, and yet their mandate requires (and rewards) finite thinking for fixed terms.

Governance is not their lane. It is ours. And we have not been paying attention.

> Cheryl Foy teases out the tension of ethics in the blurring of leadership and governance: "Remember that presidents must navigate the tension between objectively and honestly reporting on the progress of the organization and ensuring that the board has a positive impression of the president's performance. This is a conflict of interest that is mostly mitigated by having presidents who have the leadership skills and integrity to rise above their own interests when needed. Most presidents do lead with integrity, but presidents suffer from motivational blindness and the dominance of the 'want' self as much as the rest of us."[19]

Stay with the trouble

What we *have* been paying attention to, however, is the leadership crisis in higher education. It is hard to look away from the train wrecks that animate the higher ed news feeds and, increasingly, mainstream media. As American journalist Jeffrey J. Selingo and his colleagues note, "Not only are presidents aging, but public flameouts are ending their tenures early. Several presidents have faced high-profile ousters in recent years."[20]

The American Association of Colleges and Universities conducted a study in 2017 that showed that 45 per cent of American presidents in the association do not last longer than four years in one institution, and only 20 per cent last longer than ten years. It is likely the same or worse in Canada.[21]

A crisis in leadership is symptomatic of a crisis in governance. Both need our attention. Strikingly, if we spend time addressing governance, many other crises might be mitigated. Moreover, good governance fulfills the social mission of the university to the broader society because it focuses on "the establishment, the guidance, and the enrichment of the living generation and the world it inherits."[22] If generativity is "a concern for establishing and guiding the next generation," then governance is generativity-in-action.

Legacy itself can be harmful if we seek to impose old systems that no longer serve the communities rather than make space for renewed and reconfigured structures and policies.

We often treat the systems as fixed, impervious, and immovable. How many times have we heard "we've always done it this way," or "we can't do that because the system won't allow it." These statements are an acquiescence of despair, of resignation, disengagement, and stagnation. It is where good ideas go to die. And it adds up to a spectacular failure of imagination.

The challenge ahead is to build a system willing to produce something that is not itself, which requires the most generous version of generative thinking possible.

> Cheryl Foy reflects, "Isn't it odd that universities who are so focused on evaluating research methodology and teaching practice, don't take the time to reflect on how they govern themselves?"

Slow down and pause

Governance is an unsexy topic at decision-making tables because it takes time.

And time – in organizations built on scarcity and deficit – is a precious resource we seem to have less and less of. When we jump from crisis to crisis, we do not have the time to slow down because our instincts tell us to speed up. If our default is the busy-ness of business, we expend a tremendous amount of energy in survival mode, which means we do not see the water within which we are immersed.

Furthermore, responding to a crisis with a finite mindset is to imagine the crisis as an isolated occurrence – a system flaw.

A challenge to be tackled. A fire to be put out. A brick wall to climb over, run around, or scale.

And yet, as we have discussed elsewhere, crisis is chronic.

American historian Edward T. O'Donnell reflects:

We're living history, surprise after surprise, after surprise. And just when we think we've had all the big surprises for a while, along comes another one. If the first two decades of the 21st century have taught us anything, it's that uncertainty is chronic, instability is permanent, disruption is common, and we can neither predict nor govern events. There will be no "new normal"; there will only be a continuous series of "not- normal" episodes that defy prediction and are unforeseen by most of us until they happen.[23]

So, what happens when we treat crisis as a feature, not a flaw?

If we step out of the urgency of our every day and sit for a moment in Sinek's infinite mindset or the immortal realm of the body politic, how does this change the way we approach crisis from a governance perspective?

What does it look like to design systems to anticipate and adapt to chronic crisis?

Rewiring necessitates that we move from default survival mode (high energy over the short term) to hope circuits (renewed frameworks, governance structures, decision-making trees, policies) that help us to better respond to harmful or destabilizing stimuli.

To do the purposeful work of governance is not merely to enact the systems and structures that we have inherited; the work ahead also requires us to ask whether the policies or statutes we encounter still serve our communities – and to ask even more decentring questions like, were they ever in service to some communities?

Educating those tasked with governance – and being clear what roles are needed when playing an infinite game – is essential if we are to anchor institutional values in practice with rules, timeline, tasks that reflect healthy governance.

YES: It is much faster to follow the policies and statutes already in place than to do the tedious work of consultations, committees, and convening bicameral bodies.

AND: There is no "pay-off" at the end. No press releases. No photo-op. No gold stars. No grand opening. No ribbon cutting.

PLUS: The work of revising governance – and rumbling on the structures, statutes, and policies that comprise an intricate system of relationships – is the opposite of low-hanging fruit.

We need to do it anyway.

Governance is a key piece of the wellness puzzle and yet is often overlooked. There are more extensive conversations to have about what our institutions are doing to create working environments that are healthy, sustainable, and sane. It is helpful here to acknowledge that we are often playing a finite game in an infinite context. Hot chocolate in the quad offers better photo-ops and instant gratification – and is much easier (and much less effective) than improving people's working conditions at the systems level.[24]

As American higher ed columnist Kevin McClure reminds us, "Morale can absolutely be improved in higher education, but it requires the type of sustained attention necessary to shift organizational culture. Leaders need to be ready to put in the work, starting with admitting there is a morale problem and actively listening to what staff and faculty are saying."[25]

Practise divergent thinking

In sixteenth-century political theory, the state as a human body was a common metaphor to understand how complex systems operated and interacted. The ideal society was thought to function like the harmonious cooperation of the various body parts, which strived for a balance of humours (fluids) in the body. The monarch was the head, the army was the arm, the commoners were the belly, and so on. It was such a compelling metaphor that several Renaissance physicians urged their kings to study the principles of medicine so they could learn how to better govern their own nations.[26]

Sixteenth-century physician William Harvey staged live vivisections of animals in public anatomy theatres (which closely resembled public theatres) to show the audience how blood circulated; his discoveries about circulatory systems were influential beyond medicine, informing economic theories of value and the theory of macrocosm/microcosm, where systems resemble other systems and merely change in scale.

Vivisection might seem archaic to a modern reader, and yet this work informed the very systems we have inherited and how we use the body as a governing principle for our organizations and ecosystems. The root of "corporation" is derived from *corporare*, which is Latin for "combine in one body." This etymology also connects us to phrases like "governing bodies" and concepts like "incorporation" and "corpus" (body). We use much of this corporeal language today to talk about organizations – so much so that the university administration is often referred to as the "corporation" in collective bargaining and other forms of negotiation with faculty and staff associations.

We are, as a community, deeply embodied.

If a university is treated as a holistic body, then all parts flourish when the body is healthy. However, the whole system is affected if one area is wounded or sick. Toxicity can migrate from one part of the body to another in this interconnected system, which makes it vulnerable to becoming sick and worsening without attention and intervention.

Commit to unlearning and relearning

So, if we can concede that something is rotten in the state of (insert your organization here), and that governance is the apparatus for how the "state" operates, what can we do about it?

This feels like a big and impossibly wicked question, and there are many people much better equipped to guide discussions on the nuts and bolts of university governance.[27]

The strengths of this book lie elsewhere, in the rewiring of mindsets so we can then rewire (and reinvigorate) the complex systems we inhabit. This project aspires to help people see the water – and future books in this series will engage in more granular planning, offering blueprints to prototype hope in particular contexts and through case studies. In the meantime, though, we can deploy interdisciplinary lenses to see with fresh eyes what is otherwise invisible in governance.

To heal an ailing body politic, Sir Philip Sidney offers us a metaphor of surgery. This sixteenth-century courtier, very much involved in the politics of his day, believed that poetry, plays, and other artistic forms have a social function that exposes wicked problems, and that surfacing social ills is an essential mechanism to maintain a healthy society. In *The Defence of Poesy*, he writes,

> The high and excellent tragedy, that opens the greatest wounds, and shows forth the ulcers that are covered with tissue; that makes kings fear to be tyrants, and tyrants manifest their tyrannical humors; that with stirring the effects of admiration and commiseration teaches the uncertainty of this world, and upon how weak foundations gilded roofs are builded.[28]

For Sidney, art has a surgical function: seeing our individual and societal flaws represented in varying forms (in this case, a play) is the most effective intervention to surface the rot, expose a festering wound, and lance the toxic poison that threatens the health of the whole body. Only then can the body (community, polity, state, nation) move towards healing and renewal.

Moreover, Sidney argues that literature invites us – through "admiration and commiseration," i.e., empathy – to fully embrace the uncertainty of the world and the mutability of fortune. Even for Philip Sidney, four hundred years ago, crisis is a feature, not a flaw.

Sidney's advice – surface the systems, expose toxicity, embrace change, treat crisis as a feature, prioritize building solid foundations over superficial pursuits – remains relevant in contemporary conversations about governance.

> University leader Jeff Hennessy notes, "As a body, faculty are the enduring element of the institution. The membership may change, but it does so slowly and there is always continuity. This also has a downside because it can allow grievances and trauma to be inherited and become part of the DNA of an institution. But generally, it is a strength to be valued. As leaders, we can lament the grindingly slow pace of change at our universities, but it is incumbent upon us to work with the collegium to make the changes that are needed to ensure long-term health and endurance. Collegial governance is vital, and short-circuiting it is not in the long-term interests of the university."[29]

Build intentional (and integrated) community

If the university is a body, it has two heads.

Or, to be more specific, the university has bicameral governing bodies – the board of governors and the academic senate. These two bodies have different yet critical responsibilities for the organization's long-term health.[30] The senate is the highest governing body in all academic matters, chaired by the university president or sometimes a faculty member elected as secretary of senate.[31] The board of governors (sometimes called the board of trustees) oversees all non-academic matters, financial sustainability, and external relations, as well as risk management.

> Cheryl Foy offers this helpful overview: "In Canada, shared governance (governance in which there is a board responsible for non-academic or business matters, and in which academic matters are decided by academics) is implemented through three different models: unicameral (UofT), bicameral (most universities), and tricameral (University of Saskatchewan and University of Montreal). In the unicameral model, the involvement of academics in academic decision-making is accomplished through the bodies that sit under the University Council (which also has academics on it). In the tricameral model, the third body is often explicitly and solely focused on the public interest."

These systems are especially hard to understand for external board members and those in government. The bicameral system – the most common model in Canada – sets universities apart from other kinds of organizations in corporate, government, and not-for-profit sectors. Ensuring that these two bodies talk to one another – and also stay out of each other's business – is always a delicate balance. In principle this is a shared governance model, and yet in practice the levels of trust, communication, and collaboration are always in flux. There are also strange overlaps and odd examples of cross purposes that expose the peculiarity of the academic enterprise. What these dual bodies share in common, though, is the responsibility of taking an infinite mindset.

In some ways, we have lost sight of the game we are playing and the roles of the players. Presidents are not all-powerful, boards are not puppeteers, senates are not gatekeepers, and no one person holds all the decision-making power. Unionized environments and faculty associations make it almost impossible to fire someone. Ironically, the most precarious jobs with the least stability – beyond the contingent and precarious faculty – are the provosts and the presidents, who can be dispatched at the will of the board.

Moreover, collegial governance – oft quoted and yet rarely understood – has become a lightning rod in labour strife and job action at many institutions across Canada. Disgruntlement extends beyond financial compensation, and many organizations have found themselves at an inflection point about how decisions are made and by whom.

> American higher education scholar Jeffrey Buller puts it this way: "A lot of times [external board members] who come from a very hierarchical environment, like the corporate world, think that power flows down ... But if you just take a look at the academic side of the institution, how we actually make decisions, you've never had a president come in and say, 'from now on, we're going to teach organic chemistry this way.' That just doesn't work. We do things as a distributed organization ... And the number of times I've heard a faculty member say, in response to a dean who's come in and done things that the faculties don't like, 'we're just going to wait this guy out.' Faculty members have a power and that is the power of time because presidents come and go, deans come and go, students come and go, but the faculty are usually there forever, so they can slow walk anything."[32]

Reimagine authority and expertise

We cannot blame the salmon for behaviour shaped by the dams. When we empower systems rather than empowering humans to change systems, resistance is inevitable. How do we engage all members of our community in a shared vision of what is possible? As we imagine better systems, we must reimagine authority and expertise if we are going to heal a sickening body politic.

Shakespeare shares a valuable lesson on governance. King Lear learns that the best medicine is for leaders to "expose thyself to feel what wretches feel."[33] Those in power must work harder to understand how the poor and disenfranchised weather the proverbial storm through radical empathy while also inviting people from diverse backgrounds into the upper echelons.

At the play's outset, Lear's court is a safe space for his subjects to be brave. He has a licensed fool whose primary role is to speak truth to power; his most trusted advisor Kent challenges his decisions; and his favorite daughter Cordelia is preferred because she refuses to flatter.

As soon as Lear banishes his truth-tellers, his descent is rapid and inevitable.

His kingdom – and his mind – becomes unhinged.

In sixteenth-century governance, truth-tellers played a unique role in maintaining the health of the body politic: royal courts and noble households employed licensed jesters to speak plainly – to expose excess, greed, and corruption – without fear of reprisal. Henry VIII's fool Will Sommers was scathing in his condemnations of the king's greed and yet so beloved that he appears in royal family portraits.

Renaissance fools were socially marginalized *and* highly valued because they presented differing perspectives and gave voices to unrepresented community members that would not otherwise interact with those at the centres of power.

Lear's revelation – that otherwise excluded voices must be permitted to speak uncomfortable truths and those responsible for governance must listen – comes too late for him to heal the body politic he was tasked with maintaining.

However, it is not too late for us.

We have an opportunity to renovate governance structures to include diverse stakeholders who can sit at tables with the job protection necessary to speak up and speak out. We need to intentionally design governing bodies – boards and senates – that are not ruled with an expectation of conformity and compliance; rather we need consent and consensus, compassion, and contestation embedded in the systems. Together we need to stay with the trouble to expose the structural inequalities and systemic racism we have inherited, internalized, and will reproduce unreflectively unless there is a commitment to rewiring.

We must invite members of underrepresented and historically excluded groups to existing governing bodies while also ensuring that these invitations do not deplete or put at risk already exhausted humans doing hard hope work within systems that enact harm.

We must listen to our students, especially those who have been excluded from conversations.

We must listen to contingent and precarious faculty who are shouldering a disproportionate amount of the labour.

We must listen to, and value, differing perspectives at our boards and senates as a fundamental principle of collaborative governance.

We must ensure that our existing tables are spaces that reflect equity, diversity, and inclusion.

And we must ensure that these spaces are safe for truth-tellers.

> As Cheryl Foy reminds us, "The current focus of corporate governance outside the university sector is on increasing diversity and on environmental sustainability, among other equity issues. Governance is about stakeholders – ensuring that those whose interests are affected are considered when decisions are made. The board members of universities are fiduciaries (trustees) of the university and owe duties of care and loyalty to their universities."

Concluding thoughts

Audre Lorde tells us that "there are no new ideas still waiting in the wings to save us ... There are only old and forgotten ones, new combinations, extrapolations and recognitions from within ourselves."[34]

In the spirit of Lorde's invitation, I want to think through new combinations of old ideas via Renaissance physician William Harvey's discovery of the power of macrocosm/microcosm: his theory – of how systems resemble other systems and differ only in scale – was revolutionary in the early modern period and can help us revolutionize our own organizations.

What would it look like if we scaled the principles of well designed, inclusive classrooms – based on community, consent, compassion, curiosity, collaboration – and used them to design governance systems?

What happens if we start our meetings like we start our classes?

What happens if each governance committee co-designs a "syllabus" annually?

What happens if we hold office hours for colleagues?

What happens if we administer annual "teaching evaluations" to leadership and governance members?

What happens if we make space for questions, place value in not knowing the answers, and pause to see if everyone is following as we move through agendas, motions, discussions, and voting procedures?

What happens if we focus on development rather than deliverables, processes over products, at every level?

What happens if we educate those responsible for governance about infinite mindsets, fiduciary duty, and systems thinking?

We are already well versed in pedagogical design; it is possible to import this approach into committee meetings and boardrooms, at senate and in hiring meetings, at negotiation tables and on taskforces.

Is it really so radical to superimpose these principles from a classroom microcosm onto the institutional macrocosm?

I want us to imagine systems that encourage humans to be curiosity-driven, make room for failure and learning, build upon each member's best capacities, embrace complexity, value multiple and diverse perspectives, co-construct meaning, and invite transformation through careful, respectful dialogue.

This challenge requires confident leaders, competent governors, compassionate members of faculty and staff, committed students – and a shared investment in consent and consensus.

It is not an easy ask because we must unlearn ways of operating amid permacrisis while navigating well-worn systems that were not originally designed for this kind of work. Moreover, it asks those who are closest to the centres of power – and who benefit from these systems – to be willing to adopt learner positions and, by extension, be willing to transform.

Those are some big asks.

And yet.

We must ask, "if not now, when?"

Will we wait until the body has become houseless and unfed, starved and poisoned to a point where no intervention, surgical or otherwise, can save it? Or do we double down on the wellbeing of all at the systems level by exposing the festering ulcer? When do we address the things that are making us sick, sit in the discomfort, and embark on a healing journey that focuses on flourishing?

The choice is obvious if we acknowledge that we are all part of the same body.

It is time to start governing that way.

Chapter 9

How Do We Fund
Hope University?

i have learned some things about abundance.
it is self-perpetuating. each moment in which i have claimed abundance has simply increased my comfort with claiming abundance,
and has made scarcity then more unbearable, as a personal mindset or a worldview.
– adrienne maree brown[1]

In the higher education sector – and society more broadly – we perpetuate
narratives of scarcity, lack, and crisis. And yet, as American author and emergent design strategist adrienne maree brown reminds us, we live in a time
of abundance.

When we discuss how to fund Hope University, the conceptual and practical definitions of "what is enough" test the limits of our imaginative capacities. How do we live with a mindset of abundance in systems that perpetuate
scarcity?

Yes, the current funding models are broken.

Yes, universities are chronically underfunded.

Yes, financial exigency is a real and increasingly urgent threat.[2]

These issues require extreme upstream thinking at all levels of government
– from policymakers to the public sphere – first to acknowledge that the financial models are no longer adequate and then commit to reimagining
(soul-) sustaining, equitable systems.

For those downstream, the dams – flawed federal and provincial funding formulas, shrinking government grants, metrics fixation, performance-based funding, government overreach – appear insurmountable, intractable, monolithic.

If we go farther upstream, the factors that inform how money is allocated are downright dizzying. Just dipping a toe into this fast-moving and ever-changing current of resources sends me reeling: from when the federal budget is announced to who is named (or left out); how the provinces align (or do not); the elected government's shifting values around higher education and cyclical urgency of competing sectors like health care or the economy; length of time in office that determines spending timelines; and a hundred other confounding and converging forces.

How do we keep swimming when the undercurrent of crisis threatens to pull us under?

Where do we even begin?

With us.

Surface the systems

First and foremost, we need to pause, and then we need to surface the systems.

The university's financial state informs every single one of our professional identities and shapes daily decisions and relationships. It lurks on the edges of our consciousness, always in the peripheral of our purview, and yet it is frequently framed as an indictment to justify current systems rather than an invitation to imagine new paradigms.

Imagine this familiar scenario: several provosts are invited to participate in a program to hire a handful of their students part-time. Pocket change for most and it fulfills the strategic mission of their individual universities (in this case, transformative and inclusive work-integrated learning, digital literacy, student-centred approach to twenty-first-century learning).

It is an easy win.

And yet, without pausing, one of the provosts will inevitably exclaim, "I have zero money and I am too busy putting out fires." If they had slowed down and stepped out of the busy-ness of business, they might have realized that this student-focused program was the fire extinguisher for at least a few burning issues in their institutional landscape. The myopic nature of this response is characteristic of the stories we are telling about funding in universities: No money and all crisis.

Practise divergent thinking

It would be easy to blame that provost for short-sightedness, and yet they have internalized and now reproduce crisis – without a pause or reflection – because the pressure from upstream is unrelenting.

The salmon and the dam metaphor has helped me locate myself in what otherwise feels like an impervious and mystifying ecosystem. With divergent thinking, we can look at the systems with fresh eyes and ask ourselves, "Do we blame the salmon or the dam?"

We often think of students (and sometimes faculty) as the salmon, struggling against structural barriers and slogging through administrative quagmires. However, this metaphor demands that we exercise empathy for salmon of wide varieties: depending on position and context, the provost is a salmon worthy of love and empathy. Even the university is a salmon in the dam of provincial government funding.

> It serves us well to remember that sometimes we are the salmon and at other times we are the bear devouring it. Our role at any given moment depends on our position within the system. Even if we are more comfortable identifying as the salmon, sometimes our context positions us as the dam. Or the bear positioned just upstream. Recognizing the fluid nature of these positions exercises critical empathy muscles.

> Strategic enrollment leader Jock Phippen muses, "It's funny, because we complain about institutions, but we're also comforted by them. We need boundaries, not barriers. [Hope University] is a shift that requires the right people, or people willing to unlearn and crack open their minds to a new kind of system."

How do we honour the boundaries that guard against chaos while surfacing the barriers that gatekeep meaningful change?

If we look at our institutions as ecosystems, many salmon are failing to thrive. Taking a systems-level approach rather than an individual approach redistributes blame, builds empathy, and illuminates points of intervention. Although policies, structures, and infrastructure comprise systems that in turn shape behaviour, very few systems are intentionally designed for humans to flourish.

Instead, we sometimes find ourselves working against our natures, getting in the way of ourselves, and pooling in all the wrong places while fighting each other for ever-diminishing resources.

Once we separate the salmon from the dam, how do we dismantle the dams that no longer serve us, renovate the leaky dams, and shore up the dams that keep our communities safe and bounded? And, at the same time, how do we build salmon ladders for the fish who are failing to thrive right now?

Change your language, change the world

The stories we tell ourselves and others about funding (resource control, access, allocation, reporting) are as invisible as the water we are immersed in. Deploying the conceptual tool of storytelling helps us understand the eddies and currents that are sometimes imperceptible and nevertheless have a strong pull.

One intervention available to all of us, regardless of context, is to be attentive to our language; our words create the cultures of scarcity or abundance that animate localized and institutional spaces.

Below I share two formative experiences from two different collegial governance tables that informed how narratives of scarcity are perpetuated and circulated; these vignettes might help us to better see the water within which we are immersed.

When I was a brand-new faculty member, I sat at two different tables: faculty council and the board of governors. Both "alike in dignity" (to borrow the phrase from *Romeo and Juliet*),[3] they were, at that time, the moral and operational centres of the institution.

The faculty council meetings were run by the "British Mafia" (as we called them in whispers): senior, predominantly white men who held court, wielding the collective agreement as their holy text. With forensic precision, they identified evidence of infringement upon, or violation of, members' rights. They relied on a recurring narrative at this table: namely, the belief that the university was hiding money and operating without transparency or accountability.

They conjured a vivid image of dragons guarding a treasure hoard in the bowels of our central administration building. This story, which could have been plucked from the pages of *Beowulf* or the annals of Geoffrey of Monmouth, persuaded me (as a willing, naïve audience member) to be suspicious and – more subtly – afraid.

While the dragons were entirely a product of my imagination, the stories of avarice and secrecy had real consequences on how we as faculty and staff conducted ourselves – in the relationships we built, the decisions we made, and the biases we reproduced in the everyday interactions of working life.

In what, retrospectively, was a jarring juxtaposition, I also sat on the board of governors at the same time; the BoG was run by a seasoned, savvy board chair and a benevolent, effortlessly sophisticated chancellor. The newly streamlined board was – despite good intentions – still predominantly white and populated by well-meaning alumni who were, for the most part, accountants, lawyers, and "C suite" executives.[4]

Rather than holding court, this group ran corporate meetings; they wielded financial statements and budget reports as secular texts to identify (again with forensic precision) student enrollment numbers, accumulated interest on debt, and areas of lost revenue. A recurring narrative at this table was the ever-looming spectre of financial crisis, operating from year to year in suspense and uncertainty.

The board of governors' conversations conjured for me a different hoard; instead of hidden funds guarded by the corporation, the treasure was the horde of students from untapped recruitment markets.

For universities with a larger percentage of funding drawn from tuition dollars than government grants, the ever-elusive international students (from emerging or established global economies) are often treated as the solution for declining funding or domestic tuition freezes. Paired with an ambitious and often unachievable strategic enrollment plan, we were always looking to the future to pull us out of present precarity – and never fully getting there.

> A retired administrative leader reflects, "When I was VP [academic], I can tell you: nothing kept me up more nights than finances. It was always there. It was always trying to fill a quart jar with a pint of water. It was always a constant struggle. We were always trying to look at how to increase revenue. I'm constitutionally opposed to the constant penny pinching and trying to find efficiencies. It is important, and can certainly save bacon occasionally, but it's not really a solution to anything. You can maybe say 5% of it might be greater efficiencies without damaging the mission. The solution is one of two things: increase in revenue, which is very difficult. Or – as you say – live in abundance in a situation of scarcity, which is to lower human material expectations. So, the answer is: a combination of both [gratitude and abundance] and new revenue sources."

In both stories and at both tables, we never had enough.
Who was to blame?
That differed depending on the decision-making table.
Faculty council blamed the administration. The board blamed missing students and disengaged faculty. Regardless, the salmon always got the blame. And the effect on the salmon was damning.

Slow down and pause

Scarcity culture is perpetuated with statements like,
We never have enough people.
We never have enough staff.
We never have enough students.
We never have enough government grants.
We never have enough resources.
We never have enough …

And, as we have previously discussed, this inevitably moves from "we never have enough [insert X]" into "I am not enough."[5]

As a junior faculty member, I internalized these two versions at two different tables about the same story – that we do not have enough. My default response was to ask, "What can I do? Can I work harder? Can I teach more students? Can I teach *pro bono*? Can I build things to attract more students? Can I help with recruitment?" A rush of adrenaline in crisis takes us to the limits of our "surge capacities."[6] It is addicting. We stay later, work harder, develop elaborate plans, rally the proverbial troops, and forge alliances with unlikely allies. We feel essential, irreplaceable, and needed. Crisis gives us the impression we have tapped into a greater purpose.

We are addicted to scarcity because it makes us feel relevant.

However, it is also burning us out, making us sick, and bolstering the systems that are chronically in crisis.

When crisis becomes chronic, we live in a state of "permacrisis," the Collins dictionary word of the year for 2022 and a term, according to British journalist David Shariatmadari, "that perfectly embodies the dizzying sense of lurching from one unprecedented event to another, as we wonder bleakly what new horrors might be around the corner."[7]

> American higher education thought strategist Jeffrey Buller reflects, "I once worked for a president at a small college for whom everything was a crisis. And what would really happen is that that attitude just permeated from the president's office on down and everyone was in a state of anxiety all the time. To the point where, for some of us, it almost became comic, because we'd be told one day, we've got to work on this now because here's a crisis and so we scurry off and do something and then by the time we brought back our solution, well, that's not the case anymore. [You are told,] 'Now the crisis is *this*.' So, you're constantly spinning wheels. That [became] one of my mantras as an administrator is that most things just aren't a crisis."

On a practical front, as individuals and as systems, we cannot live in a state of permacrisis: it degrades the bonds, relationships, and connections that make up the fabric of our communities.

The result is individual and corporate brokenness.

> Canadian journalist David Moscrop writes, "the speed and frequency at which we meet and process bad news day-to-day is unprecedented and overwhelming, producing a sort of daily deluge of doom that our tiny bipedal minds are not particularly well-adapted to process. It's easy to become exhausted and distraught – indeed to become hopeless. But hopelessness, while both understandable and rational, is also counter-productive."[8]

If crisis and tumult are now the new normal, and uncertainty is the only thing we can anticipate, what hope circuits do we need to rewire? Instead of bouncing from one crisis to the next, responding as things arise (natural disaster, global pandemic, financial crisis, protests and unrest, labour strife, declining enrollment, leadership changes, and the list goes on), what happens when we approach this as a design challenge?

Our first response to crisis might be to speed up; however, as Nigerian scholar Bayo Akomolafe reminds us, "The times are urgent; let us slow down."[9] The provost too busy putting out fires is lurching from one crisis to another, too busy to imagine that a second, learned response – to slow down and pause – is possible. If we slow down, we can, as poet Rainer Maria Rilke urges us, live in the questions for which we do not have the answers; if we keep asking the questions, one day we will live our way into an answer.[10]

I want to live in the question about how we might do things differently if we treat crisis as a feature, not a flaw. And, in parallel, I want to live into the question of what an abundance mindset looks like amid a scarcity culture.

Reimagine expertise and authority

I am not an economist. I do not have the level of financial literacy to solve university budgets' wicked problems and complex challenges. Nevertheless, I know how living in financial crisis makes me feel, and I know how my behaviour and energy are often shaped by stories I hear, internalize, and reproduce. Using the conceptual tools to pause, surface the systems, and stay with the trouble enables me to locate agency, which is when hope circuits kick in.

Higher education has witnessed deep funding cuts over the past twenty years. Financial exigency and financial sustainability are top of mind for every university, whether a small college or a large, comprehensive institution.

Government grants, tuition, infrastructure, operating budgets, research funding, industry partnerships, foundations, and philanthropy constitute complex pieces of a funding model that almost always projects shortfalls, threatens cuts, or sees universities just squeak by. Indeed, much ink has been spilled trying to build a sustainable financial model. The consensus seems to be that the current model is broken. We are less clear on what the new paradigm might look like.

> A retired senior administrator reflects, "Part of the problem is that there is a constant absolute financial pressure, no matter how well you dig yourself out of a hole. A government-funded system is always going to every year ratchet things up more. And if you, in response, make savings and cut corners, then that becomes the basis of the funding formula going forward. So, it's a constant kind of pressure for greater efficiencies, not sustainability. People just get tired and run out of energy too."

Smart people are working on this problem. Still, no one seems to have clear, actionable, audacious solutions – at least not yet.

Putting forward another unactionable "plan of action" is not the focus of this book, and you are better served reading the work of Canadian higher education thinker Alex Usher, futurist Ken Steele, RBC's John Stackhouse, or the researchers at Universities Canada and other think tanks who are dedicating time, energy, and expertise to such matters.

Take a systems-level approach

It is worth acknowledging that very few people within the systems have the levels of financial literacy needed to contribute meaningfully to decisions about funding. Highly specialized terminology and incredibly complex spreadsheets are presented at decision-making tables where diverse representatives are expected to make informed decisions, often well beyond their expertise or disciplinary knowledge.[11]

As a junior faculty member, I was too embarrassed to admit I did not know what "fiduciary duty" was or understand the difference between a centralized and a decentralized budget. I did not think there was room for asking "stupid questions" for fear of slowing down the Rubber-Stamping Machine run by Very Busy People. Instead, I nodded, smiled, and then frantically googled terms like ROI, KPI, EBIT as soon as I left the meeting rooms.[12]

When I reflect on the faculty council meetings now, I realize the old guard did not share their vast institutional knowledge. The hoarding of institutional memory about the systems and structures means that we unwittingly – and sometimes indifferently – reinforce and perpetuate this self-exclusionary form of gatekeeping. They were themselves dragons guarding institutional memory even as they conjured imaginary ones as adversaries.

In graduate school and as an early-career professor, I was never taught how universities were funded and run. Indeed, my willingness to believe that a dragon guards a hoard of treasure (whether that takes the form of hidden funds or institutional knowledge) is as naïve as it is unfounded. It is to our detriment when we do not develop financial literacy at an organizational level.

How do we stop blaming the salmon and start focusing on the dams? To be clear, each individual within a system has a degree of power and agency – relational, positional, and symbolic. However, taking a systems-level approach helps focus our energy on the dams.

> As one mid-career staff reflected, "I am increasingly intolerant of strategic plans that champion the importance of building resilient universities without a clear plan to intervene in systems that are sustained through precarity; the language of resilient universities cannot be doublespeak for building financially viable, fiscally stable systems on the backs of the most precarious partners: students, contract faculty, underpaid staff, undervalued faculty."

Stay with the trouble

So, what *do* we know?

Universities are risk-averse organizations designed to mitigate potential financial, operational, and reputational threats. They carry minimal risk themselves. Until recently, for example, provincial governments in Canada provided surety[13] that guaranteed lower interest rates since universities were unlikely to default on their loans. They used to be a safe bet because governments would, the assumption went, bail them out. However, the stakes have changed. In 2022, Laurentian University was the first publicly funded university in Canadian history to file for bankruptcy.

They will not be the last.

> Consider the point made by Tom Chase, long-time provost and educational leader: "I think we've reached a juncture where post-secondary institutions will start to fail in large numbers, first slowly and then at an accelerated pace. (We will always have the Harvards, Torontos, MITs, Pekings, and Oxfords, but the outlook is rather bleaker for lesser institutions, and completely bleak for whole sectors such as liberal arts colleges, denominational colleges, institutions in areas in which the school leaving population is in irreversible decline, and more.)"

While many small, primarily undergraduate institutions and liberal arts colleges in Canada have been precarious for decades, we might start to see other types of universities – for example, comprehensive institutions that have grown quickly, or are top heavy, or overenrolled in international students, or overextended in STEM or professional programs – falter as the PSE sector shifts.

Since funding for higher education happens at the provincial level, different rules apply to different universities: some universities are allowed to carry debt, and some are not. All institutions need ratings from credit agencies. Usually, the "backstops" of the government mean it is a safe credit debt; therefore, universities can secure lower interest rates on debt. The idea of universities as a "safe bet" changed dramatically when the Ontario government did not immediately intervene with a rescue package for Laurentian University. This loss of trust between and amongst the credit agencies, the provincial governments, and the universities will have long-term impact on the PSE sector in Canada.

> Tom Chase offers a clear-eyed assessment of the financial landscape in light of the duplication of resources with diminishing returns: "In

part through a refusal to re-examine curricula, and to share curricular resources, inter-institutionally we have made ourselves dependent on an underclass of ill-paid contingent teachers, so that an increasingly stratified faculty body can continue to enjoy privileges and remuneration unlike anything enjoyed by those who do the bulk of the teaching, and whose revenue sustains the institution."

There is abundance and waste, lack and scarcity.

Canada is not the only higher education ecosystem under threat. The financial situations are precarious from the UK to Australia and the US. Some universities are amalgamating to consolidate and save – a global trend driven by budgetary matters.

In Canada, provincial governments are not funding universities to the same extent as they were. In 2010, government grants were a more significant proportion of operating revenues than contributions to tuition and other fees. However, more than a decade later, government grants are now on par with tuition and other fees. General operating revenues have decreased by 9 per cent, whereas operating expenses have increased by 7 per cent. Tuition fees make up the difference.[14]

When we treat students as revenue streams and data points on an excel spread sheet aimed at balancing budgets, we internalize narratives of students as units, not as three-dimensional learners.

When we treat students as numbers and as units, we choose scarcity over abundance. Students become commodities instead of learners and customers instead of collaborators. They become "bums in seats" (a disgusting phrase that we need to expunge from our lexicon immediately) and become a group more often spoken *about* rather than spoken *with*.

When we use fiscal resilience to justify dehumanization and dismemberment, this threatens our ability to deliver on the social contract to a broader society.

Yes: every person should have access to high-quality education.

And: tuition should be publicly funded, accessible and inclusive, subsidized or free.[15]

Plus, we need to be financially responsible, transparent, and accountable.

These three statements above are often put into opposition with one another instead of doing the more complex work of seeing where they might align.

Yes. And.

Build intentional community (not incidental commodities)

While students are being treated as revenue generators, faculty and staff are being treated as resource drains. When unconscious bias, narratives of crisis, mindsets of scarcity, and excel sheets converge, we have a perfect storm.

- These excerpts from interviews expose a prevailing rhetoric of crisis and scarcity.
- "Trust barometer! Profs used to be the most trusted and now are the least trusted."
- "More user pay and less government investment equals higher expectations at the same time as faculty are disengaging because they are burnt out."
- "There is little faculty renewal and so there are fewer professors at the lower ranks. Staff at full professor have the highest salaries, which has a huge burden on the budget."
- "There is an increase in full-time academic numbers from 1970 to 2018 (20% versus 36%), where the number of assistant profs was 36% and is now 19%, and no mandatory retirement has caused this."

In conversations with senior leaders, attitudes around the aging professoriate are informed by loss and deficit.

- "Universities need academic renewal with equal numbers of full, associate, and assistant professors and junior instructors. At many tables, the questions raised are, 'Is the staffing model outmoded? Is it time for a significant shift?' We can no longer afford the model."
- "At 71, you collect a full pension and full salary without paying into the pension, which makes for a 'triple whammy.'"
- "There has been a demographic flip in the professoriate. Many senior faculty are still doing the job, but 15–20% of the faculty are research inactive. A full prof costs the university $30,000/course if they teach a full-time (four-course) load at the top of salary scale with inactive research."

In these narratives, professors are an incurred, fixed cost in the operating budget. As such, in some circles people openly discuss faculty in terms of diminishing returns: the assumption is that faculty and staff get older, more expensive, less "productive." This paints a dire picture.

Well-meaning staff, administrators, and board members – generous in so many other spheres – talk with frustration about professors as lazy, entitled, and privileged. Many of the external thought leaders I interviewed point to the current unionized and tenure structures as flawed: professors cannot be fired or forced to retire, and there are few incentives and fewer disincentives to innovate, adapt, and grow.

This sentiment is seeping into the public consciousness: the salmon are always to blame in this story.[16]

We need to rumble over these narratives and determine whether these stories help or hinder us in imagining a new paradigm of higher education where everyone can flourish.

What we do know: the current funding models have an alarming toll on professors, students, and the quality of education we can deliver. We now have a choice: perpetuate scarcity and permacrisis or adopt an abundance mindset.

This does not mean gaslighting ourselves or turning a blind eye to genuine and complex funding issues.

This does mean pausing and looking for abundance where others see scarcity.

What do we have to unlearn?

Universities are not businesses.
If we were a business, then one interviewee reflects, "we would be really fucking bad at it. There are some fantastic business models out there that we could learn from, but universities are not wired that way."

Instead, universities are publicly funded social institutions.
As Lisa Dickson notes, "universities are like fire stations." Both focus on the health, safety, and well-being of our communities through the delivery of preventative, educational, solutions-based public services. One might recall the provost from earlier in the chapter who spends their days putting out

fires. This is a potentially troubling metaphor in the light of performance-based funding. If universities were businesses, Lisa Dickon muses, "you imagine a scenario where they aren't putting out enough fires, so they hire arsonists to pad their numbers and justify their budgets."

Universities are not revenue-generating enterprises.

If we believe universities are businesses, then we define students as customers. By that logic, an education is a credential one can buy. Treating humans as cost or revenue privileges the transactional over the transformative. It also informs every aspect of how we educate. Shannon Murray remarks, "If a student really needs to take a year off, change programs, or transfer schools and I know that is the best decision on their journey, I must guide them accordingly. What is best for the student is not always best for the university bottom line."

When we obsess over revenue as a series of data points on an Excel sheet without a nuanced understanding of value (or a critical treatment of metrics), we effectively turn our backs on the foundational values of what universities represent and what we can achieve.

Universities have an ethical contract to the broader society.

Let us renew our commitment that, in Canada, universities are publicly funded social institutions with an ethical contract to build nuanced, thoughtful citizens who uphold, maintain, and contribute a just and civil society. And let's stop buying the story that we can't because we must be fiscally responsible. Otherwise, as American novelist and satirist Kurt Vonnegut remarks, "We'll go down in history as the first society that wouldn't save itself because it wasn't cost-effective."[17]

The assumption has been that the university's social mission and budgetary requirements somehow work in opposition.

If our initial instinct is to turn down purpose-driven approaches because of funding, then we lack the imagination to see missions for what they are … missions. We must challenge why missions and finances are deployed as binaries in existing normative structures instead of mutually aligned in both principle and long-term trajectory.

We have a choice: set up a false binary – an either/or – or live into the "yes/and" question.

Collectively we are guilty of a failure of imagination.

One faculty member remarked, "Universities aren't supposed to be revenue generating. They are funded through grants from the government. They are revenue neutral at best. We should be investing at the government level in sustainable financial models. I believe PSE should be invested in and [those] contributions [have to happen] at a social and governmental level."

Live in the questions

So, what are we to do? How do we imagine new ways of funding these complex, unwieldy, broken, beautiful systems?

How do we invent electricity by candlelight?

When I asked one of my thought partners how to create a new funding paradigm, they advised that universities should diversify their revenue streams and look to external funding sources with increased partnerships with foundations, philanthropists, and corporations as well as industry partners, patents, and other forms of innovation income.

And yet, that is just adding more candles.

Creating a new paradigm asks us to live into questions together:

- Where do we locate abundance in a culture of scarcity?
- What is our purpose in relation to knowledge, money, and time?
- When do we imagine ourselves as stewards, givers, and patrons?
- When are we dragons, bears, or hoarders?
- What does it look like if we imagine new kinds of economies where value circulates differently?
- Can we sit with the big wicked complex problem of funding at a systems level and not be broken apart by its magnitude?

This chapter, more so than the others, is characterized by the gappiness I introduced in the prologue. Gappiness around funding is somewhat by design and also exposes the limitations of the project – or at the very least, pushes up against the boundaries of this first book, which is to identify the conceptual tools to build mindsets for the task ahead. The next phase of this project is to gather people with a common set of tools, shared mindsets, and diverse expertise to prototype the blueprints for rewiring universities at the systemic and structural levels.

And yet I understand that this might feel unsatisfactory for those interested in how hope circuits operate in funding spheres; what can we do now to intervene in this big, sticky, complex topic that affects all aspects of our institutions? In the hundreds of interviews I conducted, a series of concepts emerged that I share below with a disclaimer that they are imperfect and incomplete because many of the insights reproduce the conditions of existing systems. We still have work to do to invent electricity by candlelight. And so I offer them in the spirit of gappiness.

Build clear expectations and shared values.

Get clear and candid about the relationship between what we value and what we resource. Resource decisions sometimes have to do with budgets. Other times, they are about investing in people. Making sure people know when and how they can engage in the funding processes (e.g., consultation, feedback, decisions, or information sharing) requires attention and alignment. A higher educational leader I interviewed advised, "Communication around decision-making and the process of making the decision are two different things. People might not like the decisions, but if they understand the process, then relations become – or hopefully remain – honest and transparent, which engenders respect and collaboration."

Build teams that can engage in creative budgets and strategic spending.

vps finance work closely with the senior leadership team to operationalize the vision and mission of the university. They also play a critical role in educating, communicating, and sharing information about the financial health of the institution to all members of the community. As one senior administrator reflected, "The best kinds of vps finance get excited about working with provosts on creative budget spending and allocation." This excitement can be extended to partners across the university – and there is an important pedagogical and knowledge mobilization aspect to university finances that has been largely overlooked in existing structures.

Build financial literacy across the university community.

A shared vocabulary and common understanding of budget fundamentals ensures that every member of the community grasps how funding is determined and where resources are allocated. Each university is slightly different: budget allocation toward fixed and variable costs differs based on the institution. One interviewee shared, "Frustrations arise when there is no flexibility and lots of fixed envelopes. This can create discordance and discontent, especially when so much money is not spent while other areas of the institution are chronically underfunded." In climates of austerity, it is not a good look to have lots of money sitting in an account, and yet it is often unavoidable depending on the type of funding envelope. Educating people on the difference between restricted and unrestricted funds and whether they are internal or external (for example externally restricted funds include research dollars or endowment income) goes a long way to dispelling theories about dragons guarding a hoard of gold under the central administrative buildings.

Build curiosity and relentless welcome

In order to rewire existing systems, we need to understand basic budgetary concepts – capital reserves, liabilities of deferred maintenance, capital expenditures, ancillary funds, cost recovery, etc. – and the complexity of varying timelines compounded by provincial limitations and institutional idiosyncrasies. These conversations can be alienating and disorienting to many. The good news is that our institutions have expertise in the creation and sharing of knowledge. If fundamental values in higher education include curiosity and life-long learning, surely we can foster these in conversations around funding with all members of the university and the public more broadly.

Build trust and transparency.

In scarcity cultures, as we have discussed in other chapters, there is never enough, which creates workplace cultures rife with shame and fear. How do we get to the root of this fear, and build trust necessary to design a financial plan founded on shared values? The vp finance at one university suggested the following: "Show very transparent budgets. It's hard to argue how in debt we are, but it became clear after people asked, 'I need I need I need.'" We also need to trust the community to show up and engage in helpful and hopeful ways, which they do when they are treated with respect and radical welcome.

Build a big-picture view.

Every university can look for revenues in the margins while also exploring new funding opportunities. Philanthropy, foundations, federal grants, and so many other external possibilities fall under the purview of hard-working and understaffed advancement offices. And yet the best fundraisers are faculty, staff, students: nothing is more powerful to potential funding partners than people who love what they do and espouse the shared values and vision of the university. A senior finance leader shared, "Obviously, the more you have in endowment and trust the more flexibility you have, and then you get to have exciting conversations about where to focus some of that additional budget flexibility on institutional and strategic priorities."

Concluding thoughts

We need adequate tools to rewire mindsets; we then need to start prototyping what a funding model looks like through an abundance mindset. And then, perhaps, we can build a movement. There is much work to do, and many narratives to unlearn as we move from "we never have enough X" to "we are enough."

In the meantime, adrienne maree brown, who advocates for emergent strategy, reminds us that abundance costs us nothing to adopt, and can change everything:

> abundance is immediate. its not something you have to plant and wait for spring. that too of course, it grows now and in all your potential futures. but if you truly call it in, you must be ready for it, because it shows up right away, and you will want to have room for it.[18]

Let us make room for abundance.

Chapter 10

How Do We Build
Hope University?

"The person who invented electricity did so by candlelight."

This concept, seeded in the introductory chapter of this book, prompts us to think about how we create something that does not yet exist while working within existing systems that are becoming obsolete.

What tools do we need to build something entirely different?

We must start with daring imagination since discovering new ways of illuminating the world is, for the most part, validated only in retrospect. At the time, the inventors of electricity (Volta, Edison, Tesla, and so many others) must have seemed odd, even ridiculous. Candlemakers and candle users might have been baffled, even smug in their belief that candles are too ubiquitous to be replaced, having been the primary light source for centuries.

They could not have imagined their obsolescence.

Very few of us can.

What factors prevent us from daring to imagine something different?

We are "busy," so we rush to the next meeting.

We work in broken systems, so we patch things together on the fly.

We live in a state of permacrisis, so we race from one conflict to the next.

We do more with less, so we squeeze more out of diminishing budgets.

We are assessed by finite metrics while playing an infinite game, so we have little incentive to reshape what is valued.

We operate within cultures of scarcity, so we cannot even imagine the meaning of abundance.

In the meantime, though, the systems around us are changing. In social change movements, we enjoy periods of stable growth punctuated by revisionary revolutions. Thomas Kuhn's influential *The Structure of Scientific Revolutions* gives us a map of paradigm shifts in four stages:

1 Dominant paradigm ("normal science")
2 Extraordinary research
3 Adoption of the new paradigm
4 Aftermath

In this first stage, the dominant paradigm – the status quo – operates within a prevailing framework; shared norms, values, and a set of rules are derived by the paradigm, which in turn informs assumptions and behaviours. The community shares the same tools – the theoretical beliefs, values, instruments, and techniques – that make up the "disciplinary matrix." Members of this dominant community are committed to the disciplinary matrix; this commitment "is a key element in the formation of the mind-set."[1] In other words, internalizing the tools of the paradigm creates a mindset – a way of thinking and being – whereby *what you do* becomes *how you think*.

However, "anomalies" or gaps in the dominant paradigm start to accumulate. The tools can no longer account for variants or flaws in the existing matrix. When the normal tools fail to address an anomaly, thus exposing the inadequacy of an existing principle or underlying theory, we arrive at what Kuhn calls a "crisis."

The first response is to try to tweak the existing paradigm; according to Kuhn, this precipitates revolutionary change. At this stage, thought leaders begin engaging with what Kuhn calls "extraordinary research," characterized by "the proliferation of competing articulations, the willingness to try anything, the expression of explicit discontent, the recourse to philosophy and to debate over fundamentals."[2]

This is where we are.

And we still have a ways to go.

Eventually, a new paradigm emerges and is adopted, creating its own followers; however, this is neither automatic nor comfortable for the followers of the dominant paradigm. According to German theoretical physicist Max Planck, "a new scientific truth does not triumph by convincing its opponents and making them see the light, but rather because its opponents eventually die, and a new generation grows up that is familiar with it."[3]

Planck's observation is ungenerous: wait them out.

It should go without saying that death is not a viable strategy for Hope University.

Planck discounts the power of intergenerational partnership and over-looks generosity.

In my interviews, many of the old guard are the ones calling for the most radical change. The more seasoned the administrators – former presidents, provosts, and senior vps – the more they are able to step back and hold their deep frustration with flawed systems together with their deep love of the so-cial institutions, converging at "yes/and." These retired (rewired) higher edu-cation luminaries insist that we imagine more daring paradigms of higher education.

> Ross Paul, long-time university president and provost, read an early draft of my introduction and remarked, "I think this a really impor-tant project – ambitious, very thoughtful and delightful to read. It is obviously a work in progress and may benefit from considerable tightening up, although even that paradigm can and should be challenged. But my main message is – you go, GIRL! (oops, dated use of gender?)"

At first, I was nervous about sharing my early work with well-established senior university leaders: I took Sara Ahmed's warning to heart that the people closest to the centres of power (and who benefit the most) are less likely to change the systems. I was anxious that a critique of the dominant systems might be construed as a critique of those individuals who might identify as metonymic extensions of the systems.

I worried that the line between invitation and indictment might get blurred.

Nevertheless, I summoned the courage to share very rough drafts with people from all ages and stages of the academy. What surprised me the most was, without exception, the elder, more seasoned group was the most sup-portive of change to fulfill the social contract of universities in a civil society.[4]

While Planck advocates patience (play the long game and let the old fol-lowers die out), Kuhn champions persuasion to accelerate a new paradigm.

Yes: Paradigms are embedded in systems and mindsets, which makes them incredibly difficult to change.

And, there are some conditions that accelerate adoption.

- When the new paradigm offers a way to grasp the "anomalies" from the dominant paradigm that are otherwise disorienting or troublesome.
- When the new paradigm offers better explanations or frameworks for our present state of affairs.
- When the new paradigm offers a better guide for future problems that the current (dominant) paradigm is no longer capable of solving.

So, let us once again reconsider the electricity/candlelight example to elucidate the points above.

- Electricity helps solve the anomaly of candles burning down the house.
- Electricity makes greater sense in an industrial age.
- Electricity better illuminates new kinds of spaces.

As we imagine paradigm shifts via illumination, we hear echoes of Octavia E. Butler: "there is nothing new under the sun, but there are new suns."[5]

Responding to Octavia E. Butler, Princeton professor of African studies Ruha Benjamin asserts, "What we're after is not escapism, but a kind of visionary realism that holds in tension the deep injustices that are etched into the contemporary landscape with an unapologetic (some call it 'crunk') commitment to creating something different – more just and more joyous – for ourselves and for our children's children."[6]

And this is why we hope. And why we build. And why we illuminate.

Take a systems-level approach

Returning once more to the electricity analogy, this new "disruptive technology" displaced candles because electricity solved problems candles created – smoky, smelly, melty, messy – while also functioning as a better tool to fulfill the original need: illumination.

The term "disruptive technologies," coined by Harvard Business School professor Clayton Christensen twenty-five years ago, has affected many sectors.[7] Disruptive innovation – two very buzzy buzzwords – happens when "a product or service takes root initially in simple applications at the bottom of a market and then relentlessly moves up market, eventually displacing established competitors."

Christensen explains that "companies pursue 'sustaining innovations' at the higher tiers of their markets because this is what has historically helped them succeed." The companies are confident because they are in a stable market with a solid product or service, so they believe they can succeed by scaling.

Their very confidence, however, means these companies "unwittingly open the door to 'disruptive innovations'" by creating "space at the bottom of the market for new disruptive competitors to emerge."[8]

Merely tweaking the same model – or offering more of it – can put the organization at risk. In other words, "electric light did not come from the continuous improvement of candles."[9]

We have seen disruptive innovation – and disruptive technology – transform a myriad of industries, changing everything from how we talk on the phone to where we watch movies and from how we shop to where we invest. Music industry executive Per Sundin, in discussing how downloading music changed consumer and industry views about music ownership, shared a key takeaway: "The first mistake we made was trying to defend our existing business model."[10]

Live in the questions

The theory of disruptive innovation, paired with the metaphor of inventing electricity, illuminates the following questions in our sector.

- Do we have an outdated business model in higher education?
- Do we have communities that are not being serviced by existing systems?
- Do we have a current model that resists change?
- Do we overlook disruptive competitors at our peril?
- Do we resist new ways of thinking even as these new models offer value?
- Do we defend our model or embrace new ideas to remain relevant?

These are troubling questions with potentially damning answers.

- We began with the premise that the current paradigm in PSE in Canada has been tweaked since the 1960s and that we have now run out of room. A new paradigm is emerging.
- We have explored elsewhere how universities struggle to serve non-traditional students and that imposter syndrome is more prevalent in historically excluded and equity-deserving groups for all members of university communities.
- We know universities have been slow to embrace upskilling, reskilling, and other flexible credentialing options.[11]
- We have, as a sector, largely ignored the transformative work being done at community colleges and other alternative educational pathways because universities have a stable market and a solid "product" that has historically served a particular base of people.
- We assumed that when MOOCs, Microsoft education accelerators, and other technologies failed to gain traction in the early 2000s, we were invulnerable: too big, too embedded, too respected to be replaced.

This final question in disruptive innovation – "Do we defend our model or embrace new ways of being?" – sets up a binary that we have been challenging throughout this book. The defend/embrace stance also takes the form of resist/transform, stagnate/generate, break apart/break open, armour up/dare bigger.

However, the question presupposes that we know who we are, are clear on our social purpose, and know how we contribute to the knowledge economy. The answers to these questions – who we are, what we do, and how we contribute – should instead determine what we defend and where we transform.

If we map this onto Kuhn's theory of paradigmatic change, we are in the stage that requires us "to debate over fundamentals."

> Canadian university president Tim Loreman reflects, "What is the university for? I mean, what is the point? The history of universities is fascinating, but development over the past fifty years has left them increasingly unrecognizable from what preceded them. This is

positive in some respects, but what have we lost? I think in many ways we no longer know what we do. Is it labour market training? Is it providing an educated citizenry? Is it redressing inequalities? Is it free pursuit of knowledge? Is it transmission of disciplinary knowledge? Is it a combination of all of these and more? I'm not sure we know, and everyone from individuals to boards to governments seem[s] to have a different understanding."

Stay with the trouble

Thomas Kuhn's "extraordinary research" stage is marked by "the proliferation of competing articulations."

And so, we have seen a proliferation of op-eds that present a deceptively pleasing theory by importing a trendy concept from the corporate sector into the PSE sphere for comparison. Pundits and public scholars almost always suggest we have something to learn from whatever entrepreneurial, innovative, or lucrative (insert: industry, business, start-up, technology) has just emerged.[12]

Here's the thing, though: universities are not businesses.

They operate under different rules and governance structures. In Canada, universities are publicly funded social institutions. The logic of revenues, products, and customers in the business world does not seamlessly apply to universities, which are – at their core – values-driven centres of knowledge sharing and knowledge creation. Why would we cede the ground and play by a set of rules where students are customers, grades are transactions, degrees are bought and paid for, and research must have practical application in industry to be funded?

And so, we must ask: what, if anything, is there to learn from the follies and failures of the corporate sector when it comes to disruptive innovation?

Or are we focused on the wrong questions?

Instead of an answer, I would like to offer a volta.[13]

In Italian, volta means "turn." It is used in poetry as a strategic switch, a reframing, a surprise twist. Just when you think you have a handle on what is happening, the volta swerves, changing momentum.

Alessandro Volta invented the first battery and paved the way for electricity. What is fascinating, though, is that candles were, in turn, reinvented.

When electricity replaced candles as the primary source of light, warmth, and illumination, candles became synonymous with ambiance, intimacy, and special occasions.[14]

Instead of obsolescence, they became more treasured.

It is here – in the volta – where we need to hold space.

American poet Phillis Levin declares, "the volta is the seat of [the sonnet's] soul." The volta has power, according to Levin, to reshape our thinking: "the arrangement of lines into patterns of sound serves a function we could call architectural ... the volta, the 'turn' that introduces into the poem a possibility for transformation, like a moment of grace."[15]

The volta offers us an antidote to fear.

Social change is often depicted via disruptive, even violent imagery. Revolution evokes upheaval and conflict, fights and factions. Activists raise the alarm to convey the urgency of immediate action to decision-makers who are not paying attention. The language of transformation is often terrifying (e.g., climate crisis, burning platforms,[16] glass cliffs[17]).

> Canadian political scientist David Hornsby explains, "We keep encountering the limitations of our current model [of higher education in Canada]. And we keep edging closer and closer to the obsolescence, to the redundancy issue. And we have to push ourselves over that edge at some point, but we need to also have the space to think, how do we want to land when we finally do hit the ground? ... We all revert to some type of urgency or violent suggestion or the notion of redundancy as a means of trying to garner attention. We are compelled to suggest that there's something alarming about this moment so that people listen."

Is violence inevitable in revolutionary change?

What if we could reconfigure radical change as something generous and generative?

What if we could choose an abundance mindset over crisis and loss?

What if we started a movement through purpose rather than panic?

Martin Luther King urges us to embrace non-violence as a tool, mindset, verb, and adjective: "Nonviolence chooses love instead of hate. Nonviolence resists violence of the spirit as well as the body. Nonviolent love is spontaneous, unmotivated, unselfish and creative."[18]

Martin Luther King also reminds us to focus on the systems, not the individuals: "Nonviolence is directed against evil systems, forces, oppressive policies, unjust acts, but not against persons. Through reasoned compromise, both sides resolve the injustice with a plan of action. Each act of reconciliation is one step close to the 'Beloved Community.'"[19]

The possibility for transformation as an experience of grace – of invitation rather than indictment – offers us a different approach to paradigmatic shifts for our institutions and as a sector.

Change your language, change the world

The volta is also part of a rhetoric of hope that informs this book.

Any efforts to rewire the architecture of systems demand we also rewire our thinking at the level of language. Rhetoric – and rhetorical devices – offers us a key toolbox to build hope circuits.

The premise of hope circuits is that we can move from default (status quo, automatic, normative) to hope (learned, intentional, mindful) through a series of conceptual tools that can change mindsets.[20] The rhetoric of hope, therefore, is not merely a pleasing or pedantic exercise; instead, it is a key mechanism in the rewiring process that creates circuitry for more divergent thinking.

It is not just the words that matter; it is the combination of words we put together that determines whether we can shape new pathways or merely reproduce older ones.

American historian and thought leader David Scobey, in a talk titled "The Gifts of a Liberal Education," advocates for "an alternative framing of liberal education that is less institutional and operational, more philosophical and discursive, less a scan of present practice and more a rethinking of what might be called the grammar of the liberal arts tradition, its enduring ethical and epistemological values. I want to offer a new take on that grammar and those values."[21]

While Scobey looks at the grammar of liberal education as a way of addressing the "paradox of shrinkage in the liberal arts tradition," I am interested in grammar's sibling, rhetoric: these two, alongside logic, form the trivium – the foundation of Western education.[22]

If grammar gives us architectural frameworks for thinking and communicating, rhetoric provides us with the tools to combine, reconfigure, and reconstitute language to build and illuminate a new paradigm.

I use rhetoric here both as the art of persuasion and as an umbrella term for rhetorical devices that pattern and animate the English language. One of the conceptual tools of hope circuits is divergent thinking, which happens when we deploy metaphor (and the constellation of devices that play with comparisons) to see and think differently.

Form always informs content.[23]

In this book, another of the conceptual tools is developing the ability to live into questions. A dominant rhetorical device in this book is "quesitio," which asks questions that prompt us to think, wonder, or explore. This device can also be used to subtly influence or persuade since questions open us up to new possibilities.[24] Rhetorical questions rarely solicit definitive answers. As American poet Mary Oliver writes,

Let me keep my distance, always, from those
who think they have the answers.
Let me keep company always with those who say
"Look!" and laugh in astonishment,
and bow their heads.[25]

Rhetorical devices have conceptual depth, clustering ideas or images to explore convergences and divergences. Metaphors, analogies, conceits, and similes are tropes that make reference to one thing as another.[26] They are superimposable. Taking concepts and shuffling them around, encouraging collisions, and finding affinity are all powerful ways to think and see differently and increase our neural plasticity.

Patterns in language – schemes – also create meaning. These offer us structures of balance, change in word order, omission, and (my favourite) repetition. "Articulus," for example, is a useful tool to articulate complex issues; "articulus" joins phrases successively as a way of accelerating the speed of the argument, offering a level of urgency that mirrors the acceleration we experience in change movements.

"Anaphora," which repeats words at the beginning of successive clauses, helps build thoughts and momentum. Just as we endeavour to move from critique towards building and illumination, the device allows us to work with concepts, repeating them in new contexts to deepen understanding.

"Anadiplosis" means "doubling" or "doubling back" and refers to the repetition of the final word in a clause at the beginning of the next clause. I love this device because it models the power of yes/and. The device keeps the idea moving, evolving, growing into new spaces and reconfigurations.

The "yes/and" is itself a volta. Doubling back to go forward.

Repetition, I often joke with students, is the key to pedagogy. And the rhetoric of hope – creating new pathways, new circuits, new connections by repeating familiar things in unfamiliar contexts – is at the heart of the re-wiring process.[27]

Rhetorology is not just a technique: it is a way of transforming through conversation with others. Coined by American literary critic Wayne C. Booth, rhetorology is a means to connect those who are stuck in conflicting positions or ideologies.

Through rhetoric, Booth suggests, we can truly listen to our opponent to find common ground:

> But unlike skillful diplomats, rhetorologists do not just try to discover the rival basic commitments and then "bargain." Nor do they just tolerate, in a spirit of benign relativism. Instead, they search together for true grounds then labor to decide how those grounds dictate a change of mind about more superficial beliefs. Any genuine rhetorologist entering any fray is committed to the possibility of conversion to the "enemy" camp.[28]

The book found its voice via rhetoric.

In the summer of 2022, I had collected hundreds of interview transcripts and written thousands of words. And yet I was finding it difficult to locate a through line because I felt overwhelmed by the abundance of data and ideas. And then along came Bassam Chiblak, a former student from my first teaching gig fifteen years earlier. He popped into my inbox looking for a job and I immediately plunked him into this book project. I needed an accountability coach, a curator, a truth-teller, and a rumble partner so that I could talk my way into Hope University. I needed him to tell me when I was onto something and, more importantly, when I was flailing.

And so we began where we left off fifteen years ago when, as a brand-new professor, I taught him and his classmates a sixteenth-century poetry course where we used rhetorical devices to unlock meaning in otherwise dense and difficult poems. In one of our first meetings for this book, Bassam reminded me of this origin story and asked me to harness the lessons I had shared so many years before. He said, "You trained as an early modern orator. Write like you talk." And that was the turning point towards rhetoric not merely as a craft to hone but as a mindset to embody.

We built the architecture of this book through rhetoric: when we were stuck on an idea or concept, it was usually rhetoric or form that got us unstuck.

Form really does inform content.

Words matter. They are the tools that take us from a moment to a mindset to a movement.

Commit to unlearning and relearning

In one of the earliest conversations about this project, community development scholar Gabrielle Donnelly and I tried to locate our discomfort with the fetishization of the word "innovation." We started a thought piece we never published, primarily because we were anxious about the critical reception of our post-critical voices. As this book draws to a close, I revisit the project's beginnings to explore the tensions between legacy and newness.

We want to take a moment to speak to those of you who are deterred by the language here that points to "innovation." We've intentionally avoided using that word because it bugs us too. Innovation is a buzzword that can begin to sound hollow. The principles we're suggesting are not "out with the old, in with the new." The perceived tension between innovation and tradition is at the heart of many of our challenges in higher education, sometimes appearing across generational lines. The approach that we're proposing places this tension in relationship at the centre of the work of imagining what our universities could be.

The ability to engage in radical imagination, find scientific discoveries, uncover inequities, or develop new equations is so much of what universities are about. We have deep and long-standing traditions of innovation. They go hand-in-hand. The way forward includes both. We are compelled to ask,

- What is fundamental to our mission that we can conserve and protect?
- Where must we be open, adapt to evolving contexts, release some deep held assumptions and practices that no longer serve?
- How can we put equity at the centre of every decision we make?
- How can the journey of decolonization open up what's possible at every level of who we are and what we do?
- What is the spectrum of leadership capabilities that are needed to guide these shifts?

In this passage above we can trace the genealogy of conceptual tools in their earliest forms:

- taking a systems-level rather than individual approach;
- surfacing the systems;
- embracing the "yes/and";
- the importance of unlearning;
- living into questions.

In the first few months of the pandemic – as so many of us wondered what a new way of being in the academy and in the world might look like – Gabrielle and I howled into a shared Google Doc with equal parts hope and disorientation.

We may have a clear sense of where we want to go but very little idea of how to get there. Challenges of this nature include transforming our campuses in ways that truly centre equity, that embody decolonization, or that take seriously the devolving wellness trends we see in students, faculty, and staff with a tangible commitment to create spaces for people to thrive both personally and collectively. This work not only involves a commitment to changes at the level of structure, policy, procedures, and resource flow but also requires tending to the underappreciated dimensions of culture change, where the hearts and minds of people are engaged in the creative potential of what universities might be. This requires work at the level of beliefs, mindsets, values, and building the capacity for collaboration, not just adding another line in a collective agreement (although we are all for those too).

These conversations germinated the earliest conceptions of Hope University: the fundamental values – abundance and wholeness, wonder and convergence – have remained constant even as the ideas transformed and developed.

Stay with the trouble

If Hope University is the concept we are building, hope circuits are the tools we deploy.

In so many interviews people expressed the powerlessness they feel in the face of seemingly impervious systems. We need tools to move us from ideation to action. Otherwise, we run the risk of stagnation and despair.

> Excerpts from junior faculty members offer a representative sample of their perception of self-determination.
> - "We're in the system, and we don't know what to do about it. It feels like then there's nothing to do."
> - "Where do we begin? There is value in at least knowing that this system we are in is not *it*."
> - "This is a scary and unsettling time because in a sense, if there's no formula that you can follow to do it. There is no roadmap. We can't point to a master plan and follow it."

Lorgia García Peña, co-founder of Freedom University and professor of Latinx studies, shares her strategies for moving from stagnation to activism:

I think often about how disempowered we tend to feel when we look at the big picture, or how exhausted and defeated we might feel when we think about national or even global problems. But the possibilities can be found in the micro, everyday lives, that we live. And by that I mean locally – and that local could be your neighborhood, it could be your building, it could be the institution that you are part of. In my case, that could be a university ... So, while I think the goal would be, to have this massive, large revolution that would create national, and hopefully global changes, I think that what we do locally matters just as much. Those local moments of resistance, when multiplied, are revolutionary, and can do a lot. They're less overwhelming and more concrete.[29]

We can build a movement by locating ourselves in our own contexts and harnessing the tools within our spheres of control.

Indeed, my long-time university president Michael Goldbloom regularly quotes American anthropologist Margaret Mead: "Never doubt that a small group of thoughtful committed citizens can change the world: indeed it's the only thing that ever has."[30]

So where do we begin?

In summits and focus groups, workshops and talks, I asked participants to identify one moment of hope they encountered that week, big or small. By workshopping their lived experiences of hope, we extracted design features of hope (which have, in turn, informed the theoretical framework of hope in this book). Then we brainstormed the tools needed to increase the frequency of hope within their own contexts. And, finally, we explored how these tools might help them respond, in the moment, to encounters where they would benefit from a hope mindset.

In these workshops we moved from a moment (what does hope look like) to design principles (why and how hope happens) to tools (what do we need to build hope) to mindset (how can we internalize hope). Here is a selection of interventions they co-created that helped them build hope circuits:

- Tag team knowledge holders and change agents to share work and risk.
- Build an integrated network of hopeful humans doing hard work – and then hold space for them.
- Understand despair and grief as part of the hope circuit, not as the antithesis of hope.
- Do not frame retreat as a failure: sometimes you have to run away to play again another day.
- Critical, reflective practice exposes how we have internalized things that no longer serve us or others.

- Look for opportunities for reformation versus revolution – with the recognition that we cannot have endless revolutions.
- Say the quiet things out loud to trusted thought partners.

Slow down and pause

One of the academy's flaws is its strength: change, for the most part, happens at glacial speed.

This pace preserves systems and structures from the ups and downs of other sectors and insulates these public institutions so that they can do the work of infinite thinking.

And yet, the publication process for moving ideas into the world – the vital peer review process – can feel like an eternity. By the time the manuscript does the rounds in external review, has new edits, goes through copy editing, has final proofs, to when we can finally hold the book in our hands can take upwards of twelve to twenty-four months. Ideas that felt fresh, contexts that felt relevant, and insights that might help others run the risk of being stale and outdated in the publication cycle.

We are back to the precarious balance between timely and timelessness I introduced in the pandemic prologue. How do we sit in the discomfort of becoming obsolete?

Ross Paul, former university president at Windsor, shared the difference between timely and timelessness in our correspondence:

In the face of all this, all we can do is our best and hope it works out. We cannot beat ourselves up when things don't go as well as intended – just learn from the experience and do better next time. Channeling Riddell, I can throw in a little-known gobbet from Shakespeare here as it was my opening speech for Act V as Cleomines (one of the two messengers who brought the oracle) in *The Winter's Tale* directed by Arthur Motyer at Bishop's in 1963. I still remember it, word for word, because it was the only major speech in my part (which included brilliant other lines like "but madam"). Speaking to Leontes, he said, perhaps a bit sycophantically (is that a word?):

Sir, you have done enough, and have performed
A saintlike sorrow. No fault could you make
Which you have not redeemed – indeed, paid down
More penitence than done trespass. At the last,
Do as the heavens have done: Forget your evil
With them. Forgive yourself.

And so, we forgive ourselves with the compassion we offer to others. And this is how we build Hope University.

Concluding thoughts

In the spirit of gappiness, this is not an ending as much as it is an invitation to adapt, adopt, discard, and reconfigure the concepts in this book for purposes hitherto unimagined. I leave you with more questions than answers, more openings than closures. By accident and by design this book offers airholes to breathe into, think into, dream into – and will only come to life when you move into these spaces and invite others to join you.

Just as Antoni Gaudí's La Sagrada Família has a blueprint that leaves space for its own undoing and remaking, this book is an opening for more conversations, for building and illuminating in your own contexts.

Indeed, the only way I could finish this book is to understand it as part of a series. If this book creates the tools to build a mindset, the following books prototype hope to offer possibility models in various contexts. There is more to be done to engage with luminaries and illuminators who have built paradigms we have not yet encountered.

Slowing down to pause, surface the systems, and understand why we behave the way we do is challenging. The act of unlearning asks us to hold opinions lightly and our values firmly. And yet, this process helps us reimagine authority, power, and expertise – and approach these positions as dynamic, malleable, and shifting. Irreverence takes weighty and impervious concepts and instead seeks delight and disruption; nothing is unassailable.

Playfulness and joy are found when we start from a place of "where do you LOVE" and not "what do you think." This kind of divergent thinking breaks open possibilities for repurposing, upcycling, reconstituting, and re-configuring existing structures.

And then we begin to build.

Toni Morrison calls us to this work over time and space:

This is precisely the time when artists go to work. There is no time for despair, no place for self-pity, no need for silence, no room for fear. We speak, we write, we do language. That is how civilizations heal. I know the world is bruised and bleeding, and though it is important not to ignore its pain, it is also critical to refuse to succumb to its malevolence. Like failure, chaos contains information that can lead to knowledge – even wisdom. Like art.[31]

It is time to get to work.

Join me.

Notes

Pandemic Prologue

1   Solnit, "Hope Is an Embrace of the Unknown."
2   See Smith, "What Shakespeare Teaches Us."
3   Smith, *This Is Shakespeare*, 3.
4   Devlin McNair, "1. Why Read Shakespeare?"
5   Smith, *This Is Shakespeare*, 4
6   Solnit, *Hope in the Dark*, xii.
7   Popova, "The Six Pillars of the Wholehearted Life."
8   Brown, "Let's Rumble."
9   Personal correspondence with author.
10 Tutu, *God Is Not a Christian*, 22.
11 Dalai Lama and McDonnell, *Heart to Heart*, 70.
12 Roy, "The Pandemic Is a Portal."
13 Brown, "The Power of Vulnerability."
14 Solnit, "Hope Is an Embrace of the Unknown."
15 Consent is defined as a "notion that we should respect one another's bound-aries, to be safe, preserve dignity, and build healthy relationships." Tatter, "Consent at Every Age."
16 Caputo, *More Radical Hermeneutics*, 55–60.
17 Loud, "Loretta Ross on Calling In the Calling Out Culture."

Chapter One

1   Clear, "3–2–1: On Systems vs. Goals."
2   Sylvester, "A Message from President David Sylvester."
3   Palmer, *The Courage to Teach*, 20–1.

4 Ibid.

5 "She was an inspiration: Quotes from Lady Bird Johnson," Lady Bird Johnson website, accessed July 2023, http://www.ladybirdjohnson.org/quotes.

Section A

1 Whitman, "Song of Myself."

2 Patel, "Teach Your Students to Be Builders, Not Critics."

3 Warner (@biblioracle), "A couple of days ago I did a thread." He develops these ideas in *Why They Can't Write*.

4 Ibid.

5 Royal Orr, interview with author, June 2023.

6 Clear, "3–2–1: On Systems vs. Goals."

7 University of Calgary, "Unstoppable: Growth through Focus," accessed 19 September 2023, https://www.ucalgary.ca/president/unstoppable-growth-through-focus.

8 brown, "We Are in a Time of New Suns."

9 Lorde, "The Master's Tools," 2.

10 Binyam, "You Pose a Problem."

11 Holst, "The Fall of the Tekt n and the Rise of the Architect," 5.

12 "Generativity," Wikipedia, accessed July 2023, https://en.wikipedia.org/wiki/Generativity.

13 David Pace, interview with author, 2022.

14 Mishler, *Yoga with Adriene*.

15 Palmer and Zajonc, *The Heart of Higher Education*, 5.

Section B

1 Cunsolo and Rezagian, "Ecological Grief."

2 Riddell, "Tackling Wicked Problems in Higher Education."

3 Fletcher, "Let the Dreaming Spires Dream Afresh."

4 Hodgman, *Vacationland*, 102.

5 Caputo, *Radical Hermeneutics*, 19.

6 I am indebted to Lisa Dickson, my resident expert on John D. Caputo, for her guidance through this concept.

7 MegaGrimer, "r/Showerthoughts."

8 Fletcher, "Let the Dreaming Spires Dream Afresh."

9 See, for example, Vedder, "2025: Google U. vs. Microsoft U.?"

Section C

1 Dickinson, "'Hope' is the thing with feathers."
2 See Dickson, Murray, and Riddell, *Shakespeare's Guide to Hope*, 11.
3 Freire, *Pedagogy of Hope*, 2.
4 Ibid.
5 Shor, *When Students Have Power*, 3.
6 "Hope Is a Discipline," Toward Freedom, 17 September 2020, https://toward freedom.org/story/archives/activism/hope-is-a-discipline/.
7 Havel, *Disturbing the Peace*, 181.
8 hooks, *Teaching Community*, xiv.
9 Gannon, *Radical Hope*, 4–5.
10 Grain, *Critical Hope*, 21.
11 Popova, "Hope, Cynicism, and the Stories We Tell Ourselves."
12 Chödrön, *When Things Fall Apart*, 9–10.
13 Akomolafe, "What Do You Do When There Is No Hope?"
14 Gabrielle Donnelly, interview with author, June 2021.
15 Dickson, Murray, and Riddell, *Shakespeare's Guide to Hope*, 11.
16 Ibid., 17–18.
17 Brown, "Armored versus Daring Leadership."
18 Riddell, "Combatting Toxic Positivity with Critical Hope."
19 Haraway, *Staying with the Trouble*, 1.
20 Ahmed, *Living a Feminist Life*, 97.
21 Brown, "Armored versus Daring Leadership."
22 Palmer, *The Politics of the Brokenhearted*, 1–2.
23 See Traister, *Good and Mad*.
24 See Chemaly, *Rage Becomes Her*.
25 See Flowers, "Refusal to Forgive."
26 See Jennings, "Anger Is the Engine."
27 "Hope Is a Discipline," Toward Freedom, 17 September 2020, https://toward freedom.org/story/archives/activism/hope-is-a-discipline/.
28 Oliver, "I Worried," 59.

Section D

1 Binyam, "You Pose a Problem."
2 Seligman, *The Hope Circuit*, 370.
3 Ibid., 376.

4 Milton, *Paradise Lost*, 2.

5 "Bayo Akomolafe: The Times Are Urgent." British author Pico Iyer, in *The Art of Stillness*, also advocates for "the urgency of slowing down." Tippett, "Pico Iyer."

6 Chödrön, *When Things Fall Apart*, 2.

7 Seligman, *The Hope Circuit*, 374.

8 Wallace tells this parable during a commencement speech in 2005 at Kenyon College; this speech is the first draft of what would later become a book titled *This Is Water: Some Thoughts, Delivered on a Significant Occasion, about Living a Compassionate Life* (2009). Wallace, "This Is Water."

9 Ibid.

10 Ravenscraft, "The Science of Inspiration."

11 Quoted by Popova, "The Handle on the Door to a New World."

12 "'Guerrilla Warfare' by Che Guevara."

13 See Meyer and Land, "Threshold Concepts and Troublesome Knowledge."

14 Gardner, "Ava DuVernay Talks Linda Fairstein with Oprah Winfrey."

15 Lorde, "The Master's Tools," 2.

16 Ibid.

17 Binyam, "You Pose a Problem."

18 Haraway, *Staying with the Trouble*, 1.

19 Simon, "Lessons from James Baldwin on Betrayal and Hope."

20 Stanton, *Finding Nemo*.

21 Battiste, *Decolonizing Education*, 100.

22 Ibid., 104.

23 Ibid., 105.

24 Milton, *Paradise Lost*, 12.

25 Tippett, "Foundations 1: Seeing the Generative Story of Our Time."

26 Winfrey, "The Powerful Lesson Maya Angelou Taught Oprah."

27 The Daily Dish, "Rainer Maria Rilke, Letters to a Young Poet," *The Atlantic*, 13 June 2007, https://www.theatlantic.com/daily-dish/archive/2007/06/quote-for-the-day/227690/.

28 Tippett, "Living the Questions."

29 hooks, *All About Love*, 215.

30 Joy Mighty, interview with author, 2022.

31 See Shor, *When Students Have Power*, 3.

Chapter Two

1 "Audre Lorde," Inspirational Quotes website, accessed January 2023, https://inspiration.rightattitudes.com/authors/audre-lorde/.
2 Binyam, "You Pose a Problem."
3 The bibliography on this website provides a wonderful variety of sources and topics. See MacInnis, "Impostor Syndrome as a Diversity, Equity and Inclusion Issue."
4 This phrase is borrowed from Brené Brown's work on shame, especially in the *Dare to Lead* podcast series she leads. She uses this concept to talk about how organizations "have a shame problem" that is pernicious and negatively affects workplace cultures. See "Dare to Lead" on Brené Brown's website, https://brenebrown.com/podcast-show/dare-to-lead/.
5 Canadian philosopher Shannon Dea: "We often refer to individual colleagues who are good-natured and pleasant as 'collegial.' Hence, some people misunderstand collegial governance likewise to connote governance characterized by 'good manners' and 'cooperativeness.'" Instead, Dea asserts that collegial governance represents the "collegium charged with the academic governance of universities." Dea, "Two Misconceptions about 'Collegial Governance.'"
6 Wong, "Freudenfreude Might Be Just What Your Friendships Are Missing."
7 Jennings, "Anger Is the Engine."
8 Palmer, *The Courage to Teach*, 207.
9 Ibid., 19.
10 Ibid., 18.
11 Ibid., 206.
12 Dickson, Murray, and Riddell, *Shakespeare's Guide to Hope*, 155.
13 Gravestock, "Does Teaching Matter?," ii.
14 Many evaluation committees – ECs – are decentralized or multi-stepped, which means they go through the department, then the division, and then the institutional review processes.
15 The evaluation processes for tenure and promotion share fundamental principles. Gravestock notes, "In general, the scope of Canadian tenure policies is quite similar in that they all tend to address the same sorts of information: tenure criteria, standards of performance, mechanisms for assessment, forms of evidence, committee structures and decision-making processes, and timelines or the tenure clock (including probationary periods)." Gravestock, "Does Teaching Matter?," 216.

16 Palmer, *The Courage to Teach*, 13.
17 "Knowledge Synthesis Grant," SSHRC, February 2015, https://www.sshrc-crsh.gc.ca/funding-financement/programs-programmes/ksg_learning-ssc_apprentissage-eng.aspx.

Chapter Three

1 Popova, "Bertrand Russell on the Secret of Happiness."
2 Dickson, Murray, and Riddell, *Shakespeare's Guide to Hope*, 11.
3 Perdomo, "Human Flourishing."
4 The essence of the word refers to the "condition of human flourishing or of living well." Duignan, "Eudaimonia."
5 "For Aristotle, *eudaimonia* is the highest human good, the only human good that is desirable for its own sake (as an end in itself) rather than for the sake of something else (as a means toward some other end)." Duignan, "Eudaimonia."
6 See Meyer and Land, "Threshold Concepts and Troublesome Knowledge."
7 Wallace, "This Is Water."
8 Akomolafe, "Making Sanctuary."
9 See Meyer and Land, "Threshold Concepts and Troublesome Knowledge."
10 Akomolafe, "What Do You Do When There Is No Hope?"
11 Operationalization is the process of turning abstract concepts into measurable observations. Researchers identify broad features with corresponding variables that represent some aspect of the otherwise abstract concept (learning); then they design an instrument to measure and evaluate. See Lee et al., "Operationalizing and Monitoring Student Support."
12 Vincent, *Beyond Measure*, 5.
13 See, for example, Farr, "Arbitration Decision on Student Evaluations."
14 Ling Lee, "What to Do with Student Evaluations of Teaching?"
15 The NCAA is a non-profit organization overseeing student athletics in about 1,100 institutions in the United States, Canada, and Puerto Rico.
16 Quoted by Brutlag Hosick, "NCAA Task Force."
17 Quoted by Rosales and Walker, "The Racist Beginnings of Standardized Testing."
18 As the authors of the Boyer 2030 Commission write, "Excellence and equity are inextricably entwined, such that excellence without equity (privilege reproducing power) is not true excellence, and equity (mere access) without

excellence is unfulfilled promise." "The Equity-Excellence Imperative: A 2030 Blueprint for Undergraduate Education at U.S. Research Universities," Association for Undergraduate Research Universities, 2022, https://wac.colostate. edu/docs/books/boyer2030/report.pdf.

19 A quotation from Indigenous studies and education professor Candace Brunette-Debassige in "Questioning Colonialism in University Administration."

20 Muller, *The Tyranny of Metrics*, 16.

21 This paradox is named after psychologist and meteorologist Lewis Fry Richardson. Tippett, "The Pause."

22 Bridle, *Ways of Being*, 102.

23 Shelley, *Prometheus Unbound*, 153.

24 Bridle, *Ways of Being*, 101.

25 Dweck, *Mindset*, 11

26 Jack and Sathy, "It's Time to Cancel the Word 'Rigor.'"

27 Dweck, *Mindset*, 12.

28 This was from her Maple League Hosts session on ungrading. Murray, "Beyond Measure."

29 brown, "2012, and scene."

30 See Arum and Roksa, *Academically Adrift*.

31 Shakespeare, "History of Henry V."

32 Smith, *This Is Shakespeare*, 4.

33 Dewey, "Creative Democracy."

34 Quoted by Popova, "The Magic of Moss."

35 Foucault, *The History of Sexuality*, 8.

36 DeRosa, "Keynote."

37 Popova, "Bertrand Russell on the Secret of Happiness."

Chapter Four

1 Akomolafe, "What Do You Do When There Is No Hope?"

2 Dickson, Murray, and Riddell, *Shakespeare's Guide to Hope*, 10–11.

3 Ibid.

4 Human flourishing is first introduced by Aristotle in *Nicomachean Ethics*, who defines it simply as "the way we are *supposed to be* as human beings." Perdomo, "Human Flourishing."

5 Akomolafe, "What Do You Do When There Is No Hope?"

6 Particle physicist and cosmologist Lawrence Krauss, in his book *Every Atom*

in Your Body Comes from a Star, explains, "So, most of the atoms that now make up your body were created inside stars! The atoms in your left hand might have come from a different star from those in your right hand. You are really a child of the stars." Quoted by Popova, "Scientists and Philosophers Answer Kids' Most Pressing Questions."

7 Kuhn, *The Structure of Scientific Revolutions*, 91.

8 Great starting points are theoretical readings like hooks, *Teaching Community*, or Giroux, *Take Back Higher Education*. More hands-on guides that help faculty and staff anchor key concepts include Moore, *Key Practices for Fostering Engaged Learning*, or Namaste and Sturgill, eds, *Mind the Gap*. An important intervention in STEM is Bunnell, Jaswal, and Lyster, *Being Human in STEM*. I recommend anything by Mays Imad, including "Pedagogy of Healing," a piece on bearing witness to trauma and resilience, and "Transcending Adversity: Trauma-Informed Educational Development."

9 The session is described in the following way: "One particular telling of the story of climate chaos is that we are collectively beyond hope: we've gone over the tipping point, we've burst through the membranes, we've passed under the sign that hangs over Dante Alighieri's hell ('abandon all hope, all ye who enter here'). It's red alert from here on out." Akomolafe, "What Do You Do When There Is No Hope?"

10 A wonderful primer is Hogan and Sathy, *Inclusive Teaching*. I am a fan of Tia Brown McNair and her book *From Equity Talk to Equity Walk*.

11 See Battiste, *Decolonizing Education*.

12 A foundational understanding of high-impact practices is Kuh's *High-Impact Practices*. See also Riddell and McLennan, "Students as Partners."

13 Herrington, Reeves, and Oliver are best known for their work on the principles of authentic learning. See "Authentic Learning Environments" and also "Immersive Learning Technologies." I have also written on authentic learning via the humanities: Riddell, "Putting Authentic Learning on Trial."

14 One of the most generous thinkers and scholars in higher education work is Peter Felten, and his book with Leo M. Lambert, *Relationship-Rich Education*, is a must read.

15 One of my favourite voices in values-based academic leadership is Beronda L. Montgomery. See her article "Academic Leadership"; read her book, *Lessons from Plants*; or listen to her being interviewed by Alan Alda on the *Science Clear+Vivid* podcast (2023): https://podcasts.apple.com/us/podcast/beronda-montgomery-lessons-from-plants/id1535702219?i=1000526686859.

16 Wright, *The Hidden Habits of Genius*, 3.

17 This runs counter to John Dewey's notion of creative democracy where there is no monolithic notion of democracy that is outside of us. See Riddell, "Can Shakespeare Teach Us to Be Better Citizens?"

18 Quoted by Nordquist, "What Is Sprezzatura?"

19 Research on the science of expertise puts an emphasis on effort over talent. "Expert performers" (people who are the best in their field and have reached levels of high performance) benefit from what Ericsson and Pool call "deliberate practice." In their book, they argue that "learning isn't a way of reaching one's potential but rather a way of developing it." Ericsson and Pool, *Peak*, xx.

20 I feel the need to clarify that my references to Susie and Heather are fallacious since both these academics are institutionally and nationally recognized as award-winning educational leaders who also happen to be experts in their disciplinary fields. Thankfully, Heather taught me the difference between causation and correlation.

21 The lawsuit at Toronto Metropolitan University (Ryerson, at the time) was one of the first of many challenges in the Canadian PSE sector: "[the] arbitrator William Kaplan stated in his ruling that expert evidence presented by the faculty association 'establishes, with little ambiguity, that a key tool in assessing teaching effectiveness is flawed.'" Farr, "Arbitration Decision on Student Evaluations."

22 See, for example, Riddell, Stoddard, and Gadoury-Sansfaçon, "Building Institutional Capacities."

23 Smith, *This Is Shakespeare*, 7.

24 "Compared to women, male instructors are perceived as more accurate in their teaching, more educated, less sexist, more enthusiastic, competent, organized, easier to understand, prompt in providing feedback, and they are less penalized for being tough graders, according to the study. In studies involving identical online course designs involving a hypothetical male or female instructor, students rate the male instructor more highly than the female one." Flaherty, "The Skinny on Teaching Evals and Bias."

25 Palmer, *The Courage to Teach*, 92.

26 Ibid., 12.

27 Critical reflection is a skill that can be learned through practice and feedback. See Dewey, *How We Think*.

28 Critical reflective practice is a process of "meaning making" that links past practice with present context in order to harness future-facing goals. If there

252 | Notes to pages 127–32

is no room for reflective practice, actions remain unconnected and experience alone might cause us to "reinforce stereotypes … offer simplistic solutions to complex problems and generalize inaccurately based on limited data." Engaging in critical reflection helps us "articulate questions, confront bias, examine causality, contrast theory with practice and identify systemic issues all of which helps foster critical evaluation and knowledge transfer." Ash and Clayton, "Generating, Deepening, and Documenting Learning," 27.

29 Palmer, *The Courage to Teach*, 2.

30 Ibid., 12.

31 This is a question my friend and co-author Lisa Dickson asks all the time, in classrooms and in workshops, conferences and writing retreats. She is also an artist and will spend time asking you questions about what you love and drawing a map of the things that bring joy. She made me a map of the things that I love and I framed it and refer to it often, especially when I need to make a decision about where I want to spend my energy.

32 I am informed here by the emerging work done by Claire Hamshire and her research team on the difference between belonging and mattering presented in pre-publication form at the Annual ISSOTL (International Society for the Scholarship of Teaching and Learning) Conference in Kelowna, BC, 3 November 2022.

33 Teaching and learning communities are diverse (institutional, regional, national, international) and take many forms (centres, institutes, associations, communities of practice, research clusters). Members of the communities also play various roles, as innovative educators, SOTL researchers, educational developers, instructional designers, student leaders: what they share in common, however, is these folks are often working in grassroots spaces with few resources and little acknowledgment.

34 Quoted by Popova, "The Overview Effect and the Psychology of Cosmic Awe."

35 In 1837, Quaker philosopher Richard Humphreys wanted to "create an institution for formerly enslaved African Americans to learn basic skills like reading, writing and math so they could become equipped for the world that they were entering as free people. The Institute eventually became Cheyney University of Pennsylvania, the first HBCU." More HBCUs were established after the abolishment of slavery: "HBCUs are golden products of the African diaspora and symbols of the strength and resilience of Black people. Their

rich culture and academic rigor have allowed them to persevere despite continued obstacles." Edmonson, "A Brief History."

36 Hemphill, "Hope, Questioning, and Getting Lost with Bayo Akomolafe."

Chapter Five

1 Jenkins, *Wonder Woman.*

2 Shakespeare, *Twelfth Night, or What You Will.*

3 Brown, "The Power of Vulnerability."

4 Quoted by Slater, "Generativity versus Stagnation," 57.

5 See, for example, Ten Thousand Coffees, an online mentorship program that seeks to scale up mentorship (https://www.tenthousandcoffees.com/solutions/mentorship-program) or Chronus, a mentorship software program (https://chronus.com)

6 Homer, *The Odyssey*, Book II, lines 223–59.

7 Ibid., lines 260–95.

8 Ibid., lines 299–300.

9 Moore and Vandermaas-Peeler, "A Constellation Model for Transformative and Inclusive Mentoring."

10 "The Science of Effective Mentorships in STEM," National Library of Medicine, accessed January 2023, https://www.ncbi.nlm.nih.gov/books/NBK 552775/.

11 Jeff Hennessy, interview with author, 2022.

12 Ibarra and Scoular, "The Leader as Coach."

13 hooks, *Teaching Community*, 127, 131.

14 A number of interviewees shared stories of parents who were academics and therefore crucial mentors for helping to sign-post and way-find university value and cultural capital for their academically focused children.

15 Hoffman, Casnocha, and Yeh, "Your Company Is Not a Family."

16 Montgomery, "My Most Memorable Mentors? Plants."

17 Palmer, *The Courage to Teach*, 17.

18 Dickson, Murray, and Riddell, *Shakespeare's Guide to Hope*, 48–9.

19 Jenkins, *Wonder Woman.*

20 Solnit, "Hope Is an Embrace of the Unknown."

21 Bridle, *Ways of Being*, 280.

22 Gordon, "How Reverse Mentorship Can Create Better Leaders."

23 Galenson, *Old Masters and Young Geniuses*, summary.

24 Moore and Vandermaas-Peeler, "A Constellation Model."

25 Palmer, *The Courage to Teach*, 72.

26 Akomolafe, "What Do You Do When There Is No Hope?"

Chapter Six

1 "Toni Morrison Quotes on Love and Dreams," Uganda Empya, accessed March 2023, https://www.ugandaempya.com/toni-morrison-quotes/.

2 Battiste, *Decolonizing Education*, 104.

3 This thinking about wyrd sisters is indebted to the countless hours I have spent rumbling wyrd-ness with the brilliant and original Lisa Dickson and Shannon Murray, and this belongs to a larger set of conversations on wyrd thinking that we are developing for another project.

4 My co-authors Lisa Dickson and Shannon Murray and I explore the power of wyrd sisters in *Shakespeare's Guide to Hope*.

5 Dickson, "Conjuring Witches and Wonder."

6 Dickson, "Education: The Wonder Engine."

7 Caputo, *More Radical Hermeneutics*, 24.

8 Chödrön, *Living Beautifully*, 11.

9 Sivers, "How to Start a Movement."

10 Clear, "3-2-1: On Systems vs. Goals."

11 Brown, "Armored versus Daring Leadership."

12 All the following italicized excerpts are from Brown, "Armored versus Daring Leadership."

13 Feltman, *The Thin Book of Trust*, 7

14 Brown, "Armored versus Daring Leadership."

15 Brach, "Inviting Mara to Tea."

16 "'Shame dies when stories are told in safe spaces' – Ann Voskamp," *Crossing Bridges Together* blog, 18 June 2020, https://crossingbridgestogether.com/blog/f/shame-dies-when-stories-are-told-in-safe-spaces—ann-voskamp.

17 Brown, "Armored Versus Daring Leadership."

18 "Toni Morrison Quotes."

19 Emezi, "This Letter Isn't for You."

Chapter Seven

1 Shakespeare, *A Midsummer Night's Dream*.

2 The terminology around higher education as an engine of democracy is inspired by discussions from Jennifer Simpson's book *Longing for Justice*, 48–55.

3 Gannon, *Radical Hope*, 19.
4 Personal correspondence, 1 February 2023. "The Paradigm Project: A Brief Overview" © David Scobey, director, *Bringing Theory to Practice* (Revised, June 2022).
5 See, for example, Allen, "For Billion-Dollar COVID Vaccines."
6 Paul Davidson, interview with author, 23 August 2022.
7 Jeffrey Buller, interview with author, 7 December 2022.
8 See, for example, *Flubber* with Robin Williams. Or the *Ghostbusters* franchise (all of them). Or Eddie Murphy's Sherman Klump in *The Nutty Professor*. Or Jeff Goldblum's character Malcolm in the *Jurassic Park* franchise. Or Indiana Jones. The depictions are mostly men who lack social skills, basic empathy, and an understanding of ethics; they are almost always outsiders in the institutional structures despite (or because of) their genius. Moreover, their research and application of theory into practice has the potential to make the world better, safer, more humane – if they could just get out of their own ways. Which they don't, and they must rely on supporting characters – often women – to show them their deep responsibilities to humanity.
9 Jeffrey Buller, interview with author, 7 December 2022.
10 See "Rise of Disinformation a Symptom of 'Global Diseases' Undermining Public Trust: Bachelet," *United Nations*, 28 June 2022, https://news.un.org/en/story/2022/06/1121572.
11 See Gawande, "The Mistrust of Science."
12 See H. Bottemanne, "Théories du complot."
13 See Cook, "The Scientific Guide to Global Warming Skepticism."
14 See, for example, the foundational *Anti-intellectualism in American Life* by Paul Hofstadter and the work that has responded to and built upon the premise that "widespread attitudes, with political behaviour, with middle-brow and low-brow responses" "gravely inhibit or impoverish intellectual and cultural life" (9). For the expressions of anti-intellectualism on the response to the COVID-19 pandemic, see Merkley and Loewen, "Anti-intellectualism and the Mass Public's Response."
15 In multiple interviews with people in the US, UK, and Australia, this fight has already been lost. Ali Muhammad, Ishamuddin Mustapha, Sharina Osman, and Umar Hassan argue "that the social responsibility of universities differs in nature from corporate social responsibility since the nature of institutional operations and objectives are inherently different from business organizations." Muhammad et al., "University Social Responsibility," 124931. For a

comprehensive overview of this topic, see Lawrence, *Reconfiguring Universities*; Benner and Holmqvist, eds, *Universities under Neoliberalism*; Busch, *Knowledge for Sale*.

16 "The ranking of universities is mainly dependent on the quality of workforce distributions and numbers of students enrolled and not the practical implications of scholarly research that encourages social engagement and sustainability issues." Muhammad et al., "University Social Responsibility," 124931. For a more fulsome discussion, see Downing, Loock, and Gravett, *The Impact of Higher Education Ranking Systems*; Hazelkorn, *Rankings and the Reshaping of Higher Education*. For an overview of the origins and effects of rankings in the US, see Deresiewicz, *Excellent Sheep*.

17 A wonderful place to start is the reflection by David Scobey, "The Paradigm Project: A Brief Overview," *Bringing Theory to Practice*, February 2022, https://bttop.org/wp-content/uploads/2022/02/Paradigm-Project-Overview.pdf.

18 Johnson, *Where Good Ideas Come From*, 163.

19 Meisenzahl, "Starting in a Garage Is Crucial."

20 Brandt, "Birth of a Salesman."

21 "Symposium," Wikipedia, accessed February 2023, https://en.wikipedia.org/wiki/Symposium.

22 I borrow this phrase from Parker, *The Art of Gathering*.

23 Sun, Livan, Ma, and Latora, "Interdisciplinary Researchers," 263.

24 See Lloyd, "Leading across Boundaries."

25 For the decline in public trust, see Knott, "Gen Z's Distrust in Higher Ed." For the decline in enrollment, see Strauss, "Some See Liberal Arts Education." "Some academic fields, however, have sustained enrollment declines for years, including the broad category that encompasses four-year liberal arts and sciences/general studies and humanities programs. It saw a 4.8 percent decline over that period, which followed a 2.7 percent decline from fall 2020 to fall 2021 and a 6.4 percent drop from fall 2019 to fall 2020." For a definition on the value of the liberal arts, see Roth, *Beyond the University*.

26 This is a classic horror scenario drawn from the 1979 horror film *When a Stranger Calls* but since reproduced in many films, including *Scream* (1996). "The Calls Are Coming from Inside the House," TV Tropes, accessed February 2023, https://tvtropes.org/pmwiki/pmwiki.php/Main/TheCallsAreComingFromInsideTheHouse.

27 Starr, "Opening Plenary."

28 Palmer, *The Courage to Teach*, 38.

29 Brown, "Imposter Syndrome."

30 Dickson, "'Bless Thy Sweet Eyes, They Bleed,'" in *Shakespeare's Guide to Hope*, 45.

31 See, for example, Badley, "Post-Academic Writing."

32 "The World's Worst Writing," *The Guardian*, 24 December 1999, https://www.theguardian.com/books/1999/dec/24/news.

33 Quoted in Birkenstein, "Reconsiderations: We Got the Wrong Gal," 269.

34 Nussbaum, "The Professor of Parody."

35 I am struck by Kelly Dombroski's observation that "while the common metaphors we might use for a good book are ones of swords and slicing ('cutting edge scholarship,' or 'piercing critique') ... what is soul-refreshing about Puig de la Bellacasa's work [is that] it seeks not to merely cut, analyse and deconstruct, but to carefully acknowledge, question, and think-with, in order to enable us to dissent within those traditions of scholarship and activism we call home." Dombroski, "Thinking With, Dissenting Within," 263. See also Puig de la Bellacasa, *Matters of Care*.

36 As Karen Barad notes, "phenomena do not occur at some particular moment in time; phenomena are specific ongoing reconfigurings of spacetimemattering." Barad, *Meeting the Universe Halfway*, 182.

37 Juelskjaer and Schwennesen, "Intra-Active Entanglements," 13.

38 Latour, "Why Has Critique Run Out of Steam?," 225.

39 This notion of mattering is influenced by Maria Puig de la Bellacasa's work in care, which deploys "assemblage thinking" to theorize care as "'something we can do as thinkers and knowledge creators,' in that what we care for as researchers has material consequences, or 'contributes to mattering the world.'" Puig de la Bellacasa, *Matters of Care*, 41, quoted in Dombroski, "Thinking With, Dissenting Within."

Chapter 8

1 Lorde, "Poetry Is Not a Luxury."

2 In *Governance as Leadership*, Richard P. Chait, William P. Ryan, and Barbara E. Taylor lament that while there is a proliferation of research on leadership, very few people talk about governance.

3 Shakespeare, *The Tragedy of King Lear*.

4 Michael Childs, interview with author, 5 December 2022.

5 brown, "We Are in a Time of New Suns."

6 David Scobey, sharing a draft of an unpublished manuscript with the author in personal correspondence, 1 February 2023. The article is titled "The Paradigm Project: A Call for Radical Renewal of Higher Education." Forthcoming, 2023, in *Change: The Magazine of Higher Learning*.

7 Paul, "University Governance and Institutional Culture," 72–3.

8 Wallace, "This Is Water."

9 This refrain, which pops up throughout the book, is drawn from Ira Shor's work in *Empowering Education*.

10 I am inspired by this term, "academic enterprise," from the work and guidance of American law scholar and former university president Frederick Lawrence. Frederick Lawrence, sharing an unpublished lecture with the author in personal correspondence ("Academic Freedom: For Whom and For What?" Jules LaPidus Lecture, Council of Graduate Schools Annual Meeting, New Orleans, 4 December 2021).

11 Sinek, "Developing an Infinite Mindset."

12 Ibid.

13 Deloitte's Center for Higher Education Excellence, *Pathways to the University Presidency*, 16.

14 This notion of sixteenth-century dual bodies is remarkably contemporary: when Elizabeth II died in 2022, "the queen is dead, long live the king" enacted the unbroken line of royal power (which explains why Charles III did not need to wait for a coronation ceremony to be named king).

15 "The King's Two Bodies: A Study in Medieval Political Theology," Library of Social Science, accessed February 2023, https://www.libraryofsocialscience. com/ideologies/resources/kantorowicz-the-kings-two-bodies/.

16 Rowe and Ashkanasy, "The Environment for Canadian Universities Is Changing." This framework is informed by Bob Tricker's *Corporate Governance*. See also Skolnik and Jones, "Governing Boards in Canadian Universities"; Jones, Shanahan, and Goyan, "University Governance"; Jones, Shanahan, and Goyan, "The Academic Senate."

17 See the "How Do We Mentor" chapter for the connection between generativity and generosity.

18 For a Canadian reflection on university president transitions, see Tamburri, "Why Grooming the Next Line."

19 Foy, "Governance Professionals Foster Board Independence and Effectiveness."

20 Deloitte's Center for Higher Education Excellence, *Pathways to the University Presidency*, 6.

21 This data is indebted to a talk provost and musicologist Jeff Hennessy gave at a panel at the University of Lethbridge Faculty Association's Collegial Governance Roundtable, Online, 24 January 2023, and shared with the author in personal correspondence, 1 February 2023.

22 This is a refresher from the "How Do We Mentor" chapter, where we defined the term "generativity" via Erikson's theory of psychosocial development in the 1950s. "Generativity," Wikipedia, accessed July 2023, https://en.wikipedia.org/wiki/Generativity.

23 Sinek, "Developing an Infinite Mindset."

24 The most read article on *EdSurge* in 2022 was Kevin R. McClure's "Higher Ed, We've Got a Morale Problem – And a Free T-Shirt Won't Fix It."

25 Ibid.

26 See Soll, "Healing the Body Politic."

27 See, for example, Canadian governance strategist Cheryl Foy's *An Introduction to University Governance*.

28 Sidney, "The Defence of Poesy."

29 Jeff Hennessy, interview with author, 2023.

30 A legislating system that has two chambers, houses, or assemblies; they work separately yet must agree on new policies and systems. Both must be involved in making legislation that constitutes the governance.

31 There are variations to this structure, including senate chaired by the provost, chaired by a faculty member, or chaired by the secretary general. Having attended multiple senates, the level of formality, the adherence to Robert's Rules of Order, and the tone and tenor of collegial discourse differs wildly. And in some cases (especially out west) the senate is called the general faculties council. Many universities also have a faculty council, which has no governing authority, and yet it's a great forum for discussing big questions.

32 Jeffrey Buller, interview with the author, 7 December 2022.

33 Shakespeare, *The Tragedy of King Lear*.

34 Popova, "Audre Lorde on Poetry as an Instrument of Change."

Chapter Nine

1 brown, "2012, and scene."

2 Which "exists when substantial and recurring financial deficits threaten the

survival of the institution as a whole." "Financial Exigency and Lay-Offs," CAUT, November 2009, https://www.caut.ca/about-us/caut-policy/lists/caut-policy-statements/policy-statement-on-financial-exigency-and-lay-offs.

3 Shakespeare, *The Tragedy of Romeo and Juliet.*

4 Filed under things I didn't learn in graduate school, the phrase "C-suite executive" is a "widely-used vernacular describing the upper echelons of a corporation's senior executives and managers. C-suite gets its name from the titles of top senior executives, which tend to start with the letter C, for 'chief,' as in chief executive officer (CEO), chief financial officer (CFO), chief operating officer (COO), and chief information officer (CIO)." When I first encountered the term, I thought it denoted mediocre middle management, since an A in a pedagogical context is the best and a C would be distinctly average. Bloomenthal, "What Is the C Suite?"

5 In Brené Brown's research, a culture of scarcity creates shame, which manifests in harmful behaviours.

6 Ann Masten, a psychologist at the University of Minnesota, defines surge capacity as a collection of adaptive systems – mental and physical – that humans draw on for short-term survival in acutely stressful situations, such as natural disasters. Masten: "When it's depleted, it has to be renewed. But what happens when you struggle to renew it because the emergency phase has now become chronic?" Haelle, "Your 'Surge Capacity' Is Depleted."

7 Shariatmadari, "A Year of 'Permacrisis.'"

8 Moscrop, "A Year-End Reflection."

9 "Bayo Akomolafe: The Times Are Urgent."

10 The Daily Dish, "Rainer Maria Rilke, Letters to a Young Poet," *The Atlantic,* 13 June 2007, https://www.theatlantic.com/daily-dish/archive/2007/06/quote-for-the-day/227690/.

11 It is worth noting that I have benefitted tremendously from a decade of guidance from an exceptional VP finance, Isabelle Goyette, who takes complex reports and breaks them down methodically, takes the time to explain clearly, and delivers a master class on how to understand university finances. She also provides multiple pathways, options, and scenarios to help board members make informed decisions based on the university's vision and strategic plan.

12 ROI stands for return on investment. KPI is shorthand for key performance indicators, which are used as a dashboard, financial or otherwise, to assess impact. EBIT, "Earnings Before Interest and Taxes, and also referred to as the

operating income, is an equation that measures the operating profits of a particular company. It does so by subtracting the operating expenses and cost of goods that were sold from the total revenue of the company." "Understanding EBIT," Profit, accessed March 2023, https://www.profit.co/blog/kpis-library/finance/understanding-ebit/.

13 "The person who gives the guarantee is called the 'surety'; the person in respect of whose default the guarantee is given is called the 'principal debtor,' and the person to whom the guarantee is given is called the 'creditor.' A guarantee may be either oral or written." Kenton, "Surety."

14 CAUBO's *University Manager* magazine is a great resource and helps us look at financial factors across the country: https://www.caubo.ca/knowledge-centre/university-manager/.

15 When asked about the ideal features for Hope University, many participants in focus groups repeatedly identified free tuition as one of the top features.

16 See, for example, Lewitt, "Teachers Deserve No More."

17 Quoted by Baker, July 2019.

18 brown, "2012, and scene."

Chapter Ten

1 "Thomas Kuhn," *Stanford Encyclopedia of Philosophy*, 31 October 2018, https://plato.stanford.edu/entries/thomas-kuhn/.

2 Kuhn, *The Structure of Scientific Revolutions*, 90.

3 Quoted in ibid., 150.

4 It is important here to recognize my own privilege as a cis-gendered, able-bodied, hetero, white, middle-aged settler with a full professorship. I benefit from systems and structures in real, material, and symbolic ways. I also sought out leaders known for their generosity and vision. This is not a representative sample. It was never intended to be. My interviewees are on the edges of someone else's centre, and are the centre of someone else's edges. What this project seeks to do is build and illuminate, look for the sparks between ways of knowing where we locate the tools necessary to build a new paradigm.

5 Quoted in Benjamin, "But ... There Are New Suns!" 103.

6 Ibid.

7 Christensen and Bower, "Disruptive Technologies."

8 Christensen, "Disruptive Innovation."

9 This insight is attributed to American business analyst and author Oren Harari when he refers to Edison's invention of the electric lightbulb. Quoted in Easton, "Electric Light Did Not Come."

10 Ibid.

11 See, for example, Braxton, "Lessons Learned."

12 This is a valuable strategy if we are building and illuminating an idea by creating a cluster of concepts and exploring where they converge to spark insights. This is a dangerous strategy if we are drawing a straight line between concepts that flattens what is otherwise complex and nuanced with a warning or exhortation.

13 Alessandro Volta developed the first electrical battery in 1799 and paved the way for new forms of illumination.

14 I am indebted to Dr Ginger Grant, dean of research at Humber College, for this insight about candle rebranding in an interview we had about this book project in November 2022.

15 Levin, "Introduction," xxxix.

16 See, for example, Ziegler, "Nokia CEO Stephen Elop."

17 See, for example, Caprino, "The 'Glass Cliff' Phenomenon."

18 King, "Six Principles of Nonviolence Handout."

19 "The King Philosophy – Nonviolence 365," the King Center, accessed March 2023, https://thekingcenter.org/about-tkc/the-king-philosophy/.

20 What language we use – and what stories we choose to tell – is often intuitive, invisible, automatic. American psychologist Steven Pinker, in *The Language Instinct*, argues that "language is a human instinct, wired into our brains by evolution like web-spinning in spiders or sonar in bats." Pinker, *The Language Instinct*, abstract.

21 Scobey, "The Gifts of Liberal Education."

22 The trivium and the quadrivium are the basis of a liberal education dating back to late Roman antiquity and were foundational to medieval and early modern education.

23 For Canadian communication theorist Marshall McLuhan, the "medium is the message." McLuhan, *Understanding Media*, ix.

24 I discuss this at length in the pandemic prologue via Oxford Shakespeare professor Emma Smith.

25 Oliver, *Evidence*, 62.

26 There are also devices for wordplay and puns, substitutions, overstatements and understatements, and semantic inversions.

27 I am indebted to book coach Bassam Chiblak for rumbling on rhetoric with me. From our first discussions of this book, he told me to write like an orator and harness all the rhetorical devices that I love (and which are essential to my disciplinary training in the early modern literary period).

28 Booth, "Confessions of an Aging, Hypocritical Ex-Missionary."

29 Lyon, "Lorgia García-Peña (Q&A)."

30 This is widely attributed to Margaret Meade and circulates in various books, talks, and websites, including "Never Doubt That a Small Group of Thoughtful Committed Citizens Can Change the World: Indeed It's the Only Thing That Ever Has. Margaret Meade," National Museum of American History, accessed March 2023, https://americanhistory.si.edu/collections/search/object/nmah_1285394.

31 Quoted by Popova, "No Place for Self-Pity."

Bibliography

Ahmed, Sara. *Living a Feminist Life*. Durham: Duke University Press, 2017.

Akomolafe, Bayo. "Making Sanctuary: Hope, Companionship, Race and Emergence in the Anthropocene." Bayo Akomolafe. 15 March 2019. https://www.bay oakomolafe.net/post/making-sanctuary-hope-companionship-race-and-emerg ence-in-the-anthropocene.

— "What Do You Do When There Is No Hope? A Talk with Bayo Akomolafe & Toni Spencer." YouTube. 1 June 2020. https://www.youtube.com/watch?v=JI xymPgLk8s.

Allen, Arthur. "For Billion-Dollar COVID Vaccines, Basic Government-Funded Science Laid the Groundwork." *Scientific American*, 18 November 2020. https://www.scientificamerican.com/article/for-billion-dollar-COVID-vaccines-basic-government-funded-science-laid-the-groundwork/.

Andrew, Emily (@eandreweditor). "Door's Open, Authors!" Twitter. 19 April 2022, 9:10 a.m. https://twitter.com/eandreweditor/status/1516403927159390210.

Arum, Richard, and Josipa Roksa. *Academically Adrift*. Chicago: University of Chicago Press, 2011.

Ash, Sarah L., and Patti H. Clayton. "Generating, Deepening, and Documenting Learning: The Power of Critical Reflection in Applied Learning." *Journal of Applied Learning in Higher Education* 1, no. 1 (2009): 25–48.

Badley, Graham Francis. "Post-Academic Writing: Human Writing for Human Readers." *Qualitative Inquiry* 25, no. 2 (2017): 180–91.

Baker, Peter. July 2019, "commented on," Abbas Nawar Al-Musawi. "What Are the Reasons for Paying Attention to Environmental Costs?" ResearchGate. 2 July 2019. https://www.researchgate.net/post/What_are_the_reasons_for_paying_ attention_to_environmental_costs.

Barad, Karen. *Meeting the Universe Halfway: Quantum Physics and the Entanglement of Matter and Meaning*. Durham: Duke University Press, 2007.

Battiste, Marie. *Decolonizing Education: Nourishing the Learning Spirit*. Saskatoon: Purich Publishing Limited, 2013.

"Bayo Akomolafe: The Times Are Urgent, Let Us Slow Down." YouTube. 26 April 2019. https://www.youtube.com/watch?v=9qWaWGHNvy0.

Benjamin, Ruha. "But ... There Are New Suns!" *Palimpsest: A Journal on Women, Gender, and the Black International* 6, no. 2 (2017): 103–5.

Benner, Mats, and Mikael Holmqvist, eds. *Universities under Neoliberalism*. New York: Routledge, 2023.

Binyam, Maya. "You Pose a Problem: A Conversation with Sara Ahmed." *The Paris Review*, 14 January 2022. https://www.theparisreview.org/blog/2022/01/14/you-pose-a-problem-a-conversation-with-sara-ahmed/.

Birkenstein, Cathy. "Reconsiderations: We Got the Wrong Gal – Rethinking the 'Bad' Academic Writing of Judith Butler." *College English* 72, no. 3 (2010): 269–83.

Bishundat, Devita, Daviree Velázquez Phillip, and Willie Gore. "Cultivating Critical Hope: The Too Often Forgotten Dimension of Critical Leadership Development." *Special Issue: Integrating Critical Perspectives into Leadership Development* 2018, no. 159 (2018): 94.

Bloomenthal, Andrew. "What Is the C Suite? Meaning and Positions Defined." Investopedia, 25 July 2022. https://www.investopedia.com/terms/c/c-suite.asp.

Booth, Wayne C. "Confessions of an Aging, Hypocritical Ex-Missionary." LDS-Mormon. Accessed March 2023. https://www.lds-mormon.com/booth.shtml/.

Bottemanne, H. "Théories du complot et COVID-19: Comment naissent les croyances complotistes?" *L'Encéphale* 48, no. 5 (October 2022): 571–82.

Brach, Tara. "Inviting Mara to Tea." Tara Brach. 12 June 2012. https://www.tarabrach.com/inviting-mara-to-tea/.

Brandt, Richard L. "Birth of a Salesman." *Wall Street Journal*. 15 October 2011. https://www.wsj.com/articles/SB10001424052970203914304576627102996831200.

Braxton, Sherri. "Lessons Learned: Implementing Digital Badging Strategies." Evolllution, 15 February 2023. https://evolllution.com/programming/credentials/lessons-learned-implementing-digital-badging-strategies/.

Bridle, James. *Ways of Being*. New York: Farrar, Straus and Giroux, 2022.

brown, adrienne maree. "2012, and scene." adrienne maree brown. 31 December 2012. https://adriennemareebrown.net/2012/12/31/2012-and-scene/.

– "We Are in a Time of New Suns." On Being. 23 June 2022. https://onbeing.org/programs/adrienne-maree-brown-we-are-in-a-time-of-new-suns/.

Brown, Brené. "Armored Versus Daring Leadership, Part 1 of 2." Brené Brown. 5 April 2021. https://brenebrown.com/podcast/brene-on-armored-versus-daring-leadership-part-1-of-2/#transcript.

– "Imposter Syndrome." Brené Brown. 11 October 2021. https://brenebrown.com/podcast/imposter-syndrome/.

– "Let's Rumble." Brené Brown. 1 May 2019. https://brenebrown.com/articles/2019/05/01/lets-rumble/.

– "The Power of Vulnerability." TEDx. 23 December 2010. https://www.ted.com/talks/brene_brown_the_power_of_vulnerability.

– "Trust in Emergence: Grounded Theory and My Research Process." Brené Brown. Accessed January 2023. https://brenebrown.com/the-research/.

Brunette-Debassige, Candace. "Questioning Colonialism in University Administration." *University Affairs*. 11 January 2022. https://www.universityaffairs.ca/opinion/in-my-opinion/questioning-colonialism-in-university-administration/.

Brutlag Hosick, Michelle. "NCAA Task Force Backs Removal of Standardized Test Score Requirement." NCAA, 15 October 2021. https://www.ncaa.org/news/2021/10/15/general-ncaa-task-force-backs-removal-of-standardized-test-score-requirement.aspx.

Bunnell, Sarah L., Sheila S. Jaswal, and Megan B. Lyster. *Being Human in STEM: Partnering with Students to Shape Inclusive Practices and Communities*. Oxon: Routledge, 2023.

Busch, Lawrence. *Knowledge for Sale: The Neoliberal Takeover of Higher Education*. Cambridge, MA: MIT Press, 2017.

Caprino, Kathy. "The 'Glass Cliff' Phenomenon That Senior Female Leaders Face Today, and How to Avoid It." *Forbes*, 20 October 2015. https://www.forbes.com/sites/kathycaprino/2015/10/20/the-glass-cliff-phenomenon-that-senior-female-leaders-face-today-and-how-to-avoid-it/.

Caputo, John, D. *More Radical Hermeneutics*. Bloomington: Indiana University Press, 2000.

Chait, Richard P., William P. Ryan, and Barbara E. Taylor. *Governance as Leadership*. Hoboken, NJ: Wiley, 2004.

Chemaly, Soraya. *Rage Becomes Her: The Power of Women's Anger*. New York: Atria Books, 2018.

Chödrön, Pema. *Living Beautifully: With Uncertainty and Change.* Boulder: Shambhala Publications, 2013.

– *When Things Fall Apart: Heart Advice for Difficult Times.* Boulder: Shambhala Publications, 1997.

Chris Gardner. "Ava DuVernay Talks Linda Fairstein with Oprah Winfrey during 'When They See Us' Event." *The Hollywood Reporter*, 10 June 2019. https://www.hollywoodreporter.com/news/general-news/ava-duvernay-oprah-winfrey-talk-linda-fairstein-they-see-us-1217039/.

Christensen, Clayton, and Joseph L. Bower. "Disruptive Technologies: Catching the Wave." *Harvard Business Review*, January 1995. https://hbr.org/1995/01/disruptive-technologies-catching-the-wave.

– "Disruptive Innovation." Clayton Christensen. Accessed March 2023. https://claytonchristensen.com/key-concepts/.

Clear, James. "3-2-1: On Systems vs. Goals, Identity-Based Habits, and the Lessons of Life." James Clear, 2 January 2020. https://jamesclear.com/3-2-1/january-2-2020.

Cook, John. "The Scientific Guide to Global Warming Skepticism." *Skeptical Science*, 8 December 2010. https://skepticalscience.com/The-Scientific-Guide-to-Global-Warming-Skepticism.html.

Cunsolo, Ashlee, and Kiemia Rezagian. "Ecological Grief: The Mental Toll of The Climate Emergency." The Canadian Climate Institute, 10 July 2021. https://climateinstitute.ca/ecological-grief/.

Dalai Lama, and Patrick McDonnell. *Heart to Heart: A Conversation on Love and Hope for Our Precious Planet.* New York: Harper One, 2023.

Damon, William. *The Path to Purpose.* London: Free Press, 2009.

Dea, Shannon. "Two Misconceptions about 'Collegial Governance.'" *University Affairs*, 16 April 2021. https://www.universityaffairs.ca/opinion/dispatches-academic-freedom/two-misconceptions-about-collegial-governance/.

Deloitte's Center for Higher Education Excellence in conjunction with Georgia Tech's Center for 21st Century Universities. *Pathways to the University Presidency: The Future of Higher Education Leadership.* Deloitte University Press, 2017. https://www2.deloitte.com/content/dam/insights/us/articles/3861_Pathways-to-the-university-presidency/DUP_Pathways-to-the-university-presidency.pdf.

Deresiewicz, William. *Excellent Sheep: The Miseducation of the American Elite and the Way to a Meaningful Life.* New York: Free Press, 2014.

DeRosa, Robin. "Keynote." Presentation, POD Annual Conference, online, 18 November 2022.

Devlin McNair, Maria. "1. Why Read Shakespeare?" Shakespeare for All. Accessed February 2023. https://www.himalaya.com/courses/2649672.

Dewey, John. "Creative Democracy – The Task Before Us." Accessed January 2023. https://www.philosophie.uni-muenchen.de/studium/das_fach/warum_phil_ueberhaupt/dewey_creative_democracy.pdf.

– How We Think: A Restatement of the Relation of Reflective Thinking to the Educative Process. Boston: D.C. Health, 1933.

Dickinson, Emily. "'Hope' is the thing with feathers." Poetry Foundation. Accessed January 2023. https://www.poetryfoundation.org/poems/42889/hope-is-the-thing-with-feathers-314.

Dickson, Lisa. "'Bless Thy Sweet Eyes, They Bleed': The Ethics of Pedagogy and My Fear of Lear." In Dickson, Murray, and Riddell, Shakespeare's Guide to Hope, Life, and Learning, 43–54.

– "Education: The Wonder Engine, TEDxUNBC." YouTube. 27 March 2020. https://www.youtube.com/watch?v=sCiGPiMnDo8.

Dickson, Lisa, Shannon Murray, and Jessica Riddell. Shakespeare's Guide to Hope, Life, and Learning. Toronto: University of Toronto Press, 2023.

Dombroski, Kelly. "Thinking With, Dissenting Within: Care-Full Critique for More-Than-Human Worlds." Journal of Cultural Economy 11, no. 3 (2018): 261–4.

Downing, Kevin, Petrus Johannes Loock, and Sarah Gravett. The Impact of Higher Education Ranking Systems on Universities. New York: Routledge, 2021.

Duignan, Brian. "Eudaimonia." Britannica. 27 January 2023. https://www.britannica.com/topic/eudaimonia.

Dweck, Carol. Mindset: The New Psychology of Success. New York: Penguin Random House, 2006.

Easton, Chris. "Electric Light Did Not Come From The Continuous Improvement of Candles." LinkedIn. 19 May 2017. https://www.linkedin.com/pulse/electric-light-did-come-from-continuous-imrovement-candles-easton/.

Edmonson, Jasmine. "A Brief History: The Rise of Historically Black Colleges and Universities." Louisiana State University. Accessed March 2023. https://www.lsu.edu/intlpro/apa/blog_posts/2021/hbcus_a_brief_history.php.

Emezi, Akwaeke. "This Letter Isn't for You: On the Toni Morrison Quote That Changed My Life." Them, 7 August 2019. https://www.them.us/story/toni-morrison.

Ericsson, Anders, and Robert Pool. Peak: Secrets from the New Science of Expertise. New York: HarperCollins, 2016.

Erikson, Erik, and Joan Erikson. "On Generativity and Identity." *Harvard Educational Review* 51, no. 2 (1981): 249–69.

Farr, Moira. "Arbitration Decision on Student Evaluations of Teaching Applauded by Faculty." *University Affairs*, 28 August 2018. https://www.universityaffairs.ca/news/news-article/arbitration-decision-on-student-evaluations-of-teaching-applauded-by-faculty/.

Felten, Peter, and Leo M. Lambert. *Relationship-Rich Education: How Human Connections Drive Success in College*. Baltimore, MD: Johns Hopkins University Press, 2020.

Feltman, Charles. *The Thin Book of Trust: An Essential Primer for Building Trust at Work*. Bend: Thin Book Publishing, 2008.

Flaherty, Colleen. "The Skinny on Teaching Evals and Bias." *Inside Higher Ed.* 17 February 2021. https://www.insidehighered.com/news/2021/02/17/whats-really-going-respect-bias-and-teaching-evals.

Fletcher, Tom. "Let the Dreaming Spires Dream Afresh." *Tortoise Media.* 24 September 2021. https://tomfletcher.global/articles/details/141.

Flowers, Rachel. "Refusal to Forgive: Indigenous Women's Love and Rage." *Decolonization: Indigeneity, Education & Society* 4, no. 2 (2015): 32–49.

Foucault, Michel. *The History of Sexuality, Vol. 2: The Use of Pleasure.* New York: Vintage Books, 1984.

Foy, Cheryl. "Governance Professionals Foster Board Independence and Effectiveness." Strategic Governance, 14 November 2022. https://universitygovernance.ca/governance-professionals-foster-board-independence-and-effectiveness/.

– *An Introduction to University Governance.* Toronto: Irwin Law Inc, 2021.

Freire, Paulo. *Pedagogy of Hope: Reliving the Pedagogy of the Oppressed.* London: Bloomsbury, 1994.

Galenson, David. *Old Masters and Young Geniuses: The Two Life Cycles of Artistic Creativity.* Princeton: Princeton University Press, 2016.

Gannon, Kevin. *Radical Hope: A Teaching Manifesto.* Morgantown: West Virginia University Press, 2020.

Gauld, Tom. "Tom Gauld Stared into the Abyss, and Now They Meet for Regular Chats." *The New Scientist,* 11 May 2022. https://www.newscientist.com/article/2319695-tom-gauld-stared-into-the-abyss-and-now-they-meet-for-regular-chats/.

Gawande, Atul. "The Mistrust of Science." *The New Yorker,* 10 June 2016. https://www.newyorker.com/news/news-desk/the-mistrust-of-science.

Giroux, Henry, and Susan Searls Giroux. *Take Back Higher Education: Race, Youth, and the Crisis of Democracy in the Post-Civil Rights Era*. London: Palgrave Macmillan, 2004.

Gordon, Patrice. "How Reverse Mentorship Can Create Better Leaders." TEDX, November 2020. https://www.ted.com/talks/patrice_gordon_how_reverse_mentorship_can_help_create_better_leaders.

Grain, Kari. *Critical Hope: How to Grapple with Complexity, Lead with Purpose, and Cultivate Transformative Social Change*. Berkeley: North Atlantic Books, 2022.

Gravestock, Pamela. "Does Teaching Matter?" University of Toronto. 2011. https://tspace.library.utoronto.ca/bitstream/1807/31764/6/Gravestock_Pamela_S_201111_PhD_thesis.pdf.

"Guerrilla Warfare by Che Guevara." NC State University. Accessed January 2023. https://faculty.chass.ncsu.edu/slatta/hi216/documents/cheexcerpt.htm.

Haraway, Donna. *Staying with the Trouble: Making Kin in the Chthulucene*. Durham: Duke University Press, 2016.

Havel, Václav. *Disturbing the Peace: A Conversation with Karel Huizdala*. New York: Knopf Doubleday Publishing Group, 1991.

Hazelkorn, Ellen. *Rankings and the Reshaping of Higher Education: The Battle for World-Class Excellence*. New York: Palgrave Macmillan, 2011.

Hemphill, Prentis. "Hope, Questioning, and Getting Lost with Bayo Akomolafe." *Finding Our Way*, season 2, episode 3 (2022). https://podcasts.apple.com/ca/podcast/s2-ep3-hope-questioning-and-getting-lost-with/id1519965068?i=1000519932046.

Herrington, Jan, Thomas C. Reeves, and Ron Oliver. "Authentic Learning Environments." In *Handbook of Research on Educational Communications and Technology*, edited by J. Michael Spector, M. David Merrill, Jan Elen, and M.J. Bishop, 401–12. New York: Springer, 2014.

– "Immersive Learning Technologies: Realism and Online Authentic Learning." *Journal of Computing in Higher Education* 19 (2007): 80–99.

Hodgman, John. *Vacationland: True Stories from Painful Beaches*. New York: Penguin Random House, 2017.

Hoffman, Reid, Ben Casnocha, and Chris Yeh. "Your Company Is Not a Family." *Harvard Business Review*, 17 June 2014. https://hbr.org/2014/06/your-company-is-not-a-family.

Hofstadter, Paul. *Anti-intellectualism in American Life*. New York: Vintage Books, 1963.

Hogan, Kelly A., and Viji Sathy. *Inclusive Teaching: Strategies for Promoting Equity in the College Classroom*. Morgantown: West Virginia University Press, 2022.

Holst, Jonas. "The Fall of the Tekt n and the Rise of the Architect: On the Greek Origins of Architectural Craftsmanship." *Architectural Histories* 5, no. 1 (2017): 5.

Homer, *Odyssey*. Perseus. Accessed January 2023. http://www.perseus.tufts.edu /hopper/text?doc=Perseus%3Atext%3A1999.01.0136%3Abook%3D13.

– The Odyssey, Book II. Poetry in Translation. 2004. https://www.poetryintrans lation.com/PITBR/Greek/Odyssey2.php.

hooks, bell. *All About Love: New Visions*. New York: HarperCollins, 2000.

– *Teaching Community: A Pedagogy of Hope*. New York: Routledge, 2003.

Ibarra, Herminia, and Anne Scoular. "The Leader as Coach." *Harvard Business Review*, November 2019. https://hbr.org/2019/11/the-leader-as-coach.

Imad, Mays. "Pedagogy of Healing: Bearing Witness to Trauma and Resilience." *Inside Higher Ed*, 7 July 2021, https://www.insidehighered.com/views/2021/ 07/08/how-faculty-can-support-college-students%E2%80%99-mental-health- fall-opinion.

– "Transcending Adversity: Trauma-Informed Educational Development." *To Improve the Academy* 39, no. 3 (Spring 2021). DOI: https://doi.org/10.3998/tia.170 63888.0039.301.

Jack, Jordynn, and Viji Sathy. "It's Time to Cancel the Word 'Rigor.'" *Chronicle*. 24 September 2021. https://www.chronicle.com/article/its-time-to-cancel-the- word-rigor.

Jenkins, Patty, dir. *Wonder Woman*. 2017; USA: Warner Bros. Pictures.

Jennings, Willie. "Anger Is the Engine of Hope Now." *Reflections*. June 2020. https://reflections.yale.edu/article/seeking-light-notes-hope/anger-engine-hope- now.

Johnson, Steven. *Where Good Ideas Come From: The Natural History of Innovation*. New York: Riverhead Books, 2010.

Glen A. Jones, Theresa Shanahan, and Paul Goyan. "The Academic Senate and University Governance in Canada." *Canadian Journal of Higher Education* 34, no. 2 (2004): 35–68.

– "University Governance in Canadian Higher Education." *Tertiary Education and Management* 7, no. 2 (2001): 135–48.

Jonson, Ben. "To the Memory of My Beloved the Author, Mr. William Shakespeare." Poetry Foundation. Accessed February 2023. https://www.poetryfoundation. org/poems/44466/to-the-memory-of-my-beloved-the-author-mr-william- shakespeare.

Juelskjaer, Malou, and Nete Schwennesen. "Intra-Active Entanglements: An Interview with Karen Barad." *Kvinder, Køn & Forskning [Women, Gender and Research]* 1, no. 2 (2012): 10–23.

Kenton, Will. "Surety: Definition, How It Works with Bonds, and Distinctions." *Investopedia*, 6 December 2020. https://www.investOp-edia.com/terms/s/surety.asp.

King, Martin Luther, Jr. "Six Principles of Nonviolence Handout." United Nations. Accessed March 2023. https://www.unodc.org/documents/e4j/Secondary/Terrorism_Violent_Extremism_Six_Principles_of_Non-Violence.pdf.

Knott, Katherine. "Gen Z's Distrust in Higher Ed a 'Red Flag.'" *Inside Higher Ed*, 12 August 2022. https://www.insidehighered.com/news/2022/08/12/survey-highlights-gen-zs-distrust-higher-ed.

Kuh, George. *High-Impact Practices: What They Are, Who Has Access to Them, and Why They Matter.* Washington, DC: AAC&U, 2008.

Kuhn, Thomas. *The Structure of Scientific Revolutions.* Chicago: University of Chicago Press, 1962.

Latour, Bruno. "Why Has Critique Run Out of Steam? From Matters of Fact to Matters of Concern." *Critical Inquiry* 30, no. 2 (2004): 225–48.

Lawrence, Frederick. "Academic Freedom: For Whom and for What?" Jules LaPidus Lecture, Council of Graduate Schools Annual Meeting, New Orleans, 4 December 2021.

Lawrence, Louise J. *Reconfiguring Universities in an Age of Neoliberalism: Creating Compassionate Campuses.* Cham, Switzerland: Palgrave Macmillan, 2017.

Lee, Walter C., et al. "Operationalizing and Monitoring Student Support in Undergraduate Engineering Education." *Journal of Engineering Education* 111, no. 1 (2022): 82–110.

Levin, Phillis. "Introduction." *The Penguin Book of the Sonnet: 500 Years of a Classic Tradition in English.* New York: Penguin, 2001.

Lewitt, Howard. "Teachers Deserve No More – Or Less – Than Private Sector Workers." *Financial Post*, 2015. https://financialpost.com/executive/management-hr/teachers-deserve-no-more-or-less-than-private-sector-workers.

Ling Lee, Theresa Man. "What to Do with Student Evaluations of Teaching?" *Academic Matters*, 8 March 2021. https://academicmatters.ca/what-to-do-with-student-evaluations-of-teaching/.

Lloyd, Christine. "Leading across Boundaries and Silos in a Single Bound." *Community College Journal of Research and Practice* 40 (2016): 1–8.

Lorde, Audre. "Poetry Is Not a Luxury." Making Learning. January 2014. https://makinglearning.files.wordpress.com/2014/01/poetry-is-not-a-luxury-audre-lorde.pdf.

– "The Master's Tools Will Never Dismantle the Master's House." *Sister Outsider: Essays and Speeches*. Berkeley: Crossing Press, 1984.

Loud, Rachel. "Loretta Ross on Calling In the Calling Out Culture." Presidio Graduate School. 10 May 2021. https://www.presidio.edu/blog/loretta-ross-on-calling-in-the-calling-out-culture/.

Lyon, Mordecai. "Lorgia García-Peña (Q&A)." *The Boycott Times*. 23 February 2021. https://boycottx.org/lgp/.

MacInnis, Cara. "Impostor Syndrome as a Diversity, Equity and Inclusion Issue." *University of Calgary Psychology Equity, Diversity and Inclusion Blog*, 12 February 2020. https://arts.ucalgary.ca/news/impostor-syndrome-diversity-equity-inclusion-issue.

Matthew (@crowsfault). "People speak of hope." Twitter. 10 March 2022, 2:21 p.m. https://twitter.com/CrowsFault/status/1502001835779014666.

McClure, Kevin R. "Higher Ed, We've Got a Morale Problem – And a Free T-Shirt Won't Fix It." *EdSurge*. 27 September 2021. https://www.edsurge.com/news/2021-09-27-higher-ed-we-ve-got-a-morale-problem-and-a-free-t-shirt-won-t-fix-it.

McLuhan, Marshall. *Understanding Media: The Extensions of Man*. New York: Signet Books, 1964.

McNair, Tia Brown, Estela Mara Bensimon, and Lindsey Malcolm-Piqueux. *From Equity Talk to Equity Walk: Expanding Practitioner Knowledge for Racial Justice in Higher Education*. San Francisco: Jossey-Bass, 2020.

MegaGrimer, "r/Showerthoughts," Reddit, 2017, https://www.reddit.com/r/Showerthoughts/comments/7h4k7f/when_people_talk_about_traveling_to_the_past_they/.

Meisenzahl, Mary. "Starting in a Garage Is Crucial to the Origin Story of Many Silicon Valley Entrepreneurs." *Business Insider*, 1 April 2020. https://www.businessinsider.com/google-apple-hp-microsoft-amazon-started-in-garages-photos-2019-12.

Merkley, Eric, and Peter John Loewen. "Anti-intellectualism and the Mass Public's Response to the COVID-19 Pandemic." *Nature Human Behavior* 5 (2021): 706–15.

Meyer, Jan, and Ray Land. "Threshold Concepts and Troublesome Knowledge." In *Improving Student Learning*, 412–24. Oxford Centre for Staff and Learning Development, 2003.

Milton, John. *Paradise Lost*. London: J.&H. Richter, 1796.

Mishler, Adriene. *Yoga with Adriene*. YouTube. Accessed January 2023. https://www.youtube.com/user/yogawithadriene.

Montgomery, Beronda L. "Academic Leadership: Gatekeeping or Groundskeeping?" *Journal of Values-Based Leadership* 13, no. 2 (2020): article 16.

– *Lessons from Plants*. Cambridge, MA: Harvard University Press, 2021.

– "My Most Memorable Mentors? Plants." *Nature*. 13 April 2021. https://www.nature.com/articles/d41586-021-00961-9.

Moore, Jessie L. *Key Practices for Fostering Engaged Learning: A Guide for Faculty and Staff*. Oxon: Routledge, 2023.

Moore, Jessie, and Maureen Vandermaas-Peeler. "A Constellation Model for Transformative and Inclusive Mentoring." Presentation, Annual ISSOTL Conference, Kelowna, BC, 3 November 2022.

Moscrop, David. "A Year-End Reflection." David Moscrop, 20 December 2022. https://davidmoscrop.substack.com/p/a-year-end-reflection.

Muhammad, Ali, Ishamuddin Mustapha, Sharina Osman, and Umar Hassan. "University Social Responsibility: A Review of Conceptual Evolution and Its Thematic Analysis." *Journal of Cleaner Production* 286 (2020): 124931.

Muller, Jerry Z. *The Tyranny of Metrics*. Princeton: Princeton University Press, 2018.

Murray, Shannon. "Beyond Measure: A Nervous Approach to Ungrading." Maple League of Universities. 9 November 2022. https://www.youtube.com/watch?v=vjbm58kncxc.

Namaste, Nina, and Amanda Sturgill, eds, with Neal W. Sobania and Michael Vande Berg. *Mind the Gap: Global Learning at Home and Abroad*. Oxon: Routledge, 2020.

Nordquist, Richard. "What Is Sprezzatura?" *ThoughtCo*, 17 November 2019. https://www.thoughtco.com/what-is-sprezzatura-1691779.

Nussbaum, Martha C. "The Professor of Parody." *The New Republic*, 22 February 1999. https://newrepublic.com/article/150687/professor-parody.

Oliver, Mary. "I Worried." *Devotions*. New York: Penguin Random House, 2017.

– *Evidence*. Boston: Beacon Press, 2009.

Palmer, Parker. *The Courage to Teach: Exploring the Inner Landscape of a Teacher's Life*. San Francisco: Jossey-Bass, 1998.

– *The Politics of the Brokenhearted: On Holding the Tensions of Democracy*. Kalamazoo: Fetzer Institute, 2005.

Palmer, Parker, and Arthur Zajonc. *The Heart of Higher Education*. San Francisco: Jossey-Bass, 2010.

Parker, Priya. *The Art of Gathering: How We Meet and Why It Matters*. New York: Riverhead Books, 2018.

Patel, Eboo. "Teach Your Students to Be Builders, Not Critics." *Inside Higher Ed*. 6 September 2022. https://www.insidehighered.com/views/2022/09/06/teach-students-be-builders-not-critics-opinion.

Paul, Ross. "University Governance and Institutional Culture: A Canadian President's Perspective." In *University Governance and Reform*, edited by Hans G. Schuetze, William Bruneau, and Garnet Grosjean, 63–76. New York: Palgrave Macmillan, 2012.

Perdomo, Daniela. "Human Flourishing: Could a Philosophical Concept Impact Health?" John Hopkins Medicine, 28 October 2021. https://biomedicalodyssey.blogs.hopkinsmedicine.org/2021/10/human-flourishing-could-a-philosophical-concept-impact-health/.

Pierre, Jon (@JonPierre2). 19 April 2018, "commented on" Shit Academics Say (@AcademicsSay). "Reviewer 2 walks into a bar." Twitter. 11 June 2020, 9:38 p.m. https://twitter.com/AcademicsSay/status/1271255491407155200.

Pinker, Steven. *The Language Instinct: How the Mind Creates Language*. New York: Perennial Classics, 1994.

Popova, Maria. "Audre Lorde on Poetry as an Instrument of Change and Feeling as an Antidote to Fearing." *The Marginalian*, 18 October 2020. https://www.themarginalian.org/2020/10/18/poetry-is-not-a-luxury-audre-lorde/.

– "Bertrand Russell on the Secret of Happiness." *The Marginalian*, 21 February 2023. https://www.themarginalian.org/2023/02/21/bertrand-russell-happiness/.

– "The Handle on the Door to a New World: Poet Jane Hirshfield on the Magic and Power of Metaphor, Animated." *The Marginalian*, 7 July 2021. https://www.themarginalian.org/2021/07/07/jane-hirshfield-metaphor/.

– "Hope, Cynicism, and the Stories We Tell Ourselves." *The Marginalian*, 9 February 2015. https://www.themarginalian.org/2015/02/09/hope-cynicism/.

– "The Magic of Moss and What It Teaches Us about the Art of Attentiveness to Life at All Scales." *The Marginalian*, 13 May 2015. https://www.themarginalian.org/2015/05/13/gathering-moss-robin-wall-kimmerer/.

– "No Place for Self-Pity, No Room for Fear: Toni Morrison on the Artist's Task in Troubled Times." *The Marginalian*, 15 November 2016. https://www.themarginalian.org/2016/11/15/toni-morrison-art-despair/.

– "The Overview Effect and the Psychology of Cosmic Awe." *The Marginalian*, 18 December 2012. https://www.themarginalian.org/2012/12/18/the-overview-effect-and-the-psychology-of-cosmic-awe/.

– "Scientists and Philosophers Answer Kids' Most Pressing Questions about How the World Works." *The Marginalian*, 5 November 2012. https://www.themarginalian.org/2012/11/05/big-questions-from-little-people/.

– "The Six Pillars of the Wholehearted Life: Parker Palmer's Spectacular Naropa University Commencement Address." *The Marginalian*, 10 August 2015. https://www.themarginalian.org/2015/08/10/parker-palmer-naropa-university-commencement-address/.

Puig de la Bellacasa, Maria. *Matters of Care: Speculative Ethics in More than Human Worlds*. Minneapolis: University of Minnesota Press, 2017.

Ravenscraft, Eric. "The Science of Inspiration (And How to Make It Work for You)." *Lifehacker*, 19 November 2013. https://lifehacker.com/the-science-of-inspiration-and-how-to-make-it-work-for-1467413542.

Riddell, Jessica. "Can Shakespeare Teach Us to Be Better Citizens?" *University Affairs*, 23 August 2019. https://www.universityaffairs.ca/opinion/adventures-in-academe/can-shakespeare-teach-us-to-be-better-citizens/.

– "Combatting Toxic Positivity with Critical Hope." *University Affairs*, 19 June 2020. https://www.universityaffairs.ca/opinion/adventures-in-academe/combatting-toxic-positivity-with-critical-hope/.

– "Conjuring Witches and Wonder: Leadership from the Edges." The Wyrd House, 28 October 2021. https://www.thewyrdhouse.com/post/conjuring-witches-and-wonder-leadership-from-the-edges.

– "Putting Authentic Learning on Trial: Using Trials as a Pedagogical Model for Teaching in the Humanities." *Arts and Humanities in Higher Education* 17, no. 4 (2017): 410–32.

– "Tackling Wicked Problems in Higher Education." Maple Business Council, 20 August 2021. https://www.maplecouncil.org/momentum-content/2021/8/20/maple-league-article.

Riddell, Jessica, and Tiffany McLennan. "Students as Partners: An Inclusive Approach to High-Impact Practices (HIPs)." In *Taking Stock 2.0: Transforming Teaching and Learning in Higher Education*, edited by Julia Christensen Hughes, Joy Mighty and Denise Stockley, 270–93. St Peters Bay: Society for Teaching and Learning in Higher Education, 2022.

Riddell, Jessica, Scott Stoddard, and Georges-Philippe Gadoury-Sansfaçon.

"Building Institutional Capacities for Students as Partners in the Design of COVID Classrooms." *International Journal of Students as Partners* 5, no. 2 (2021): 111–22.

Rosales, John, and Tim Walker. "The Racist Beginnings of Standardized Testing." National Education Association, 3 March 2021. https://www.nea.org/advocating-for-change/new-from-nea/racist-beginnings-standardized-testing.

Roth, Michael S. *Beyond the University: Why Liberal Education Matters*. New Haven: Yale University Press, 2014.

Rowe, Kelly, and Zac Ashkanasy. "The Environment for Canadian Universities Is Changing." Nous Group, 23 March 2022. https://nousgroup.com/ca/insights/canada-universities-governance/.

Roy, Arundhati. "The Pandemic Is a Portal." *Financial Times*. 3 April 2020. https://www.ft.com/content/10d8f5e8-74eb-11ea-95fe-fcd274e920ca.

RuPaul (@RuPaul). "Call's coming from inside the house is a metaphor." Twitter. 12 April 2011, 8:47 p.m.. https://twitter.com/RuPaul/status/57968018176737280.

Scobey, David. "The Gifts of Liberal Education." Robertson Memorial Lecture, University of Michigan, 2014.

– "The Paradigm Project: A Brief Overview." Bringing Theory to Practice, February 2022. https://bttop.org/wp-content/uploads/2022/02/Paradigm-Project-Overview.pdf.

Seligman, Martin E.P. *The Hope Circuit*. New York: Public Affairs, 2018.

Shakespeare, William. *History of Henry V*. Open Source Shakespeare. Accessed March 2023. https://www.opensourceshakespeare.org/views/plays/play_view.php?WorkID=henry5&Act=0&Scene=1&Scope=scene.

– *A Midsummer Night's Dream*. Open Source Shakespeare. Accessed March 2023. https://www.opensourceshakespeare.org/views/plays/play_view.php?WorkID=midsummer&Act=5&Scene=1&Scope=scene.

– *The Tragedy of Hamlet, Prince of Denmark*. Open Source Shakespeare. Accessed March 2023. https://www.opensourceshakespeare.org/views/plays/play_view.php?WorkID=hamlet&Act=2&Scene=2&Scope=scene.

– *The Tragedy of King Lear*, "Act III Scene 4." Open Source Shakespeare. Accessed February 2023. https://www.opensourceshakespeare.org/views/plays/play_view.php?WorkID=kinglear&Act=3&Scene=4&Scope=scene.

– *The Tragedy of Macbeth*. Open Source Shakespeare. Accessed March 2023. https://www.opensourceshakespeare.org/views/plays/play_view.php?WorkID=macbeth&Act=1&Scene=1&Scope=scene.

– *The Tragedy of Romeo and Juliet*. Open Source Shakespeare. Accessed March 2023. https://www.opensourceshakespeare.org/views/plays/play_view.php?WorkID=romeojuliet&Act=0&Scope=act&pleasewait=1&msg=pl.

– *Twelfth Night, Or What You Will*. Open Source Shakespeare. Accessed March 2023. https://www.opensourceshakespeare.org/views/plays/play_view.php?WorkID=12night&Act=2&Scene=2&Scope=scene.

Shariatmadari, David. "A Year of 'Permacrisis.'" Collins, 1 November 2022. https://blog.collinsdictionary.com/language-lovers/a-year-of-permacrisis/.

Shelley, Percy Bysshe. *Prometheus Unbound*. London: C. and J. Ollier, 1820.

Shor, Ira. *Empowering Education: Critical Teaching for Social Change*. Chicago: University of Chicago Press, 1992.

– *When Students Have Power: Negotiating Authority in a Critical Pedagogy*. Chicago: University of Chicago Press, 1996.

Sidney, Philip. "The Defence of Poesy." Poetry Foundation. Accessed January 2023. https://www.poetryfoundation.org/articles/69375/the-defence-of-poesy.

Simon, Clea. "Lessons from James Baldwin on Betrayal and Hope." *The Harvard Gazette*. 2 July 2020. https://news.harvard.edu/gazette/story/2020/07/james-baldwin-as-seen-against-the-backdrop-of-racial-upheaval/.

Simpson, Jennifer. *Longing for Justice: Higher Education and Democracy's Agenda*. Toronto: University of Toronto Press, 2014.

Sinek, Simon. "Developing an Infinite Mindset." Brené Brown. 18 January 2021. https://brenebrown.com/podcast/brene-with-simon-sinek-on-developing-an-infinite-mindset/#transcript.

Sivers, Derek. "How to Start a Movement." TEDx. 2010. https://www.ted.com/talks/derek_sivers_how_to_start_a_movement.

Skolnik, Michael, and Glen A. Jones. "Governing Boards in Canadian Universities." *The Review of Higher Education* 20, no. 3 (1997): 277–95.

Slater, Charles L. "Generativity Versus Stagnation: An Elaboration of Erikson's Adult Stage of Human Development." *Journal of Adult Development* 10, no. 1 (2003): 53–65.

Smith, Emma. *This Is Shakespeare*. New York: Vintage Books, 2019.

– "What Shakespeare Teaches Us about Living with Pandemics." *The New York Times*, 28 March 2020. https://www.nytimes.com/2020/03/28/opinion/coronavirus-shakespeare.html.

Soll, Jacob. "Healing the Body Politic: French Royal Doctors, History and the Birth of a Nation 1560–1634." *Renaissance Quarterly* 55 (2002): 1–28.

Solnit, Rebecca. "Hope Is an Embrace of the Unknown: Rebecca Solnit on Living in Dark Times." *The Guardian*. 15 July 2016. https://www.theguardian.com/books/2016/jul/15/rebecca-solnit-hope-in-the-dark-new-essay-embrace-unknown.

– *Hope in the Dark: Untold Stories, Wild Possibilities*. Chicago: Haymarket Books, 2016.

Stanton, Andre, dir. *Finding Nemo*. 2003; Burbank: Walt Disney Pictures.

Starr, G. Gabrielle. "Opening Plenary." Presentation, AAC&U Annual Meeting, San Francisco, 18 January 2023.

Strauss, Valerie. "Some See Liberal Arts Education as Elitist. Why It's Really Pragmatic." *Washington Post*, 5 February 2023. https://www.washingtonpost.com/education/2023/02/05/liberal-arts-education-is-pragmatic/.

Sun, Ye, Giacomo Livan, Athen Ma, and Vito Latora. "Interdisciplinary Researchers Attain Better Long-Term Funding Performance." *Communictions Physics* 4 (2021): 263.

Sylvester, David. "A Message from President David Sylvester to the St. Michael's Community." University of St Michael's College, 8 June 2020. https://stmikes.utoronto.ca/news/a-message-from-president-david-sylvester-to-the-st-michaels-community.

Tamburri, Rosanna. "Why Grooming the Next Line of University Matters More Than Ever." *University Affairs*, 2 August 2016. https://www.universityaffairs.ca/features/feature-article/grooming-the-next-line-of-university-presidents/.

Tatter, Grace. "Consent at Every Age." Harvard Graduate School of Education, 19 December 2018. https://www.gse.harvard.edu/news/uk/18/12/consent-every-age.

The CryptoNaturalist (@cryptonature). "We seldom admit." Twitter. 22 July 2022, 3:09 p.m. https://twitter.com/cryptonature/status/1550558603056136195.

Tippett, Krista. "Foundations 1: Seeing the Generative Story of Our Time." On Being. Accessed January 2023. https://onbeing.org/on-being-foundations/.

– "Living the Questions." On Being. Accessed January 2023. https://onbeing.org/series/living-the-questions/.

– "Pico Iyer: The Urgency of Slowing Down." On Being, 29 November 2018. https://onbeing.org/programs/pico-iyer-the-urgency-of-slowing-down-nov2018/.

– "The Pause." On Being. 26 November 2022. https://onbeing.salsalabs.org/the pause_20221126.

Traister, Rebecca. *Good and Mad: The Revolutionary Power of Women's Anger.* New York: Simon and Schuster, 2018.

Tricker, Bob. *Corporate Governance: Principles, Policies, and Practices.* Oxford: Oxford University Press, 2015.

Tutu, Desmond. *God Is Not a Christian: Speaking Truth in Times of Crisis.* London: Ebury Publishing, 2013.

Vedder, Richard. "2025: Google U. vs. Microsoft U.?" *Forbes*, 31 August 2020. https://www.forbes.com/sites/richardvedder/2020/08/31/2025-google-u-vs-microsoft-u/.

Vincent, James. *Beyond Measure: The Hidden History of Measurement from Cubits to Quantum Constants.* New York: W.W. Norton & Company, 2022.

Wallace, David Foster. "This Is Water by David Foster Wallace (Full Audio and Transcript)." FS. Accessed January 2023. https://fs.blog/david-foster-wallace-this-is-water/.

Warner, John. *Why They Can't Write: Killing the Five-Paragraph Essay and Other Necessities.* Baltimore: Johns Hopkins Press, 2020.

Warner, John (@biblioracle). "A couple of days ago I did a thread." Twitter. 13 January 2022. https://twitter.com/biblioracle/status/1481626250687004675.

Whitman, Walt. "Song of Myself, 51." Poets.org. Accessed January 2023. https://poets.org/poem/song-myself-51.

Winfrey, Oprah. "The Powerful Lesson Maya Angelou Taught Oprah." Oprah's Lifeclass, 19 October 2011. https://www.oprah.com/oprahs-lifeclass/the-powerful-lesson-maya-angelou-taught-oprah-video.

Wong, Brittany. "Freudenfreude Might Be Just What Your Friendships Are Missing." *HuffPost*, 6 January 2023. https://www.huffpost.com/entry/freudenfreude-in-friendships_l_63b5c468e4b0d6f0b9f7ad79.

Wright, Craig. *The Hidden Habits of Genius: Beyond Talent, IQ, and Grit – Unlocking the Secrets of Greatness.* New York: HarperCollins, 2020.

Ziegler, Chris. "Nokia CEO Stephen Elop Rallies Troops in Brutally Honest 'Burning Platform' Memo? (Update: It's Real!)." *Engadget*, 8 February 2011. https://www.engadget.com/2011-02-08-nokia-ceo-stephen-elop-rallies-troops-in-brutally-honest-burnin.html.

Zolli, Andrew. "Learning to Bounce Back." *The New York Times*, 2 November 2012. https://www.nytimes.com/2012/11/03/opinion/forget-sustainability-its-about-resilience.html.

Index